IMAGES
of America

EARLY REDLANDS

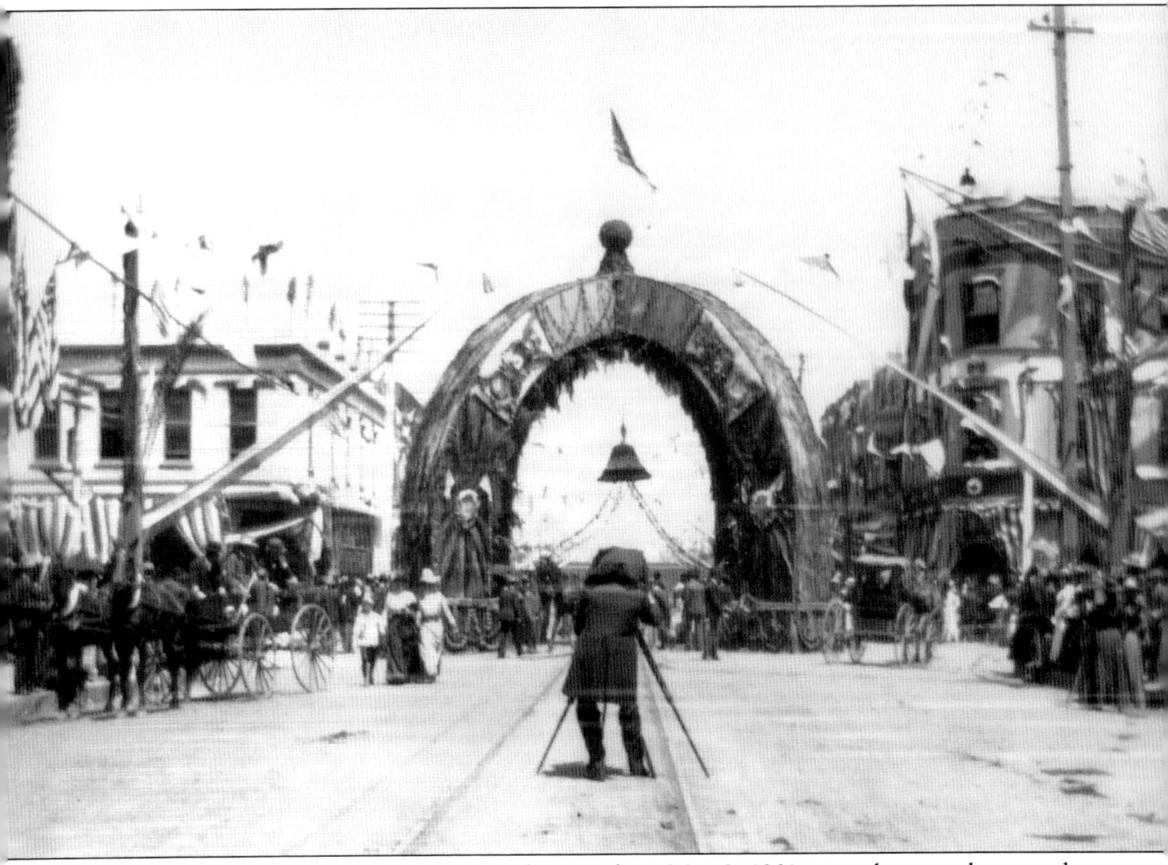

The same day that the cover photograph was taken, May 8, 1901, an unknown photographer captured this image of a professional photographer standing in the middle of Orange Street, facing north towards the double arch at the intersection of Orange and State Streets. (Courtesy of the Archives of the A.K. Smiley Public Library.)

On the Cover: Redlands always enthusiastically plunged into celebrations, including this one for the visit of Pres. William McKinley on May 8, 1901. The massive double arch was created with local materials, including palm fronds, citrus fruit, and roses. (Photograph by Elias F. Everitt; courtesy of the Archives of the A.K. Smiley Public Library.)

IMAGES
of America

EARLY REDLANDS

Ann Cordy Deegan and Maria Y. Carrillo

ARCADIA
PUBLISHING

ISBN 978-1-4671-3067-7

Published by Arcadia Publishing
Charleston, South Carolina

Printed in the United States of America

Library of Congress Control Number: 2013937628

For all general information, please contact Arcadia Publishing:
Telephone 843-853-2070
Fax 843-853-0044
E-mail sales@arcadiapublishing.com
For customer service and orders:
Toll-Free 1-888-313-2665

Visit us on the Internet at www.arcadiapublishing.com

This book is dedicated to the professional photographers of Redlands who worked between 1880 and 1920. Their passion and expertise produced images still cherished today.

Contents

Acknowledgments

This book would never have been possible without the interest and support of Dr. Larry Burgess, director emeritus; Don McCue, director; and Dr. Nathan Gonzales, archivist of the A.K. Smiley Public Library in Redlands, whose extensive knowledge of the photograph collection in the archives helped make this work possible. A special thank you is extended to the library's board of trustees, whose permission to allow the use of this extraordinary group of images was essential and encouraging.

All author royalties from this book will go to the A.K. Smiley Public Library. Without its archives, this book would never have been created, and without wonderful repositories like this one, the world would be so much the poorer in its knowledge of the past. Those who thought to donate their photographs over the years are thanked for their kindness and foresight.

Others who have helped aim this book in the right direction include our editor at Arcadia Publishing, Jared Nelson, who patiently answered our questions; Michele Nielsen, curator of history and head of the history division at San Bernardino County Museum, for brainstorming for answers when puzzled; and Alex Capuchino, a work-study student from the University of Redlands who dug through photograph files to help find images.

A big thank you is extended to our proofreaders, including Dr. Nathan Gonzales, archivist of the A.K. Smiley Public Library; Karen Keen, a lifelong Redlands resident; Jim Deegan, coauthor Ann Cordy Deegan's patient husband; and Juan Colato, the manager of Wells Fargo History Museums. Your enthusiasm has been greatly appreciated!

And to the people of Redlands who listened to our ideas and gave us feedback, thank you!

All images are courtesy of the Archives of the A.K. Smiley Public Library.

INTRODUCTION

This book started as an effort to compile a list of professional photographers who began their work in Redlands between 1880 and 1920. Their names appeared on images being cataloged and used by patrons in the archives of the A.K. Smiley Public Library in Redlands, and it quickly became apparent that knowing when they did business in town helped not only to date the photographs but also to provide insights into their trade at the time they worked. The project became fascinating as more and more photographers were identified and their stunning images were located. Sharing these findings with the public—both local patrons and those in other communities—can help identify photographers and thereby date images. The exceptional photograph collection in the archives of the A.K. Smiley Public Library proved to hold a more-than-ample supply of these images, which the library generously shared with the authors of this work.

Redlands was officially incorporated in 1888 and, although few of its photographers appear in the 1880s, this is the founding decade and is therefore used as the starting point for this work. A total of 34 professional photographers have been documented as working in Redlands prior to 1920. Not all of these photographers are illustrated in this book, as some have no identified photographs in the A.K. Smiley Public Library archives. This does not necessarily mean that their work is rare, but rather that the current holdings do not contain any images that can be linked to them. Perhaps this book will stimulate interest for families researching their own photographs and recognizing the works of professional photographers that could be donated to local institutions for others to see and use now and in the future.

The works of a professional photographer were only included if their name was commercially affixed to the image in some way or if their negatives were identified. The photographer must have placed the town name of Redlands on the photograph or be linked to the town through other historically validated information. Finally, when they lived in Redlands has been determined to a time range, understanding that this is a work in progress and that date ranges may change as more data surfaces. Chapter one describes how the authors determined who worked in Redlands as professional photographers and when. A table at the end of the book lists all currently known professional photographers linked to Redlands between 1880 and 1920 and when they worked in town.

One after another, these professionals tried their hand, succeeding and failing, staying and moving on. Flexible in response to the times, they created images to promote the town and sell land to potential settlers, provided photographs to tourists visiting by rail, served schools and graduates, and recorded events in the growing town. Truly successful ones advertised in newspapers, city directories, and school annuals while selling their services for numerous enthusiastic town promotional publications. They sold images through their own studios but also marketed through other merchants in town, including drugstores, to expand their sales.

This book is organized around the images that were taken by the professional photographers of Redlands, whether related to businesses, homes, schools, amusements, or tourism. Each chapter title is a direct quote from the period and its source is noted in its chapter. Buying a professional's photographs required disposable income, as these men and women needed to earn money to stay in town. If they could not earn enough, they moved on to other locations or occupations. Early Redlands could support them due to its growing citrus industry, its early influx of wealthy residents, and, soon, its booming tourism industry. From the 1890s until 1913, Redlands was on a roll. A devastating freeze in 1913 nearly destroyed the citrus groves, and a local recession of several years set in; however, it was partially offset by continued tourism, which helped professional photographers stay in business.

Many wealthy individuals came to Redlands at its start, bought land, and either remained here year-round or wintered over in the mild climate. This wealth helped cause a quick increase in town growth, the building of mansions (to the delight of the owners and tourists), citrus grove development, and monies to support professional photographers. Photography businesses were necessary because the townspeople and tourists needed advertising photographs. Schools expanded and new ones were built, providing opportunities for class photographs, graduation pictures, and sports team coverage, some of which ended up in the town newspapers. Lest boredom set in, opera houses, parades, visiting dignitaries, and other events also needed coverage for souvenirs and advertising. As the fame of Cañon Crest Park in Redlands spread, the railroad tours added stops and needed images for brochures and sales, and tourists wanted keepsakes to take home, such as postcards. In short, early Redlands was a good place to be a professional photographer.

These photographs are a delight to look at because of the technical and aesthetic knowledge the photographers possessed. It is hoped that readers will enjoy these images of early Redlands in and of themselves but will also appreciate their historical context. Journey now through early Redlands, courtesy of these professional photographers of the past.

One

"Compliments of Your Photographer"

Old photographs provide wonderful views of the past, and dating these images places them in a historical context. Tying a military image to a specific war increases understanding and knowledge about that event. Knowing when a business existed in town helps to explain what life was like then and what one could buy. And the pile of all those unidentified family photographs might just shrink a bit if a date can be assigned to an image.

Photographs can be dated in many ways, including style of dress, type of automobile, or photographic process. Another method is to determine when a specific professional photographer was living and working in a town. Professional photographers needed to constantly drum up new business. Advertising by name and location brought customers and allowed them to know what type of photography they could buy. What better, longer-lasting means than to put your name and possibly your address on each photograph sold?

Sometimes, these photographers worked for a year or less, which can really aid in pinpointing the date of an image. Making a list of professional photographers with dates when they worked in a town requires detective work, searching through historical documents such as government census records and voter registration files. Throughout this chapter and subsequent chapters are examples of sources that may help other communities identify photographers from the past.

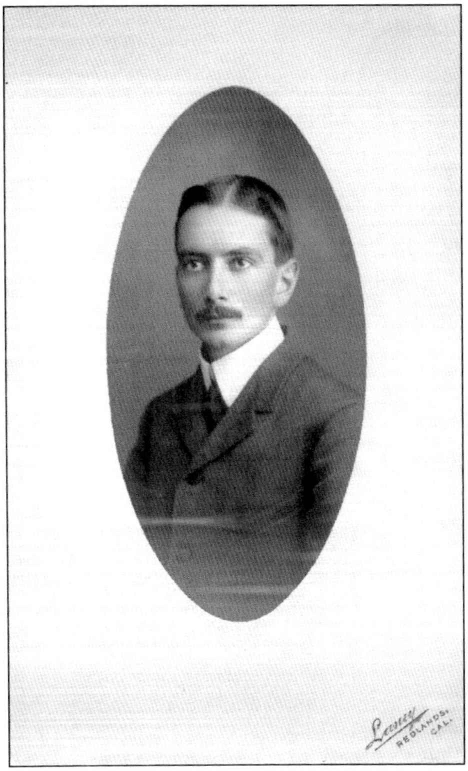

Men's portraits from 1880 to 1920 are hard to date by clothing, as their fashions changed very little. Using a photographer's name often allows dating, as seen in these images of unidentified men. The photograph at left was taken by Grace E. Laney, a professional photographer in Redlands from about November 1896 to 1904. The photograph below was taken by Perry D. Sutphen, who worked in Redlands from about 1904 to 1907. The clarity and detail in these portraits are common in a professional photographer's work. (Photographers: left, Grace E. Laney; below, Perry D. Sutphen.)

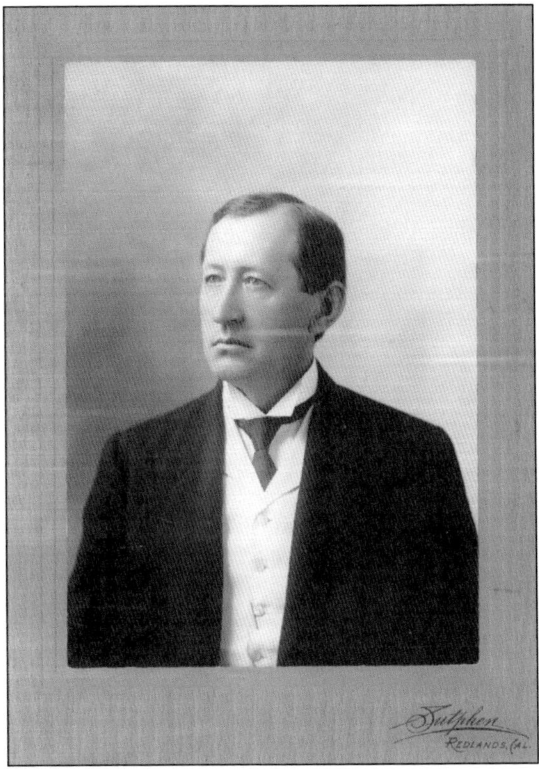

Edward Roessler worked in Redlands during the time of two presidential visits. His photographs of Pres. William McKinley (1901) and Pres. Theodore Roosevelt (1903) add to the historical record. Because he worked in Redlands from 1900 to 1904, this image of Rose Hewitt, who had married into the local Hinckley family by at least 1910, places her in her early 20s when the photograph was taken. (Photographer: Edward E. Roessler.)

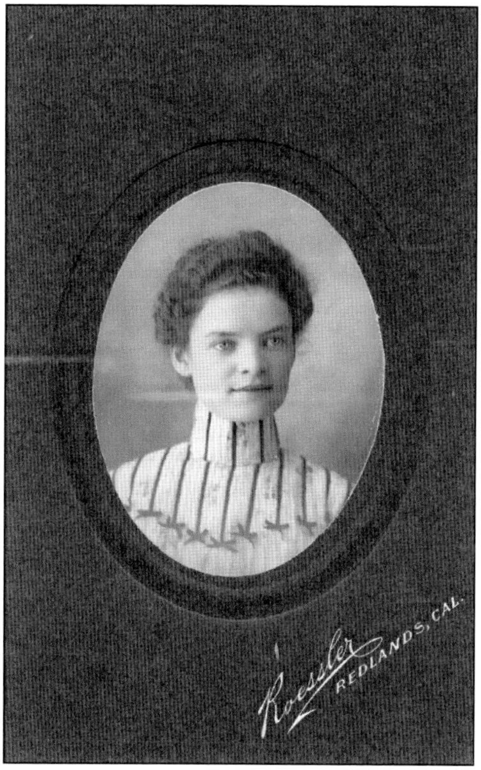

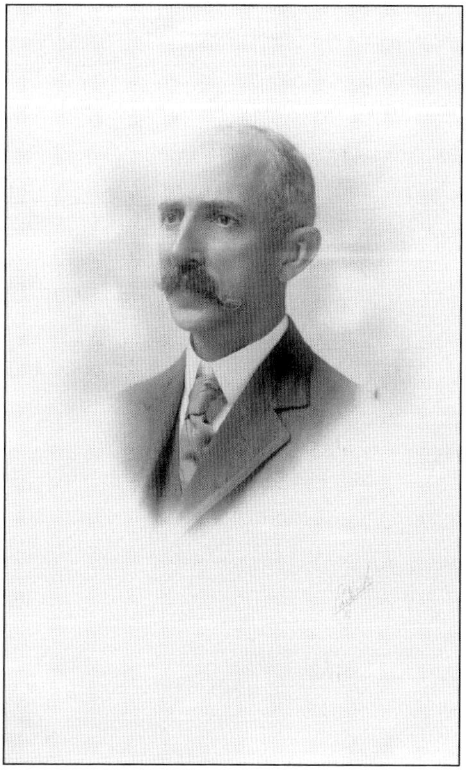

Sometimes, professional photographers stayed in Redlands only one or two years, helping to narrow the dating of photographs. D.W. Carpenter, who took this image of L. Worthington Green, appeared as a professional photographer only in the 1900 Redlands city directory. His short stay assigns a date to Green's portrait. Green was on the board of trustees of the A.K. Smiley Public Library from 1908 to 1919. (Photographer: D.W. Carpenter.)

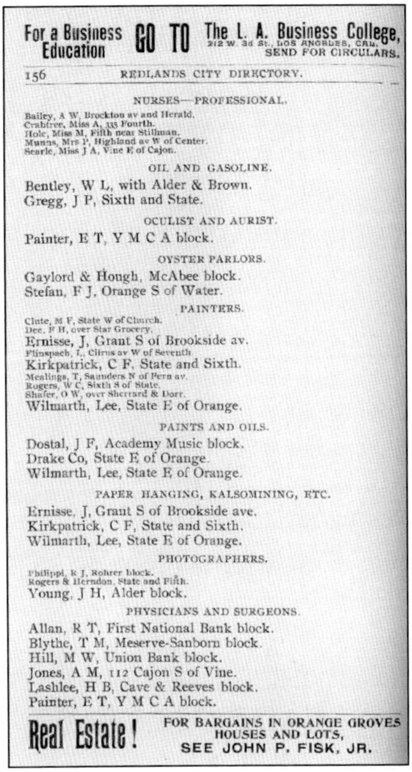
For a Business Education GO TO The L. A. Business College, 212 W. 3d St., LOS ANGELES, CAL. SEND FOR CIRCULARS.

156 REDLANDS CITY DIRECTORY.

NURSES—PROFESSIONAL.

Bailey, A W, Brockton av and Herald.
Crabtree, Miss A, 335 Fourth.
Hole, Miss M, Fifth near Stillman.
Munns, Mrs P, Highland av W of Center.
Searle, Miss J A, Vine E of Cajon.

OIL AND GASOLINE.

Bentley, W L, with Alder & Brown.
Gregg, J P, Sixth and State.

OCULIST AND AURIST.

Painter, E T, Y M C A block.

OYSTER PARLORS.

Gaylord & Hough, McAbee block.
Stefan, F J, Orange S of Water.

PAINTERS.

Clute, M F, State W of Church.
Dee, F H, over Star Grocery.
Ernisse, J, Grant S of Brookside av.
Flinspach, L, Citrus av W of Seventh
Kirkpatrick, C F, State and Sixth.
Mealings, T, Saunders N of Fern av.
Rogers, W C, Sixth S of State.
Shafer, O W, over Sherrard & Dorr.
Wilmarth, Lee, State E of Orange.

PAINTS AND OILS.

Dostal, J F, Academy Music block.
Drake Co, State E of Orange.
Wilmarth, Lee, State E of Orange.

PAPER HANGING, KALSOMINING, ETC.

Ernisse, J, Grant S of Brookside ave.
Kirkpatrick, C F, State and Sixth.
Wilmarth, Lee, State E of Orange.

PHOTOGRAPHERS.

Philippi, R J, Rohrer block.
Rogers & Herndon, State and Fifth.
Young, J H, Alder block.

PHYSICIANS AND SURGEONS.

Allan, R T, First National Bank block.
Blythe, T M, Meserve-Sanborn block.
Hill, M W, Union Bank block.
Jones, A M, 112 Cajon S of Vine.
Lashlee, H B, Cave & Reeves block.
Painter, E T, Y M C A block.

Real Estate! FOR BARGAINS IN ORANGE GROVES HOUSES AND LOTS, SEE JOHN P. FISK, JR.

City and county directories of the late 1800s and early 1900s provide names of professional photographers and their addresses. A customer would look under "Photographers" in the business directory and find the name and address of a photographer in town. In 1896, Redlands had four photographers named in the business directory, two of whom were in partnership—Rogers and Herndon.

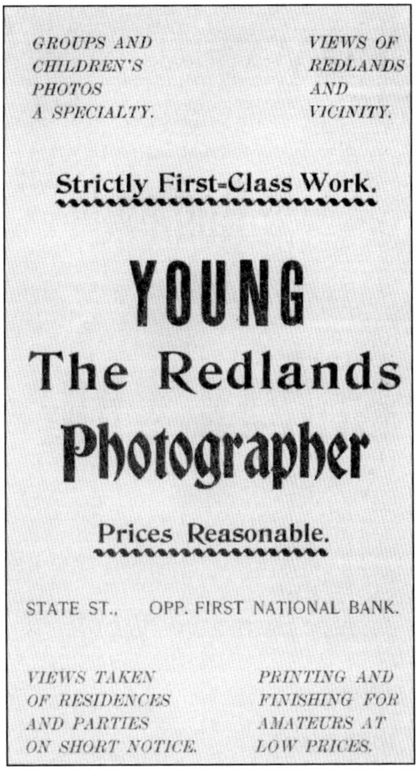

Some photographers placed advertisements in the directories that provided more information about the type of photography they did. John Young, active in Redlands from September 1895 to November 1896, put this advertisement in the 1896 Redlands city directory. To compete with at least three other professional photographers in Redlands and fewer than 4,000 people, Young offered "low prices" and "views taken of residences and parties on short notice."

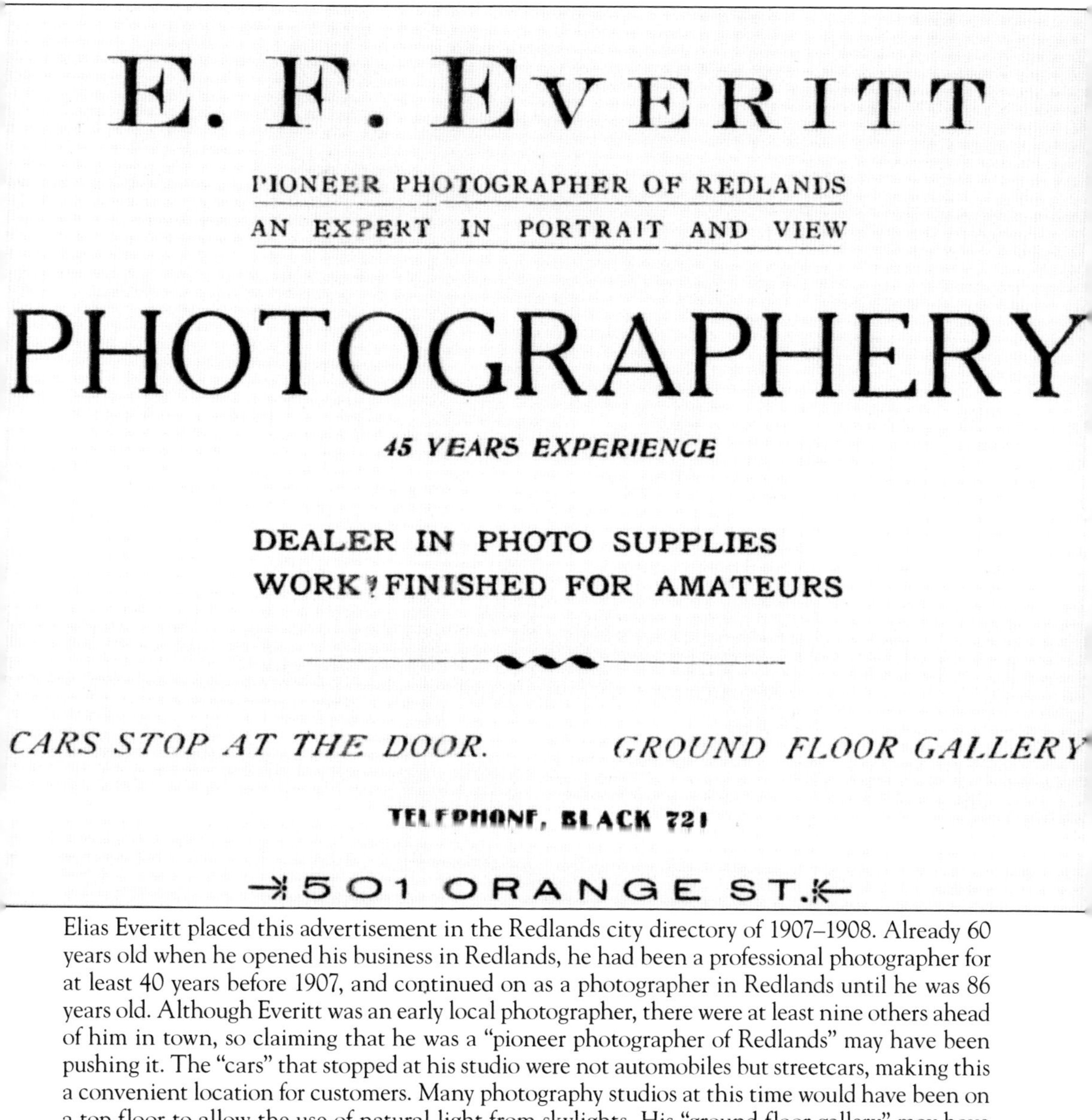

Elias Everitt placed this advertisement in the Redlands city directory of 1907–1908. Already 60 years old when he opened his business in Redlands, he had been a professional photographer for at least 40 years before 1907, and continued on as a photographer in Redlands until he was 86 years old. Although Everitt was an early local photographer, there were at least nine others ahead of him in town, so claiming that he was a "pioneer photographer of Redlands" may have been pushing it. The "cars" that stopped at his studio were not automobiles but streetcars, making this a convenient location for customers. Many photography studios at this time would have been on a top floor to allow the use of natural light from skylights. His "ground floor gallery" may have appealed to those who found stairs a challenge. Everitt was a prolific photographer and many of his images have survived into today's collections.

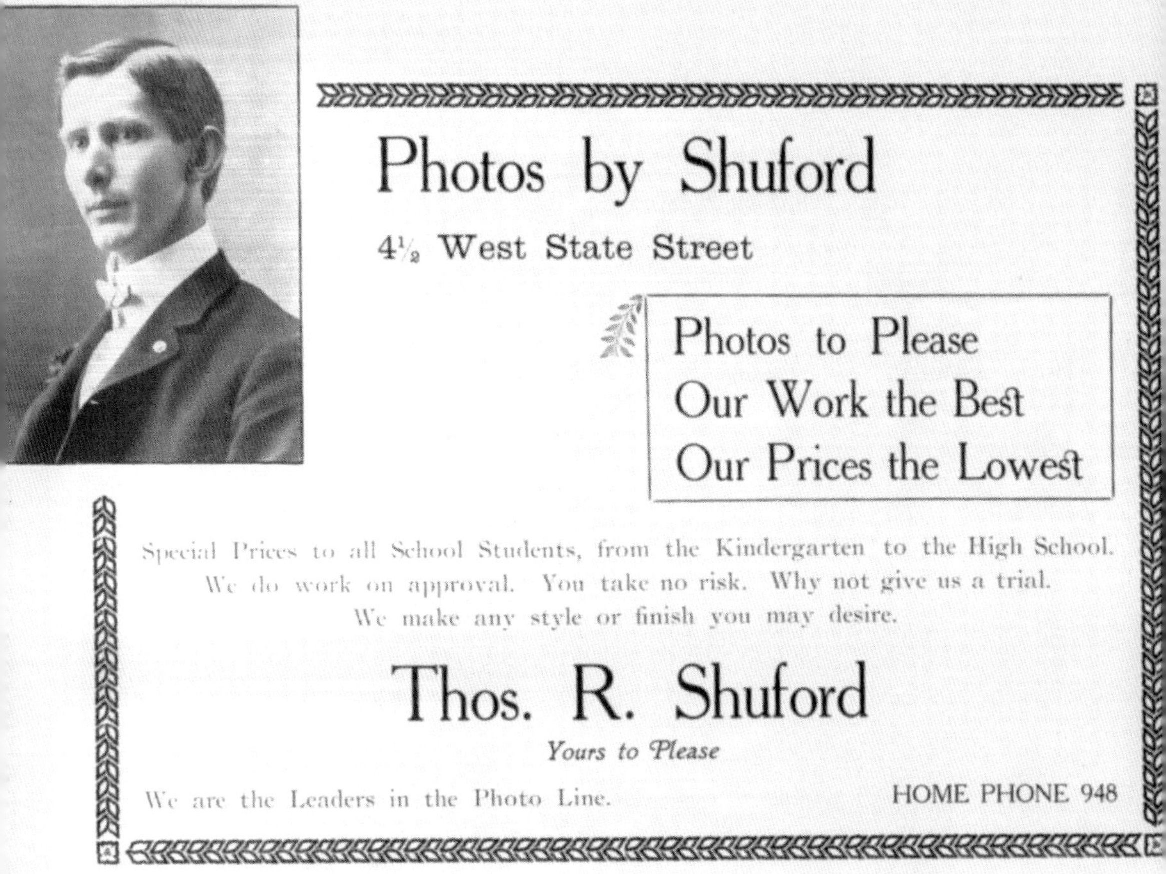

Advertisements were often sought for high school annuals to help pay for publication costs. The precise dating of these books aids in identifying when a photographer worked in town. Thomas Shuford, who was in Redlands from about 1907 to 1914, placed this full-page advertisement in the 1907 Redlands High School annual, the *Makio*. At least four other photographers worked in Redlands in 1907; they may not have agreed with Shuford's comment "we are the leaders in the photo line." School annuals contain photographs of individual students but also of athletics, plays, buildings, student organizations, and faculty. Redlands High School published its first annual in 1904, and the University of Redlands created its annual, *La Letra*, in 1915.

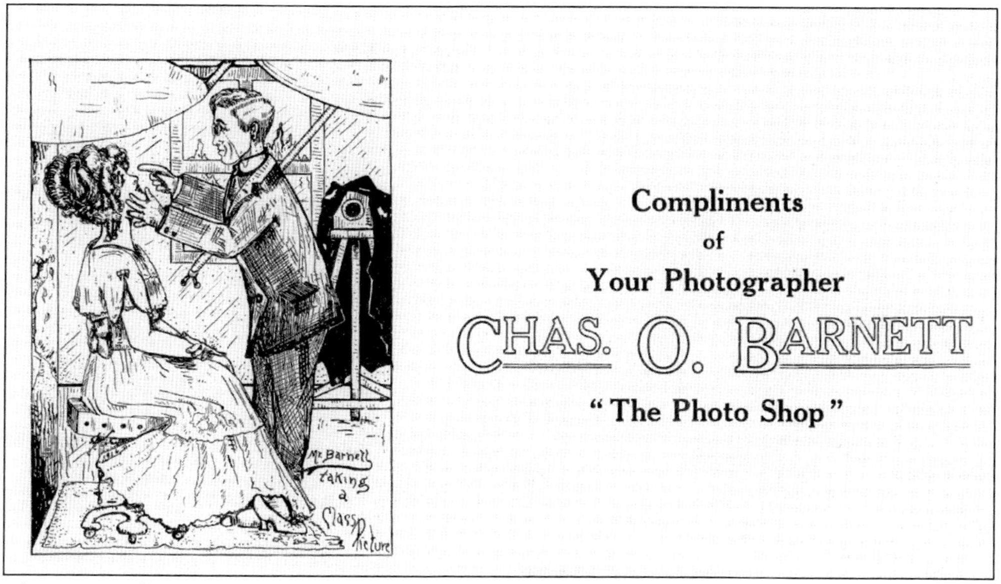

The 1914 Redlands High School annual contained this advertisement for photographer Charles Barnett and provided the title for this chapter. Barnett's name appears on numerous photographs and advertisements in annuals from 1912 through 1922. He found a profitable niche and became so well known that a student sketched him for this advertisement and labeled it, "Mr. Barnett Taking a Class Picture."

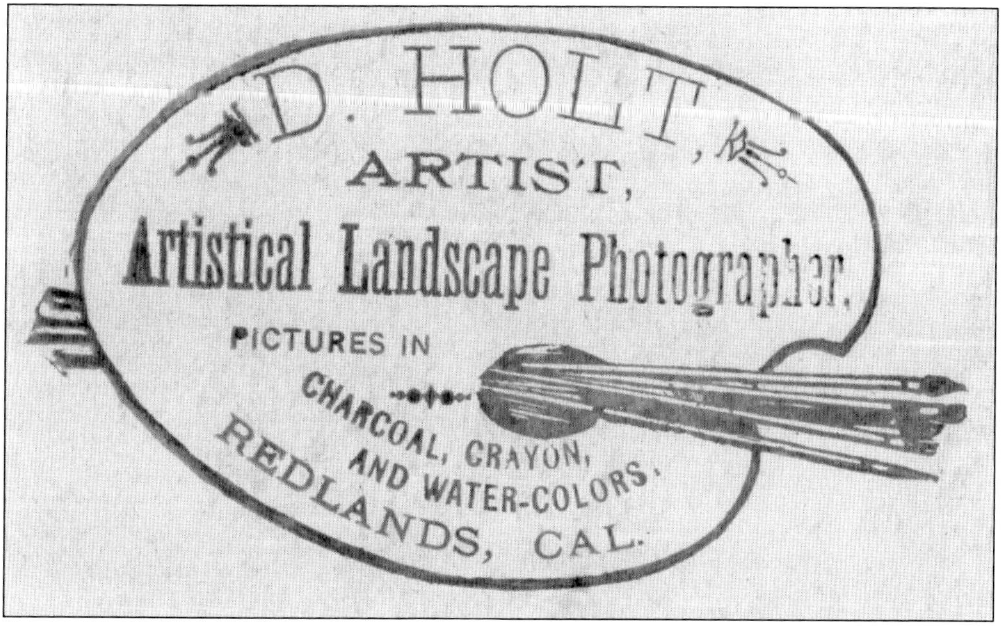

Most professional photographers used the term "photographer" as their occupation. However, the word "artist" was also sometimes used. Daniel Holt, probably the first professional photographer in Redlands, working from about 1886 to 1889, listed himself as an artist in many sources. Luckily, several of his photographs bear a stamped imprint that describes him as a photographer as well as an artist.

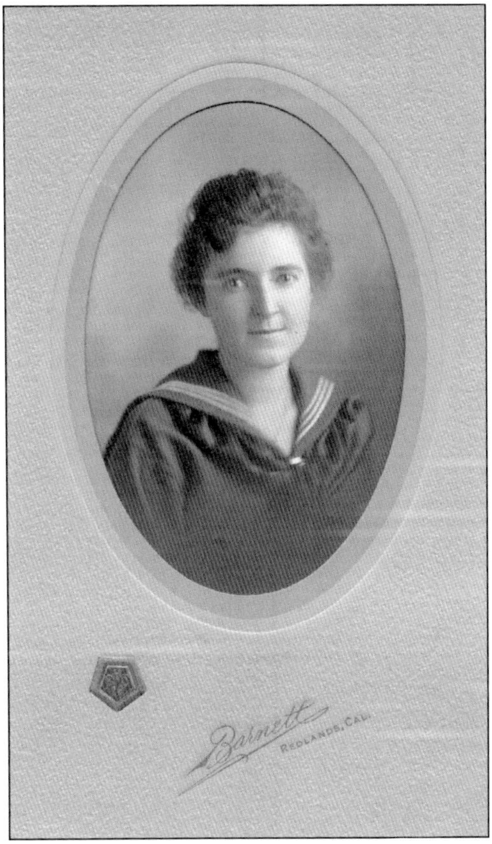

Graduating seniors have traditionally had their portrait taken by a professional photographer. Their graduation pictures may have the year embossed or printed on them, including this Charles Barnett photograph of Vera Hees, who graduated from Redlands High School in 1919. (Photographer: Charles O. Barnett.)

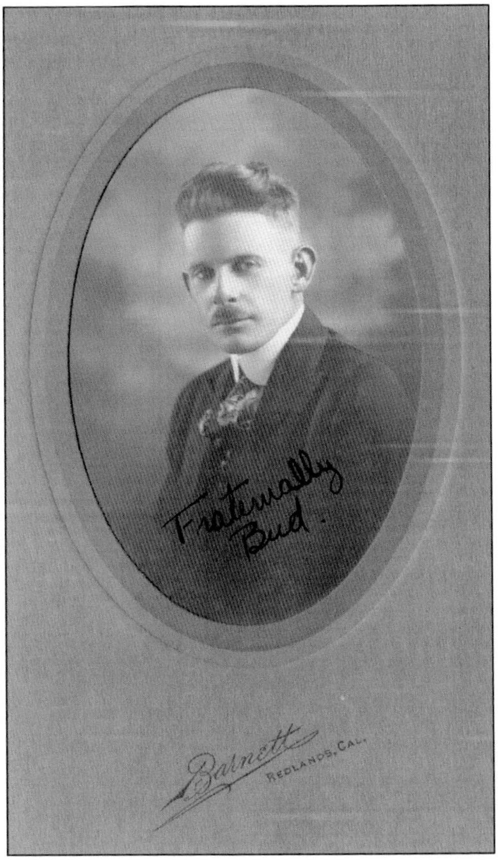

Professional photographers not only found jobs taking images of graduating seniors in universities, they also photographed members of campus groups. Jacob Walker Abbey graduated from the University of Redlands in 1921, but this photograph of him remained unidentified until it was matched to one in the 1920 annual under the Kappa Sigma Sigma fraternity. He went on to be a civil engineer with the county surveyor's department in San Bernardino. (Photographer: Charles O. Barnett.)

Newspaper advertisements and articles discussed such things as arrivals and departures of photographers. One local Redlands newspaper, *The Citrograph*, noted that Rudolph Philippi opened a new photography studio in January 1890 and included this advertisement. Philippi named his studio after his home state of Illinois. The term "give me a call" meant to visit in person, not by telephone, as no number is given and few businesses had telephones in 1890.

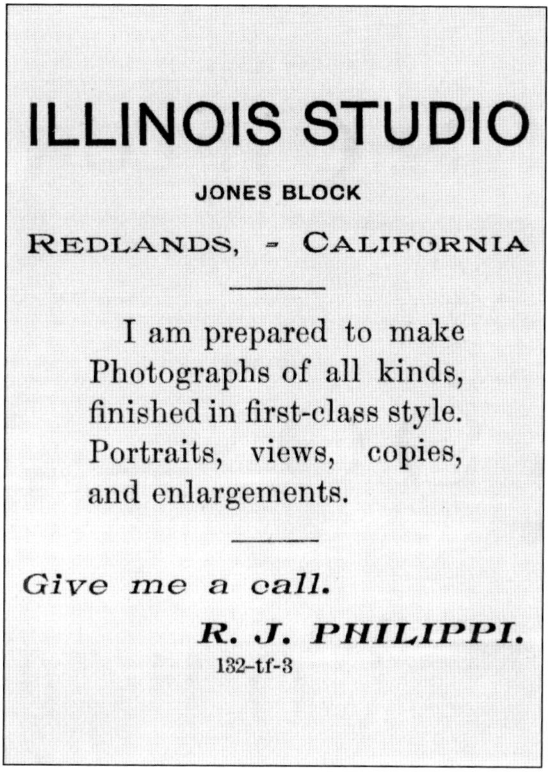

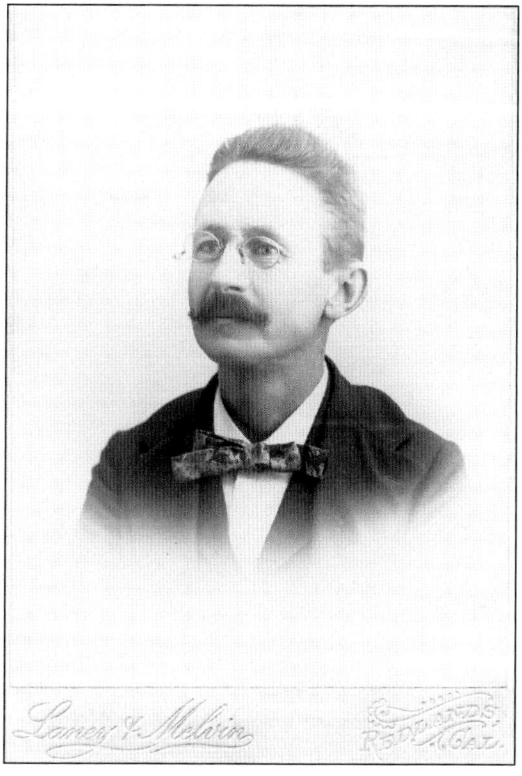

Local groups often produced illustrated publications extolling the virtues of the community. *Illustrated Redlands*, an 1897 publication, attributed most of its images to the partnership of Grace Laney and Charles Melvin, but did not place their names with any photographs. This image of Albert Brainerd, an early Redlands dentist, was found mounted on their cardstock and has been matched to a photograph in *Illustrated Redlands*, now crediting them with the portrait in the book. (Photographers: Grace E. Laney and Charles C. Melvin.)

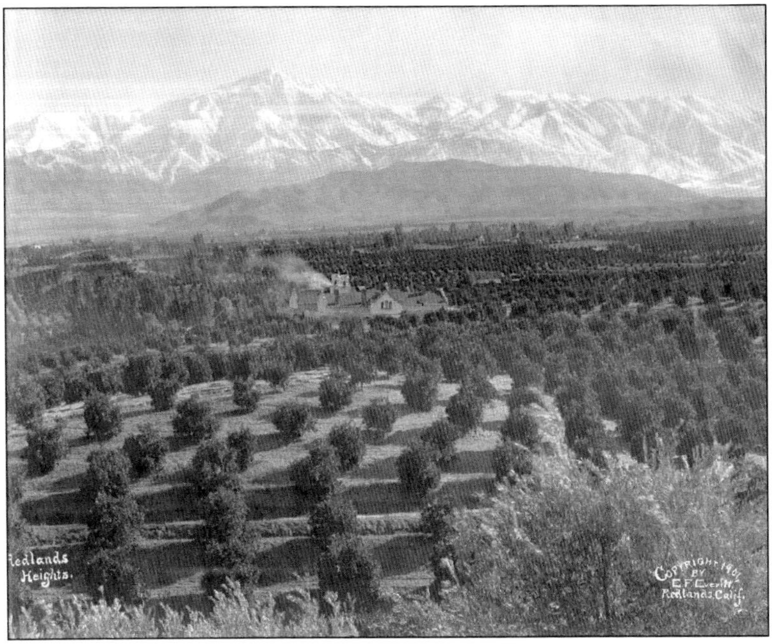

Some photographers wrote their name in black on negatives so that, when printed, the data appeared white on the image. Elias Everitt, a longtime Redlands photographer who worked from about 1897 to 1923, commonly used this technique, including on this 1901 shot of the just-built Burrage mansion in Redlands. (Photographer: Elias F. Everitt.)

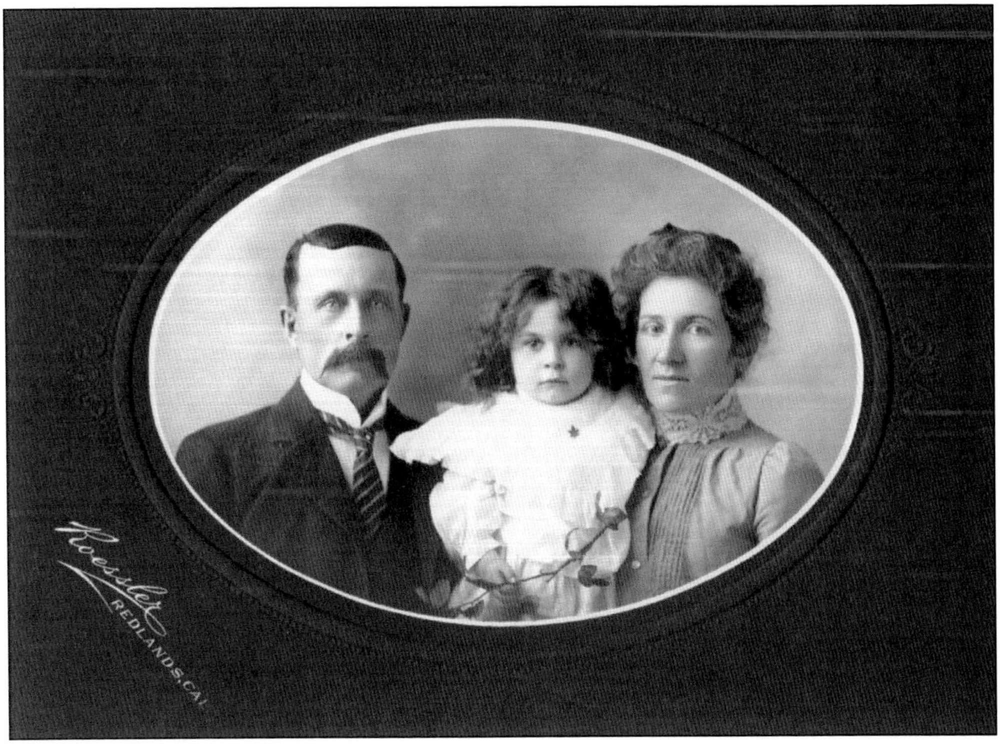

Many photographers printed their name and address directly on the front of the cardstock with the photograph mounted on the same side, making it hard for the viewer to miss. Edward Roessler took this photograph of the Heron family during his time in Redlands, from about 1900 to 1904. (Photographer: Edward E. Roessler.)

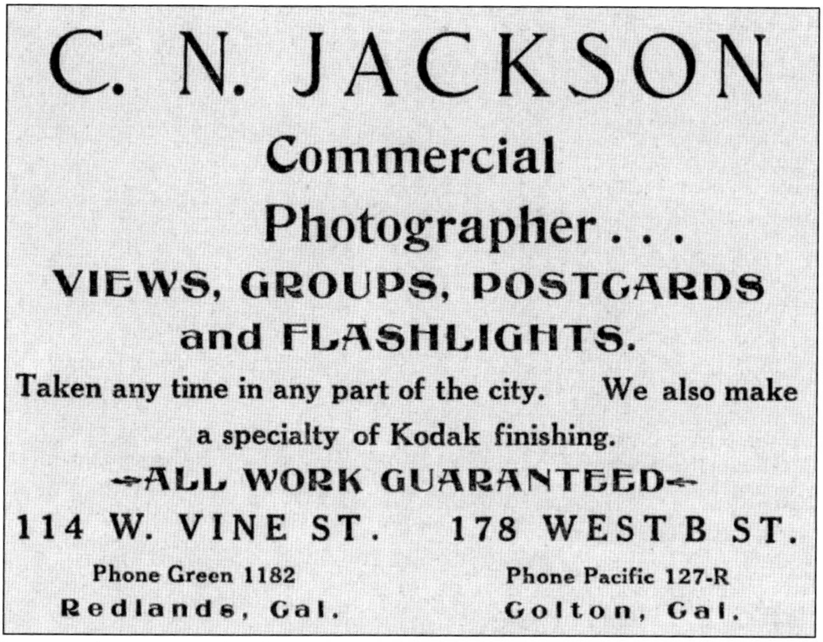

Other photographers printed information on the back of images, sometimes with extensive advertising data. Many Clarence N. Jackson photographs possess an informative advertisement on the back. He worked in Redlands from about 1912 to 1917, giving a date range to this photograph. His comment about "flashlights" did not mean the flashlights seen today or camera flash bulbs, which were not yet in use, but may have related to flash powder. "Kodak finishing" referred to developing film for amateur photographers.

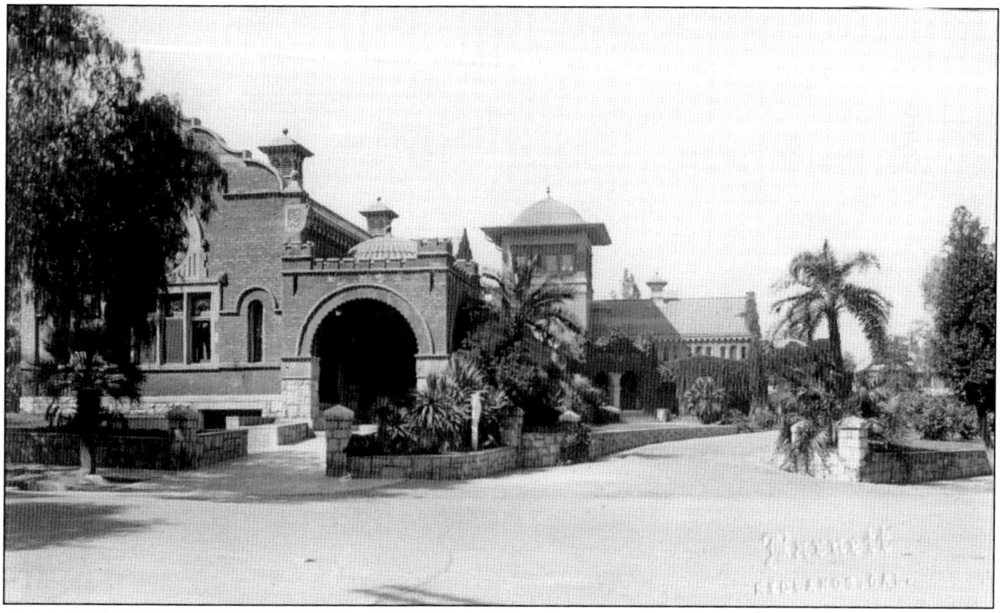

Photographers also sometimes embossed their name into an image. The embossing was often only visible by moving the photograph in the light to find the writing. This was a more subtle form of advertising, but it still showed the viewer who had taken it. Charles Barnett commonly used this method, as seen in this view of the A.K. Smiley Public Library from about 1914. (Photographer: Charles O. Barnett.)

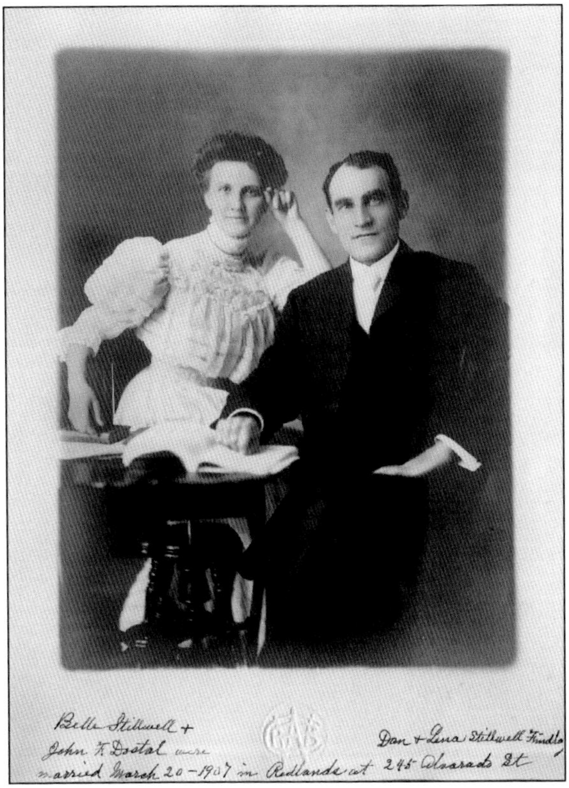

One photographer left a mystery as to his or her identity. This photograph (left) of Belle and John Dostal of Redlands shows three letters printed on top of each other at center bottom on the cardstock, "WCB," but no photographer's name. John Dostal was a prominent hardware dealer in town and this photograph was taken near the time of his marriage to Belle Stillwell, in March 1907. Only one photographer's name from between 1880 and 1920 matches these initials: William C. Butman, who worked in Redlands from about 1906 to 1911. It was confirmed that this in fact was a Butman photograph when a wedding photograph of Sumner and Alberta Grover (below) was found mounted in a folder with the front showing the same initials as the Dostal photograph, but with the cardstock of the attached photograph embossed with "Butman Redlands, California." (Photographer: William C. Butman.)

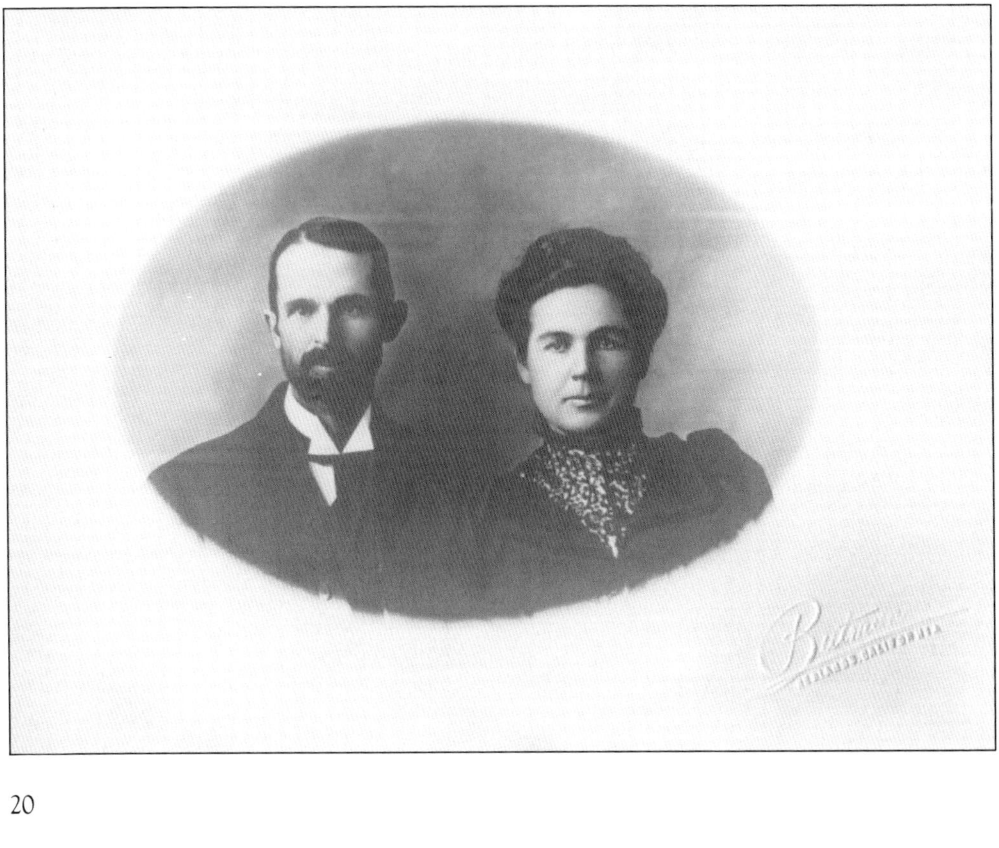

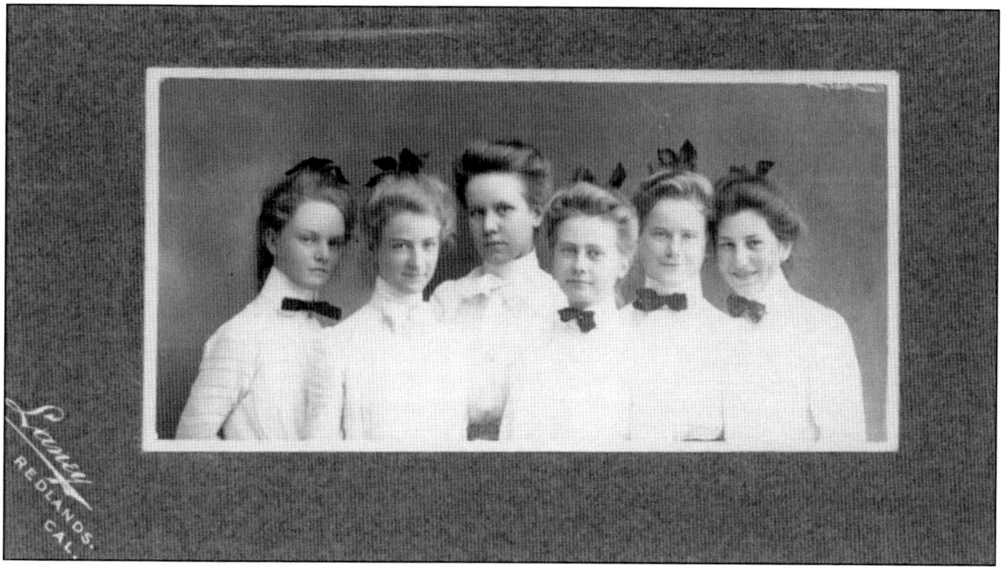

Identifying female professional photographers can sometimes be a challenge if only the last name is used on a photograph, which was a common practice. Several photographs are marked "Laney," including this photograph of a group of unidentified young ladies, or "Laney and Melvin," but was Laney a man or a woman? The charming young women above wear the Gibson Girl hairstyles and high collars that were fashionable around 1900. The advertisement below from the 1900 Redlands city directory solved this problem. "Laney" referred to Grace E. Laney, who was one of only two female professional photographers identified in Redlands between 1880 and 1920. She worked first with a partner, her brother-in-law Charles Melvin, from November 1896 to 1899, and then worked solo until leaving Redlands about 1904. (Photographer: Grace E. Laney.)

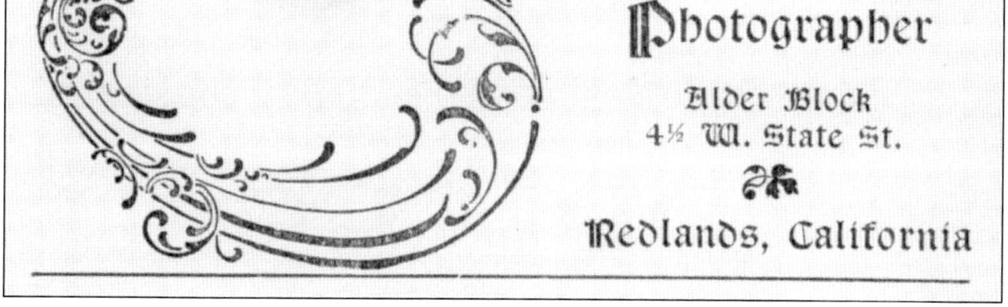

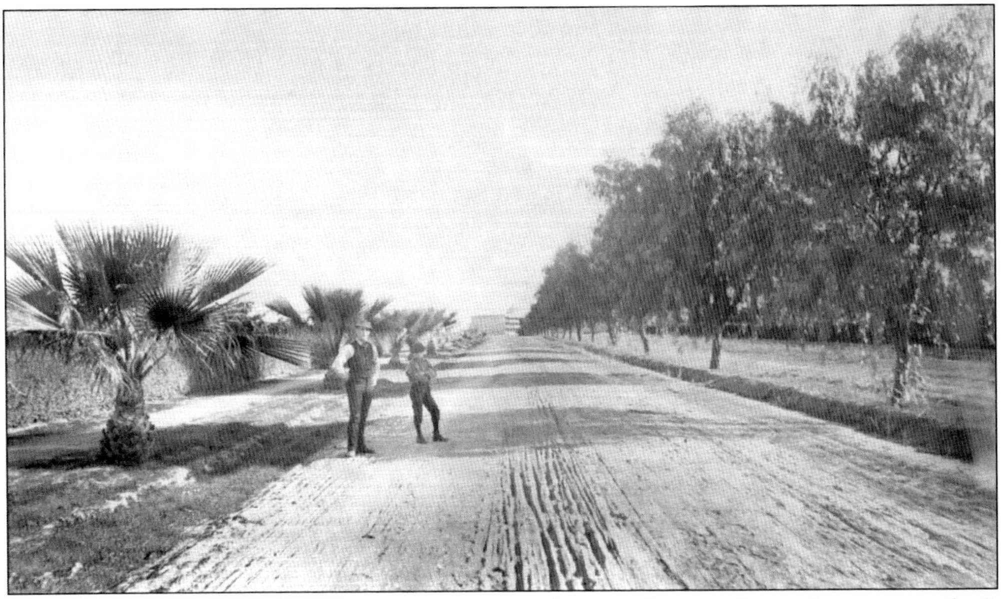

In the late 1800s and early 1900s, it was common for one photographer to buy out another's business, including their negatives. This allowed customers to return for prints, but also meant that photographs might be mounted on cardstock of the later photographer, obscuring identification of the original photographer and the date the image was taken. Daniel Holt, who was active from about 1886 to 1889, produced a photograph of Brookside Avenue (above) in Redlands that is identical to one on which Rudolph Philippi's name appears (below). Since Philippi worked from January 1890 to 1897, he probably bought some of Holt's negatives, including the one that created these images. The large three-story brick building in the distance was the Windsor Hotel, located on the northeast corner of Fourth and State Streets, which opened for business in March 1888. (Photographer: Daniel Holt.)

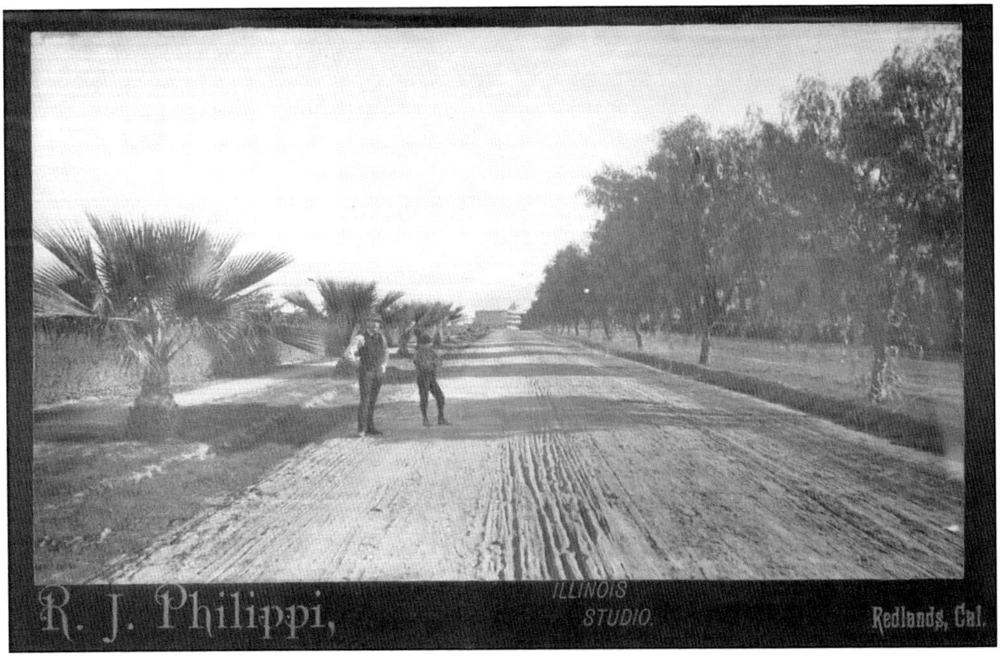

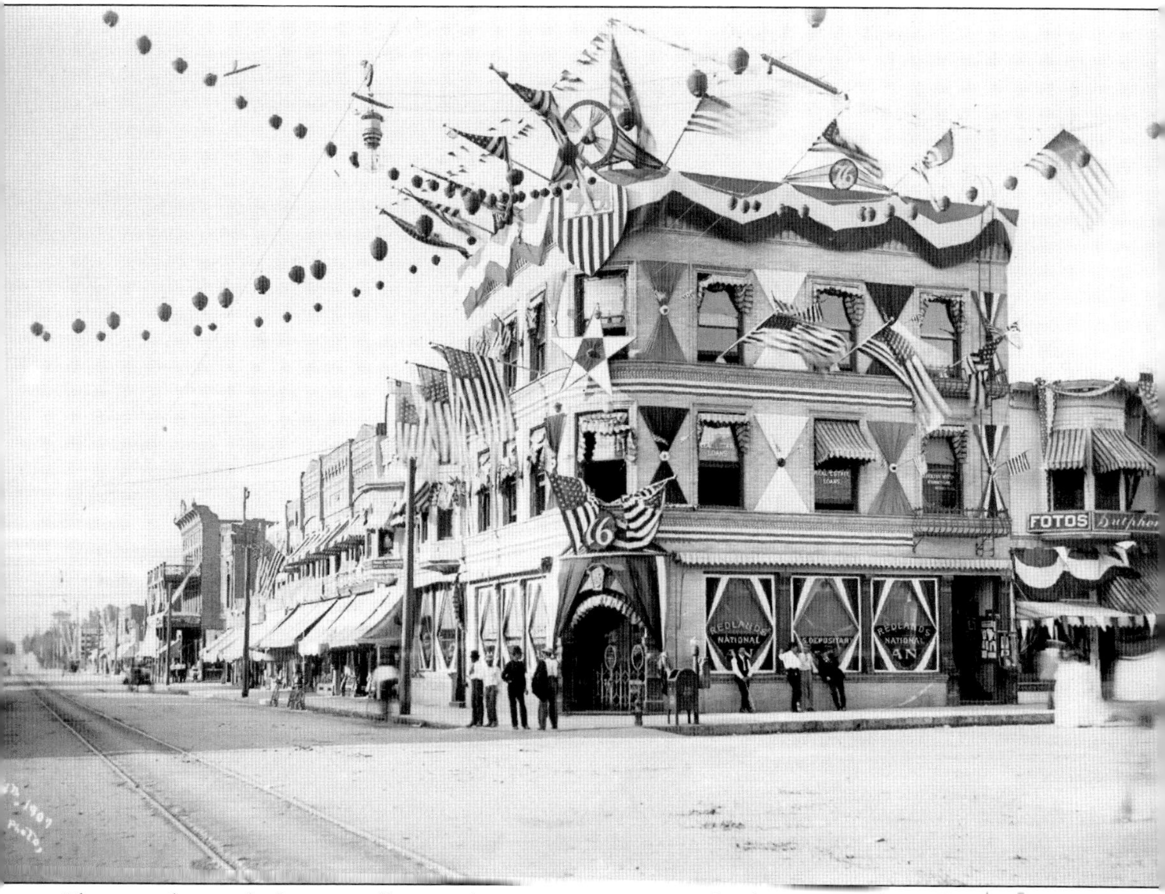

Photographic studio buying, selling, and swapping went on at a brisk pace in early Redlands. One particular studio, above a bank at 3 ½ East State Street, changed hands over and over from 1900 to 1929. Edward Roessler worked there from about 1900 to 1904, followed by Perry Sutphen from 1904 to 1907. William C. Butman was the next occupant, from 1907 through 1911, then Thomas Shuford from 1912 to 1914, and finally, Guy Fairbanks from 1914 until 1929, when the building was torn down. Several early photographs show the name of the photographer underneath the far right upstairs bay windows of this studio, including in this image taken by Elias Everitt on July 4, 1907, with Sutphen's name showing. One particularly interesting studio change was when Frank Fryett traded his Redlands studio on West State Street near Orange Street for John Young's studio in Grand Rapids, Michigan. Young moved to Redlands while Fryett went in the opposite direction to Grand Rapids. (Photographer: Elias F. Everitt.)

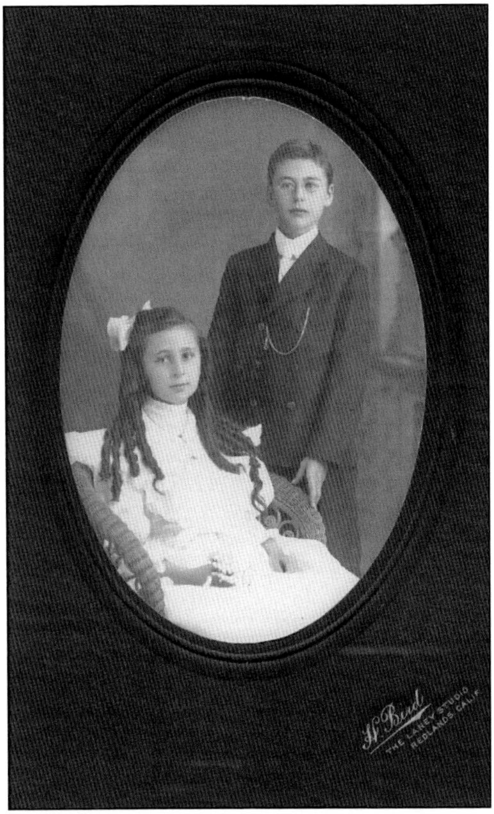

Studio names can also cause confusion. The wording "Laney Studio" appears on several photographs by Harry Bird, including this one of Ida and John Grates in October 1906. Bird bought out Grace Laney and, to advertise the new owner but keep the goodwill of those who knew Laney, he called it the Laney Studio for several years. (Photographer: Harry E. Bird.)

Mee's Studio belonged to two brothers at different times: Elbert Mee, who worked in Redlands from about 1912 to 1914, and his younger brother John Mee, who worked for Elbert around 1914 and then continued on into 1916 by himself. This full-page advertisement appeared in the 1913 Redlands High School annual, when Elbert Mee ran the studio.

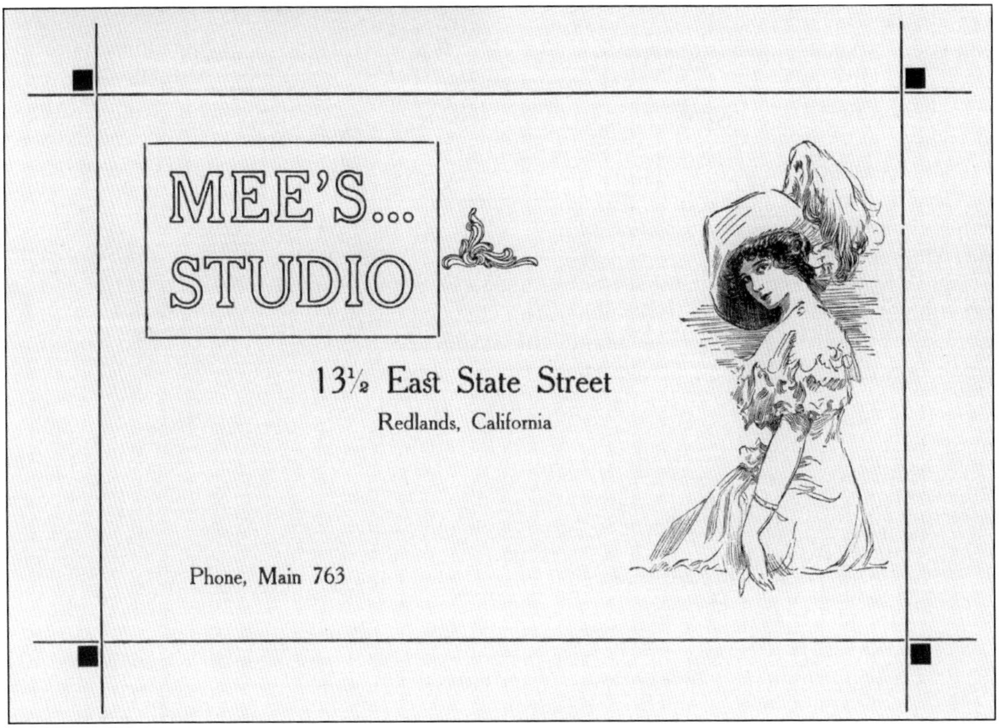

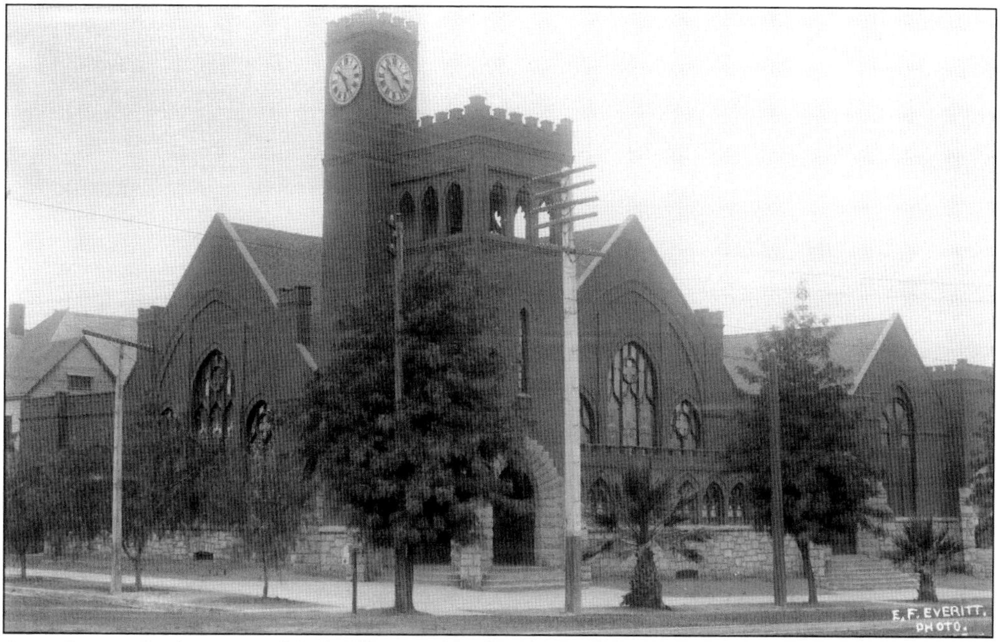

A sticker with the name "G.C. Thaxter Redlands, Calif" was found on the back of several photographs, seeming to indicate that Thaxter was a professional photographer. However, one of his photographs had two photographers' names. With Thaxter's sticker on the back and Elias Everitt's name in white on the front, who took this photograph of the First Congregational Church in Redlands shortly after 1900? (Photographer: Elias F. Everitt.)

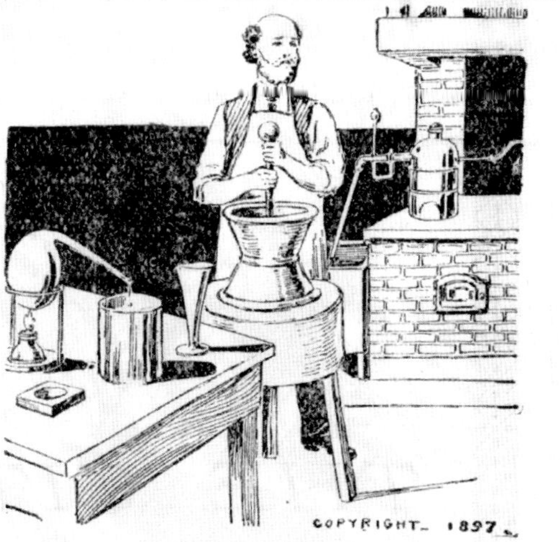
COPYRIGHT 1897

These are the Old Fashioned Tools of the Profession,
Ours are Up-to-Date,
And, by using only the Purest Chemicals and Extracts,
Make Our Prescriptions Reliable.

G. C. THAXTER,

Orange Street, - - REDLANDS.

George C. Thaxter was a druggist in Redlands from 1896 to about 1898, but not a photographer. Thaxter's drugstore advertisements appeared in local newspapers, including this one from the October 9, 1897, *Citrograph*. Perhaps Thaxter sold Everitt's prints in his drugstore with a sticker on the back to remind people where they had purchased the print. At least one 1896 advertisement for the photography team of Rogers & Herndon indicated that they sold images in local stores, including in drugstores.

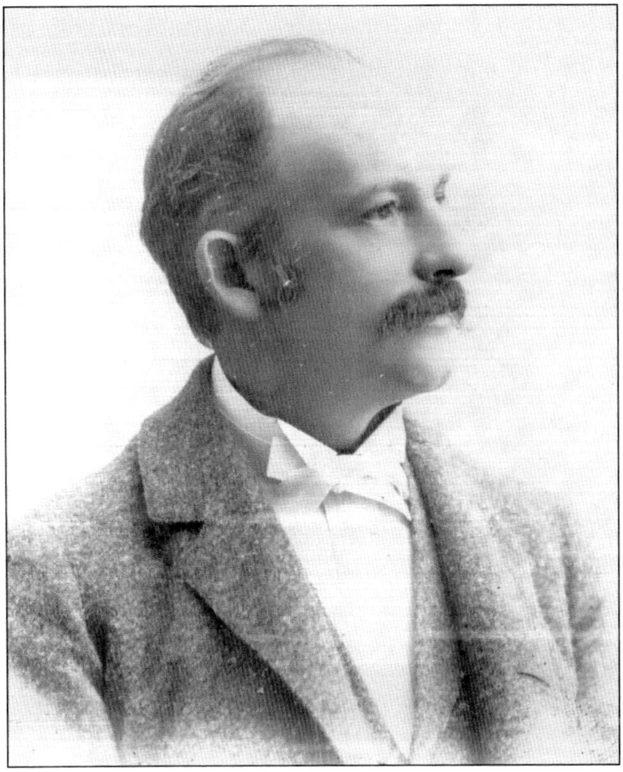

Rudolph Philippi, seen here in 1897, opened his studio in Redlands in January 1890. The local newspaper, *The Citrograph*, announced the imminent opening and commented on January 4, 1890, that "Mr. Philippi will have a very nice suite of rooms and announces his intention of fitting the rooms up in a style befitting the town with which he has cast his lot." (Unknown photographer.)

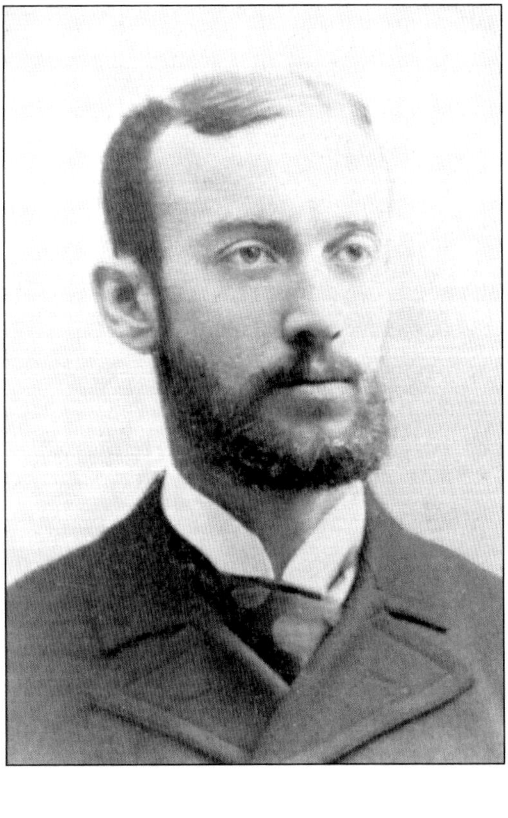

William J. Haskell worked in Redlands from about 1896 to 1900. According to the 1897 *Illustrated Redlands*, he bought out Rudolph Philippi, who then "retired" to orange growing. This image of Haskell dates from that same year. The same promotional publication also stated that he was "prepared to do the best of work in every line, making specialties of fine portraiture and views, the latter selling very rapidly, both to citizen and visitors." (Unknown photographer.)

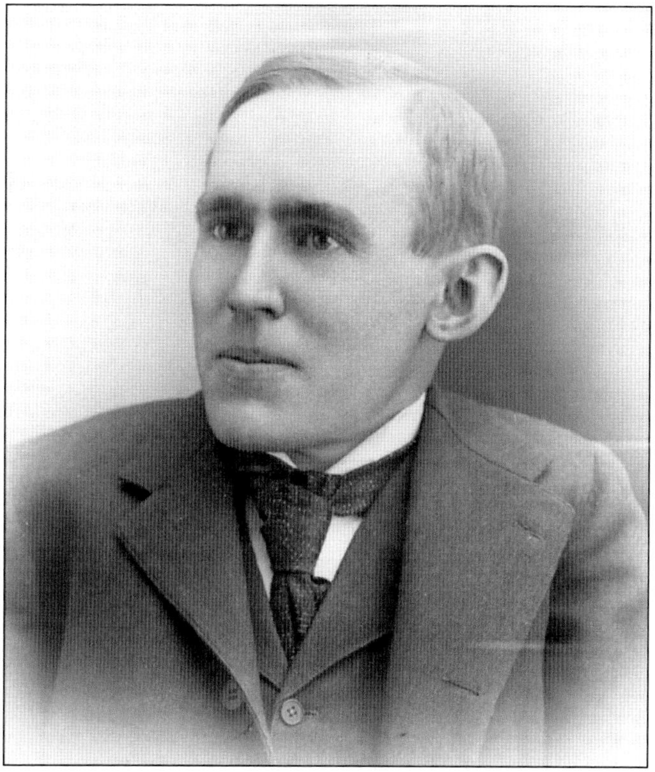

At right is Charles C. Melvin of Laney and Melvin. Below is Grace E. Laney, his sister-in-law and the other half of the photography partnership that lasted from November 1896 to 1899. Both had their portraits taken in 1897. After the partnership dissolved, she continued in Redlands until 1904. Only one other female professional photographer was in town between 1880 and 1920, Katherine Mudge, who worked from about 1914 to 1925. (Probable photographers: right, Grace E. Laney; below, Charles C. Melvin.)

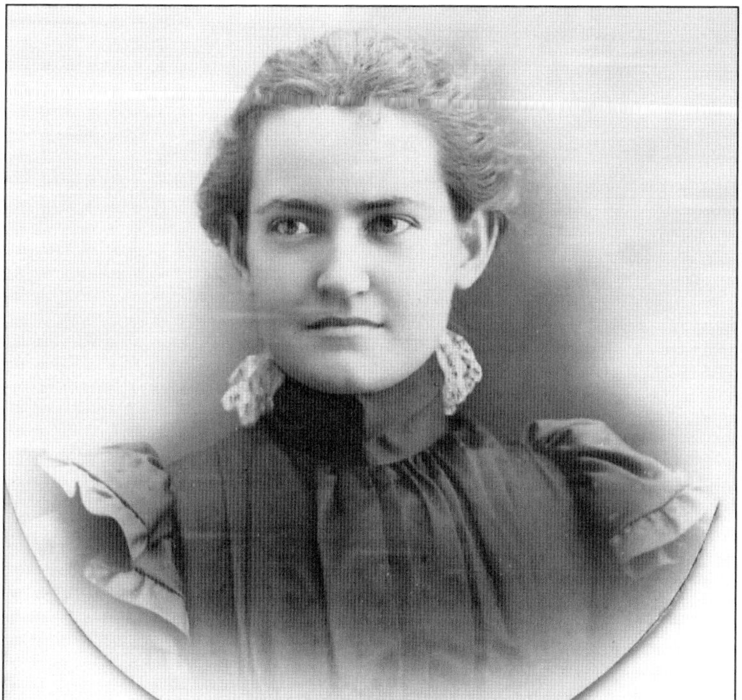

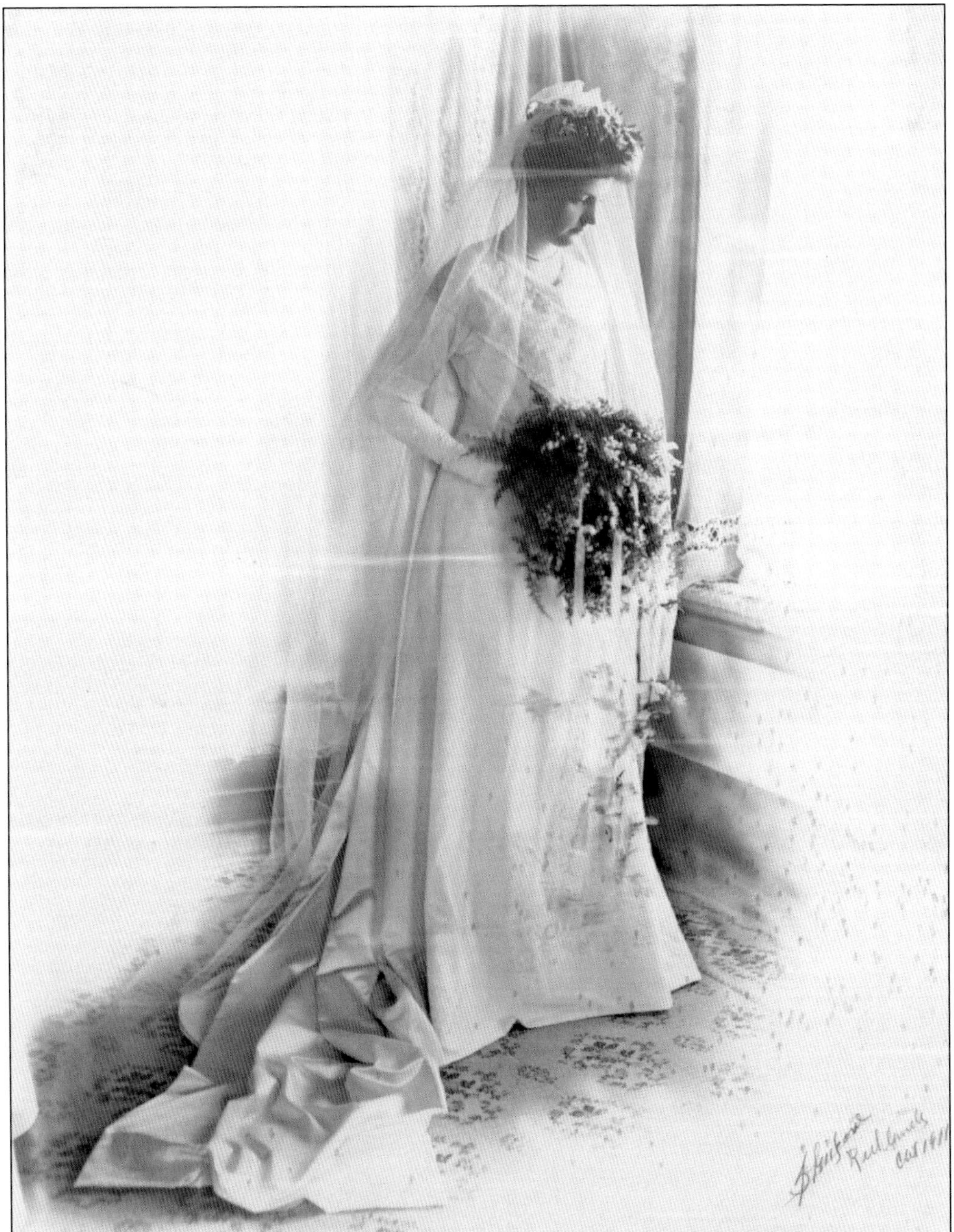

Images taken by Redlands professional photographers between 1880 and 1920 fill the remainder of this book. Their technical knowledge of aspects such as lighting and focus, along with their aesthetic sense, often resulted in stunning pictures, such as this photograph by Thomas Shuford of Irene Hornby, taken at the time of her wedding to Hugh Moran in 1911. Then as now, graduation and wedding portraits, along with photographs meant for marketing a business, provided a steady income for professional photographers. Photographs for sale to tourists, of homes and views of Redlands, were more popular in the past. Enjoy the quality and diversity of their work while learning more about Redlands and its history. (Photographer: Thomas R. Shuford.)

Two

"A Busy Business Center"

By the time of its incorporation as a town on November 26, 1888, Redlands had a growing population, a reliable source of water, close proximity to both the Southern Pacific Railroad and the Atchison, Topeka & Santa Fe Railway, and an abundance of rich, fertile soil. The new town offered limitless possibilities, of which early local boosters took full advantage. With the help of promotional pamphlets with descriptive titles like "Redlands: a perfect climate, the finest orange groves in the state, beautiful parks and fine residences," and "Redlands, California: the beauty spot of the Pacific coast," the town quickly developed into "a busy business center" with a variety of businesses to accompany the expanding populace.

Early issues of *The Citrograph* newspaper are replete with advertisements for available land, real estate agents, building materials, general merchandise stores, hotels, and businesses related to the promising citrus industry. Professional photographers filled a specific niche in the early years of town-building in Redlands, as scenic views were utilized to advertise the beauty and open land of the region and businesses commissioned commercial views to market their wares. These photographs offer viewers a glimpse of Redlands as it matured into a major citrus center, a retreat for wealthy Easterners, a health resort, a tourist center, and a place to settle and raise a family.

Like any other town, Redlands experienced a constant ebb and flow of businesses. Some, like Graham-Cope Commercial Company, found long-lived success, while others, like R.C. Shepherd Hardware, found success elusive. Such continual changeovers in business names and ownership help in dating commercial photography, with advertisements and listings in town directories and newspapers providing important clues. These resources also paint a picture of a town growing in size and scope, as new types of businesses reflect societal and technological advancements. Such changes are especially apparent in the transportation sector, where early livery stables and vendors of personal carriages and bicycles were replaced by motorcycle and automobile dealers within a short period of time just after 1900. By 1909, Redlands had seven automobile dealers and garages and one motorcycle dealer. It had also advanced from mule-drawn streetcars to electric streetcars. It is through the works of professional photographers that the town's evolution can be best understood.

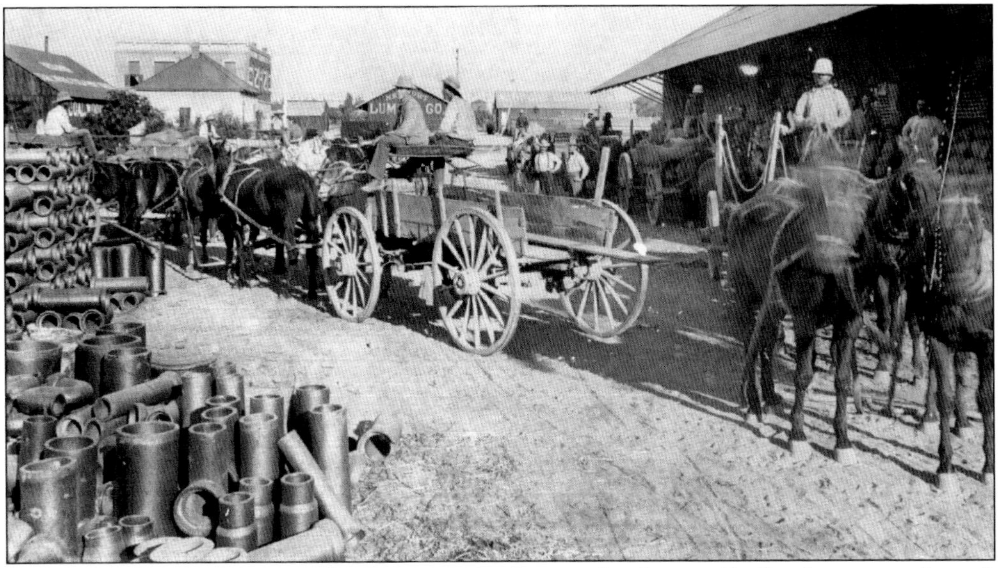

With the completion of Bear Valley Dam in 1884, the area that became Redlands was transformed. Originally dry and arid, the land became part of one of the world's top agriculturally producing regions around 1900. In 1890, the state of California produced $12 million worth of fruit, which would be the equivalent of approximately $300 million today. This 1891 image shows what was possibly the Haight Fruit Company packinghouse in Redlands, which produced both dried and fresh fruit. The company went on to ship citrus for the Redlands Orange Growers' Association. (Photographer: Rudolph J. Philippi.)

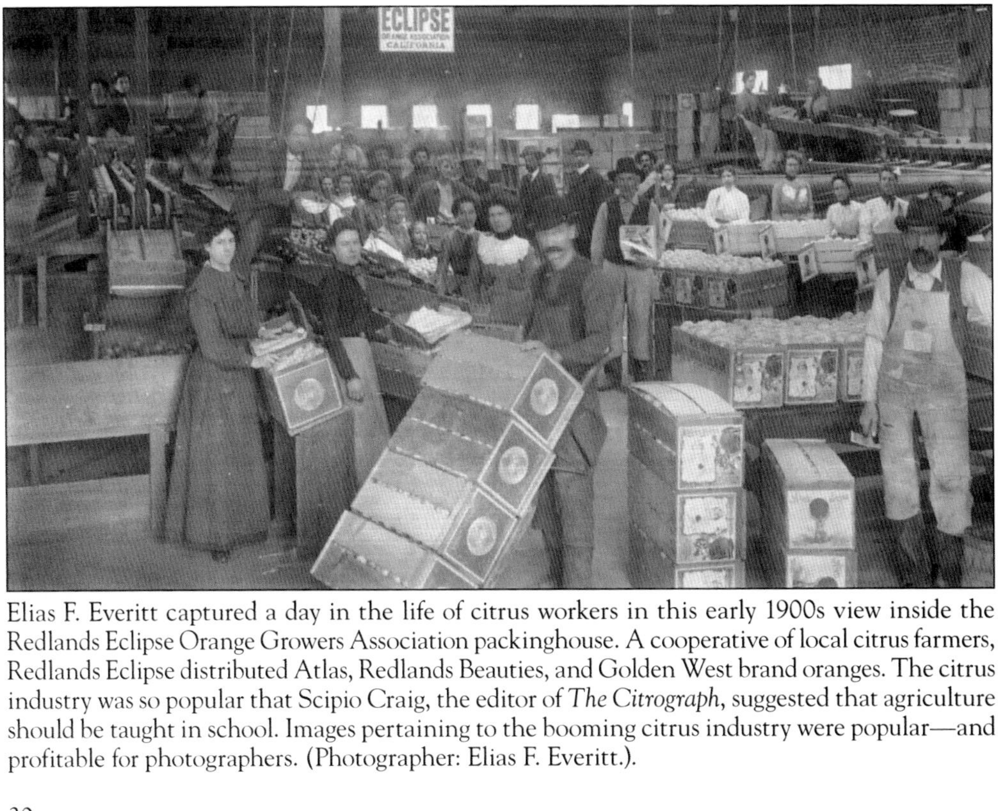

Elias F. Everitt captured a day in the life of citrus workers in this early 1900s view inside the Redlands Eclipse Orange Growers Association packinghouse. A cooperative of local citrus farmers, Redlands Eclipse distributed Atlas, Redlands Beauties, and Golden West brand oranges. The citrus industry was so popular that Scipio Craig, the editor of *The Citrograph*, suggested that agriculture should be taught in school. Images pertaining to the booming citrus industry were popular—and profitable for photographers. (Photographer: Elias F. Everitt.).

The expansion of the local transportation system allowed Redlands' citrus industry to bloom. Horse-drawn wagons transported goods locally, but it was the railroad that made the industry truly successful. The advent of ice-refrigerated cars, such as those utilized by the Pacific Fruit Express (PFE), allowed local growers to ship produce across the country. The PFE was operated by the Southern Pacific and Union Pacific railroads and began shipping produce in 1907, one year before this image of Redlands Mutual Orange Company was taken. (Photographer: Elias F. Everitt.).

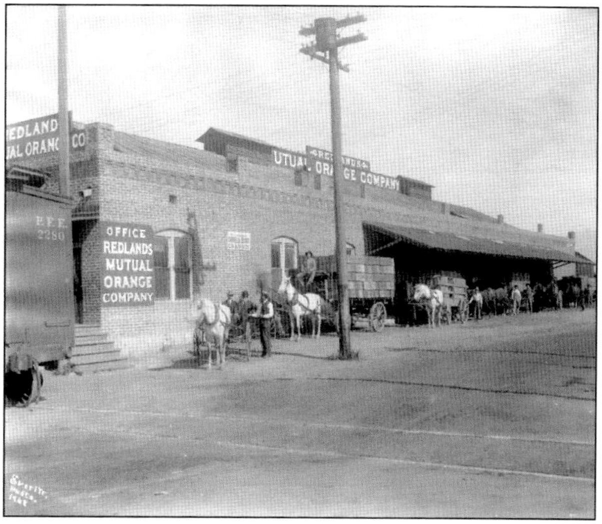

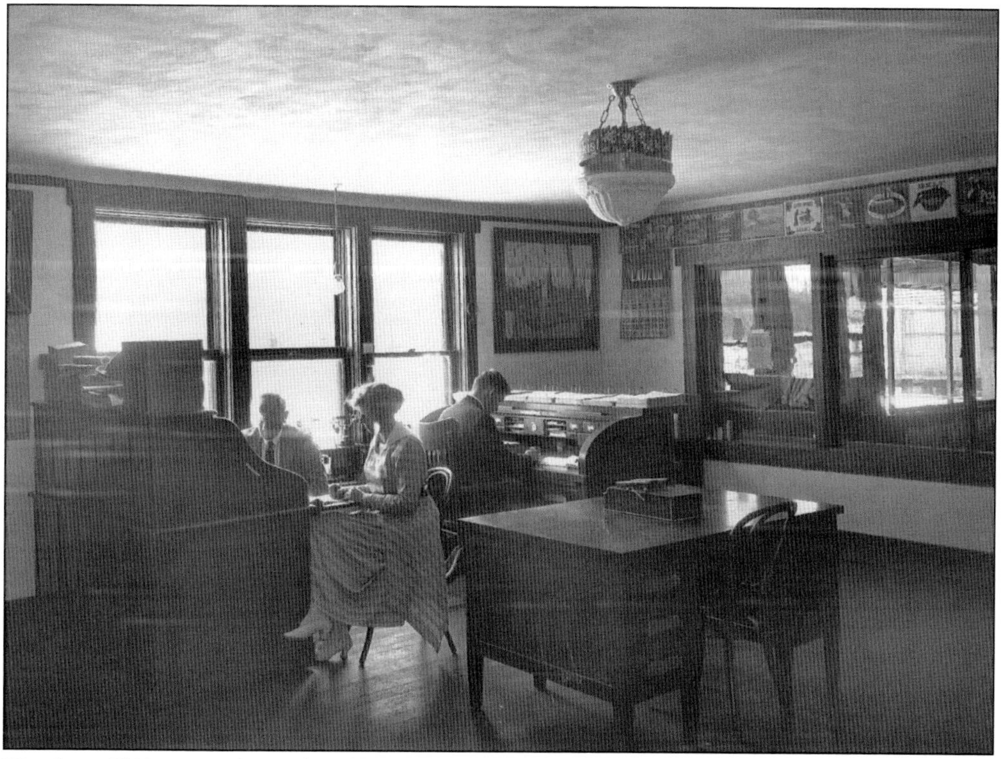

This June 1919 image shows the office of the Gold Buckle Association of East Highlands. Owned by Redlands resident James S. Edwards, the Gold Buckle Association was one of the most well-known and successful orange growers and packinghouses in the region. In a special 1908 "Progress Edition" of the *Redlands Daily Review*, it was reported that the company was using the most up-to-date technology in their packinghouse, including conveyor belts, cold storage for their fruit before shipment, and diligent fire safety guidelines. (Photographer: Elias F. Everitt.)

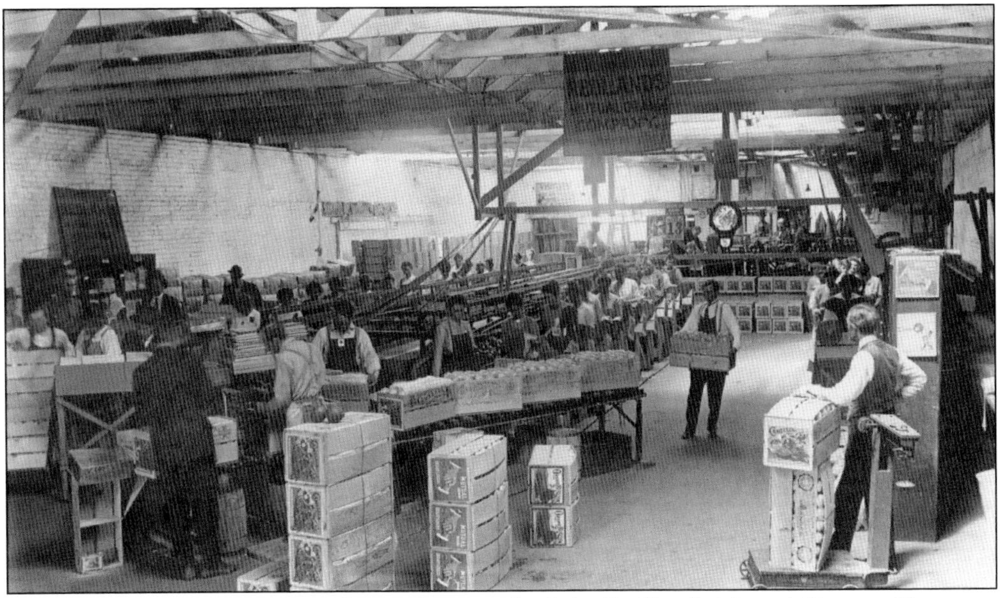

By 1915, when Clarence N. Jackson photographed the Redlands Mutual Orange Company packinghouse, citrus was one of the top agricultural commodities in California. Extending from Pasadena to Redlands, the Southern California citrus belt fell into a sharp decline after World War II, as the state's population increased and citrus groves were replaced by new communities. Since the 1980s, Redlands has fought to preserve its remaining citrus groves. (Photographer: Clarence N. Jackson.)

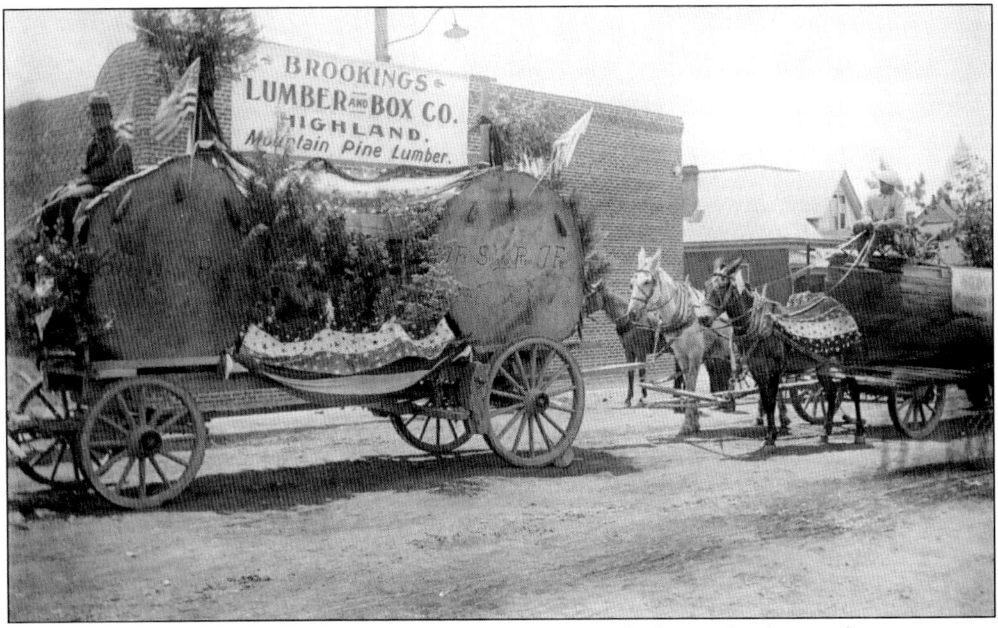

Around 1900, the Brookings Lumber and Box Company was the largest lumber producer operating in the San Bernardino Mountains. By 1911, the majority of the timber logged by Brookings was used to manufacture citrus crates for growers in Redlands and the surrounding area. Photographing special events, such as this entry into the Redlands Fourth of July parade in 1900, was lucrative for photographers. (Photographer: Elias F. Everitt.)

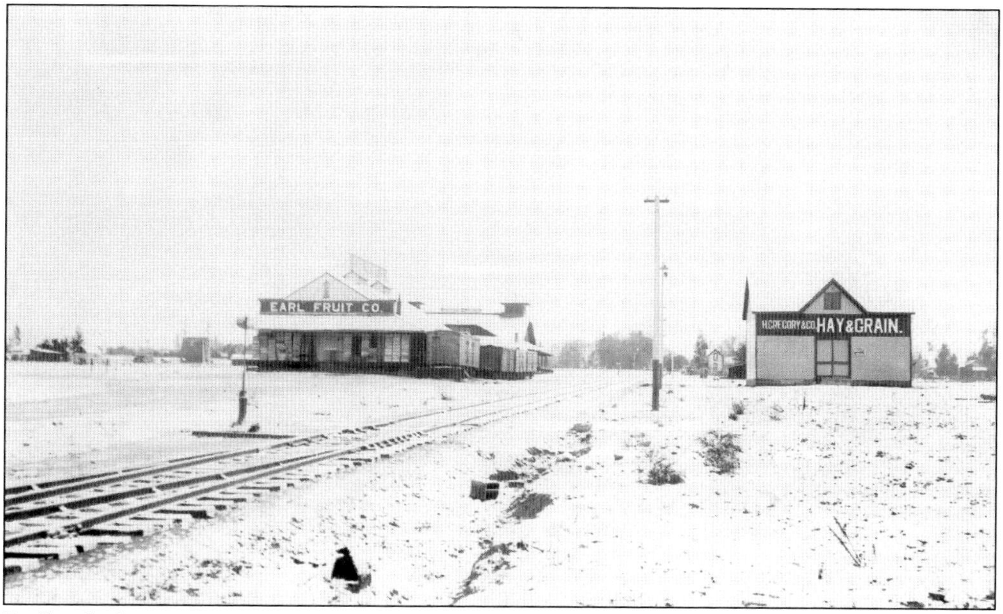

Redlands does experience snowfall on occasion, including in the 1896 scene above, captured by the yearlong photography partnership of Frederick H. Rogers and Percy Herndon. Seen in the image are the Earl Fruit Company, a national distributor that opened its Redlands office in 1889, and Harry Gregory's grain and hay business, which was established in Redlands in 1894. The photograph and the 1896 advertisement below show H. Gregory at its original location, on Orange Street near the Santa Fe Railway track, an ideal place for this business. (Photographers: Frederick H. Rogers and Percy Herndon.)

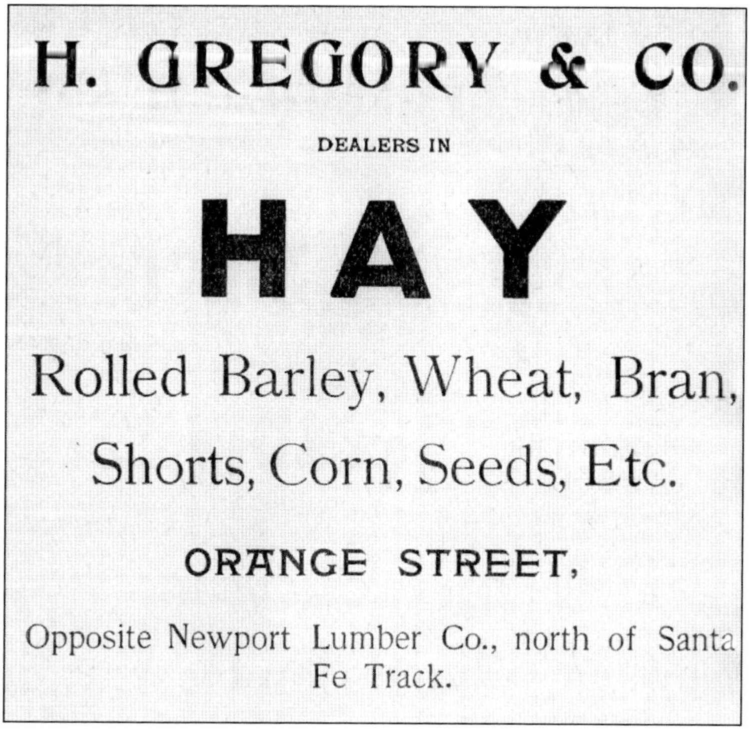

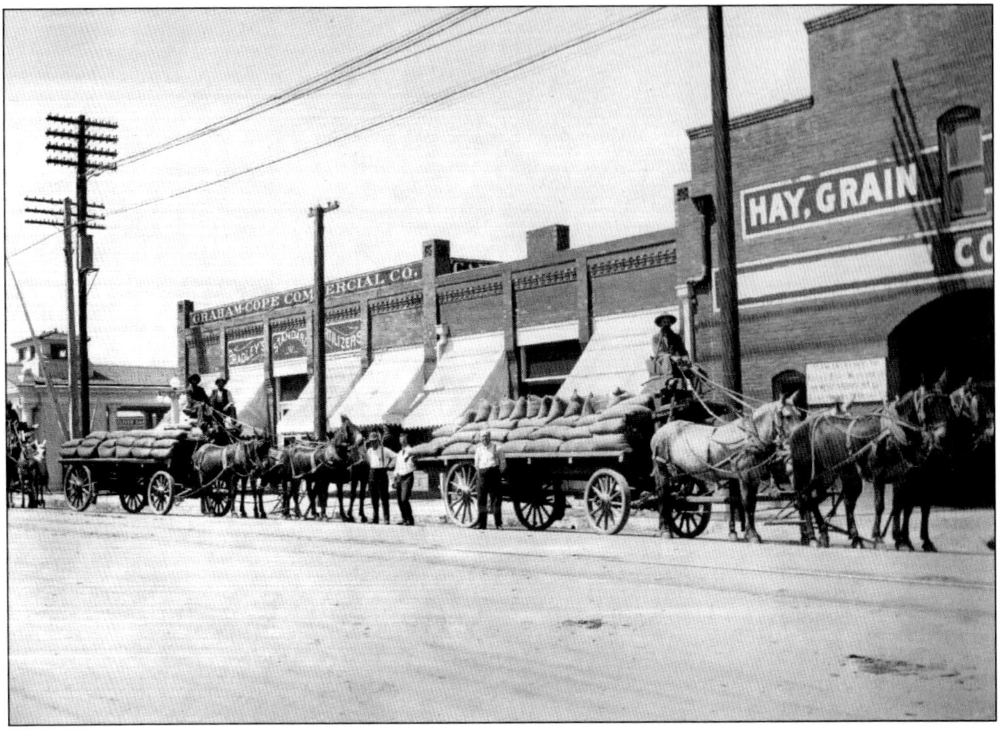

Photographs of businesses served as invaluable promotional tools. Showing the Santa Fe Railway station on the left, wagons full of merchandise, and signs for hay, grain and fertilizer, the photograph above from around 1910 of the Graham-Cope Commercial Company building does almost as good a job at advertising the company as their advertisement (below) does. Operating at the height of the citrus boom, Graham-Cope Commercial Company offered products that catered to the needs of local growers. The company became the E.M. Cope Commercial Company in 1911 and served Redlands until around 1940. (Photographer: Elias F. Everitt.)

Graham - Cope Commercial Co.

Carriages, Wagons, Harness,
Hardware, Farm Implements,
Hay, Grain, Coal, Wood.

Bradley's Fertilizers

ORANGE STREET AND SANTA FE RAILROAD

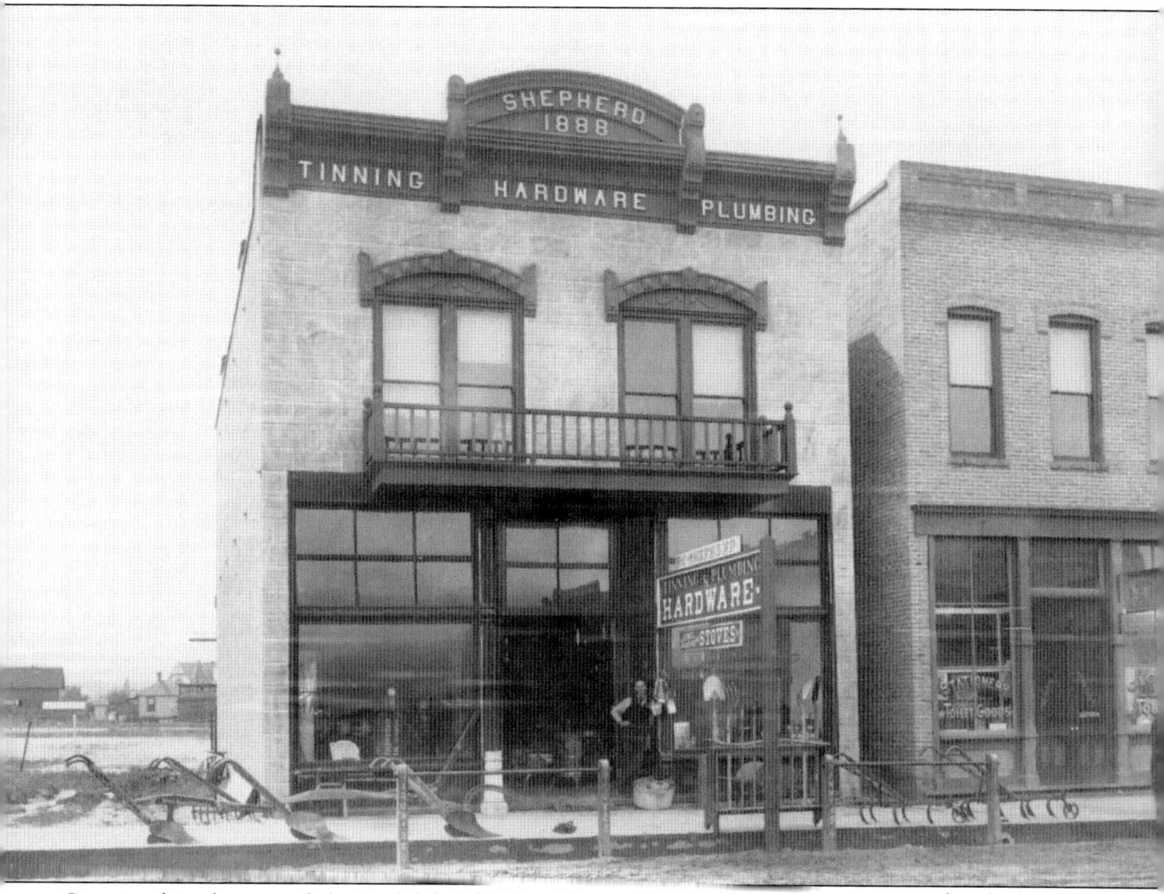

Seen in this photograph by Rudolph J. Philippi (one of Redlands' earliest photographers), R.C. Shepherd's short-lived tinning, plumbing, and hardware store opened more than a year before the town's incorporation. After selling the business in March 1890, Shepherd went on to find success as a machinist and the inventor of several items, including a water motor used for deep-well pumping. Philippi worked in Redlands from January 1890 until 1897, when he became an orange grower. Given the date that Shepherd's store closed, this may be one of Philippi's earliest photographs of Redlands. (Photographer: Rudolph J. Philippi.)

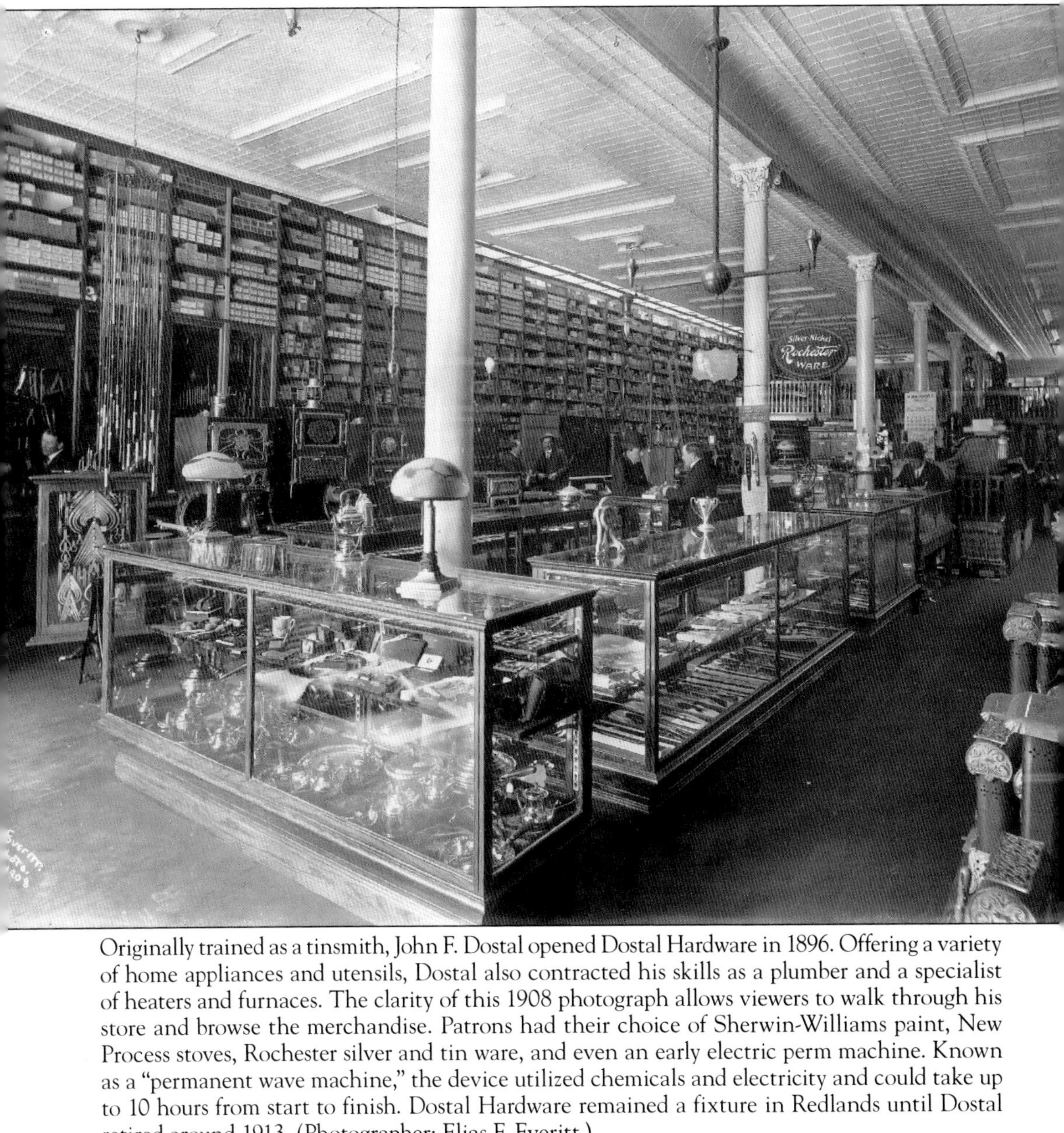

Originally trained as a tinsmith, John F. Dostal opened Dostal Hardware in 1896. Offering a variety of home appliances and utensils, Dostal also contracted his skills as a plumber and a specialist of heaters and furnaces. The clarity of this 1908 photograph allows viewers to walk through his store and browse the merchandise. Patrons had their choice of Sherwin-Williams paint, New Process stoves, Rochester silver and tin ware, and even an early electric perm machine. Known as a "permanent wave machine," the device utilized chemicals and electricity and could take up to 10 hours from start to finish. Dostal Hardware remained a fixture in Redlands until Dostal retired around 1913. (Photographer: Elias F. Everitt.)

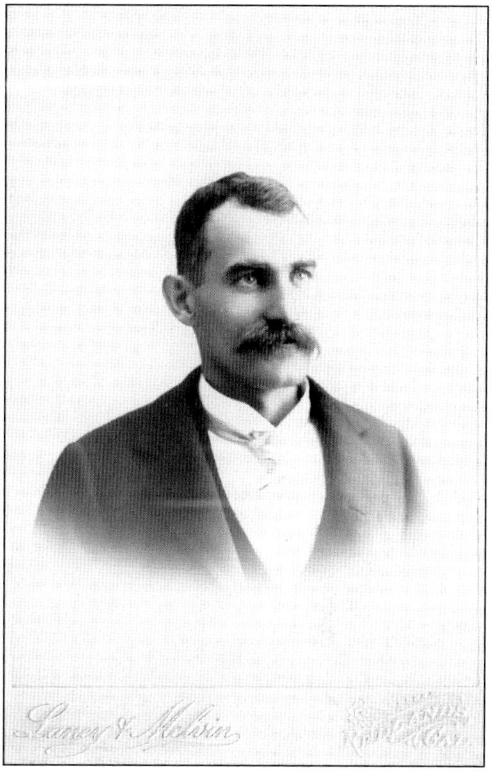

Illustrated Redlands, a promotional booklet published by the *Redlands Daily Facts* newspaper in 1897, included portraits by the studio of Grace E. Laney and Charles C. Melvin. The image at right of John F. Dostal was featured in the book along with biographical information about Dostal and his business. Although Dostal was included in the booklet, he did not advertise in the *Facts*, instead choosing to advertise in *The Citrograph* and the Redlands city directory, where the 1896 advertisement below was placed. (Photographers: Grace E. Laney and Charles C. Melvin.)

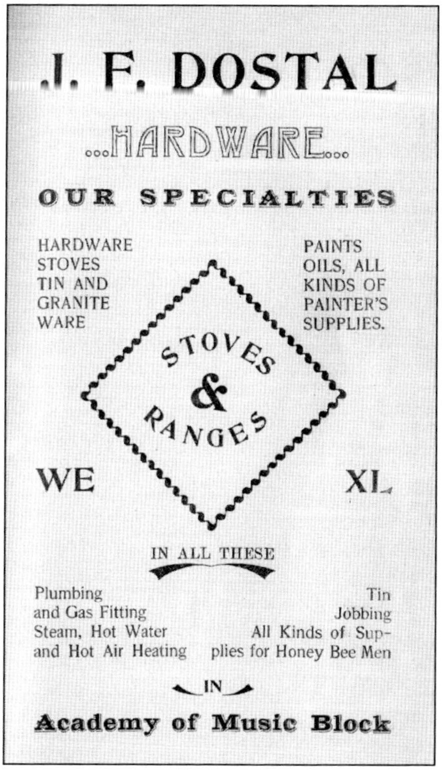

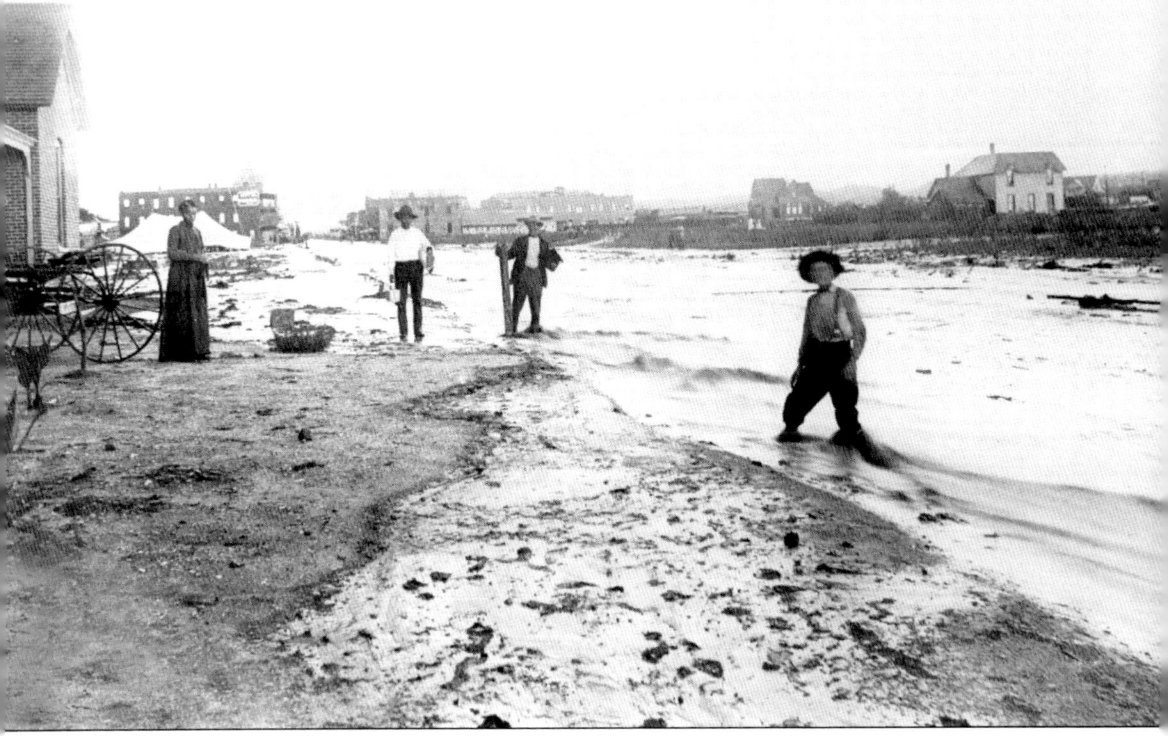

Redlands experienced heavy rainfall throughout 1891, culminating in a destructive flood on August 11 that was reported to have left 10 feet of water in some areas. Residents closest to the Mill Creek *zanja*, a well-known local irrigation canal, including one-time Redlands photographer Daniel Holt, experienced the brunt of the damage, while streets and businesses at the center of town became passageways for the water. Within an hour, the waters had subsided and residents and business owners were left with the cleanup, as this image of State Street by Joseph F. Hammond shows so vividly. Another flood in September led to many proposed changes, including the creation of a storm water commission and a storm water ditch. In the aftermath, local Native Americans were hired to help with cleanup. Little is known about Hammond, and this is the only image attributed to him that has been located in the archives of the A.K. Smiley Public Library to date. (Photographer: Joseph F. Hammond.)

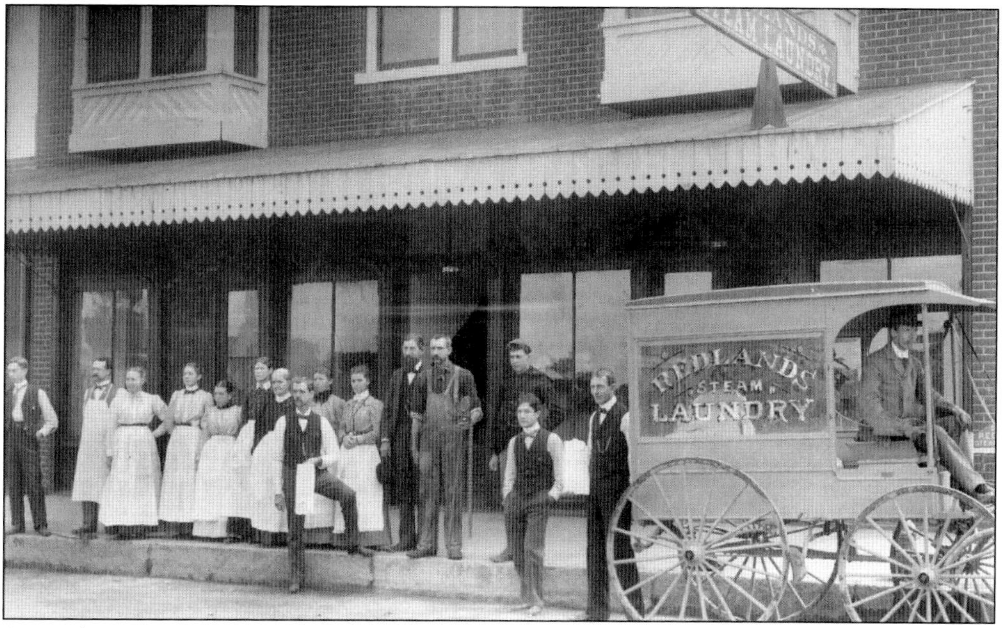

Around 1900, approximately 95 percent of laundry workers in the United States were women, the majority of whom worked in private homes. From this c. 1900 photograph of the Redlands Steam Laundry, it would appear that Redlands fit into the national statistics. Images such as this offer an interesting view into gender and labor relations at that time. (Photographer: Elias F. Everitt.)

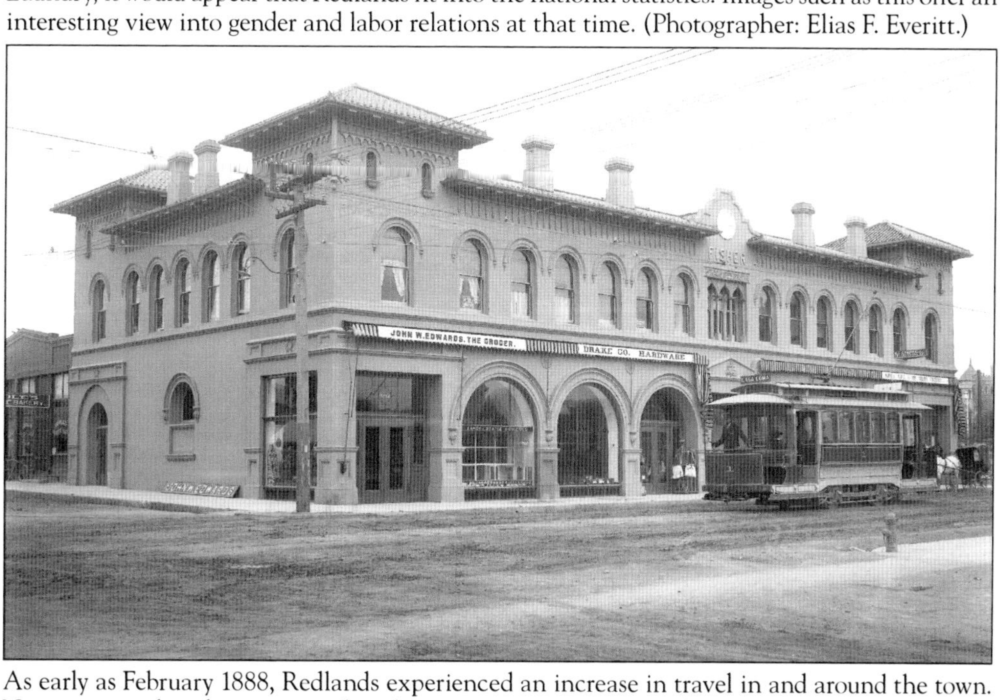

As early as February 1888, Redlands experienced an increase in travel in and around the town. New streets and roads were created, and existing streets were repaved with frequency. Residents had the convenience of the Redlands Street Railway Company beginning in May 1889, a mule-drawn car service that cost 5¢ per ride. The company electrified in late 1899 and quickly saw a need for expansion. Seen here in 1900, the Orange Street line was one of the company's original routes and eventually extended from State Street to Lugonia Avenue. (Photographer: Elias F. Everitt.)

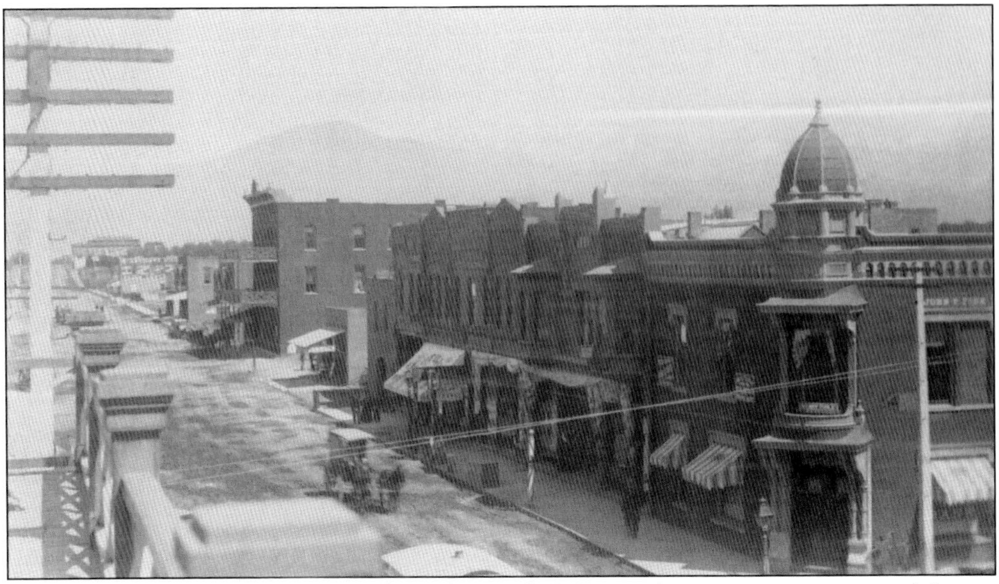

The photograph above, taken around 1895 by Frank C. Fryett, shows a growing town with horse-drawn carriages, the dominant mode of transportation of the day, and electrical and streetcar wires throughout. Looking north on Orange Street from State Street, the image shows several businesses, including the real estate offices of John P. Fisk and P.B. Fussell, the dental office of Dr. E. Bedford, the office of physician Dr. Christopher Sanborn, Meserve's Clothing House, and the Baker House Hotel. One of Redlands' first clothing stores, Meserve's served the community for 20 years before closing its doors in 1909. The advertisement below was placed in the 1901 promotional book *Souvenir of Redlands, California*. (Photographer: Frank C. Fryett.)

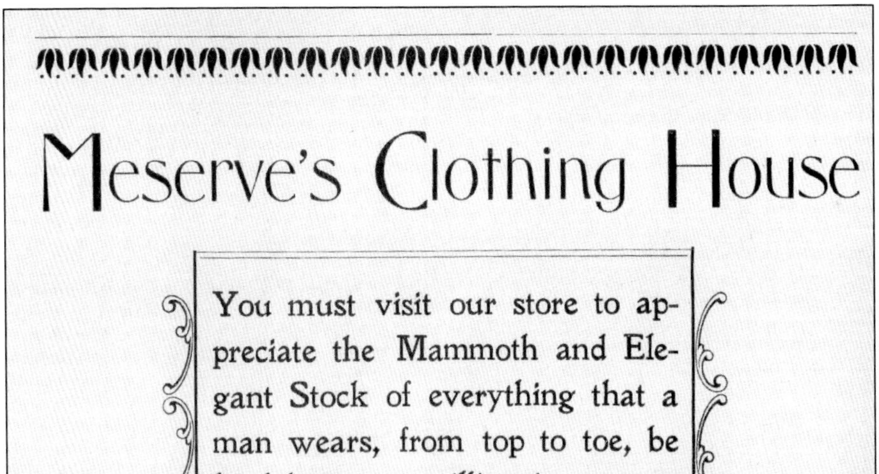

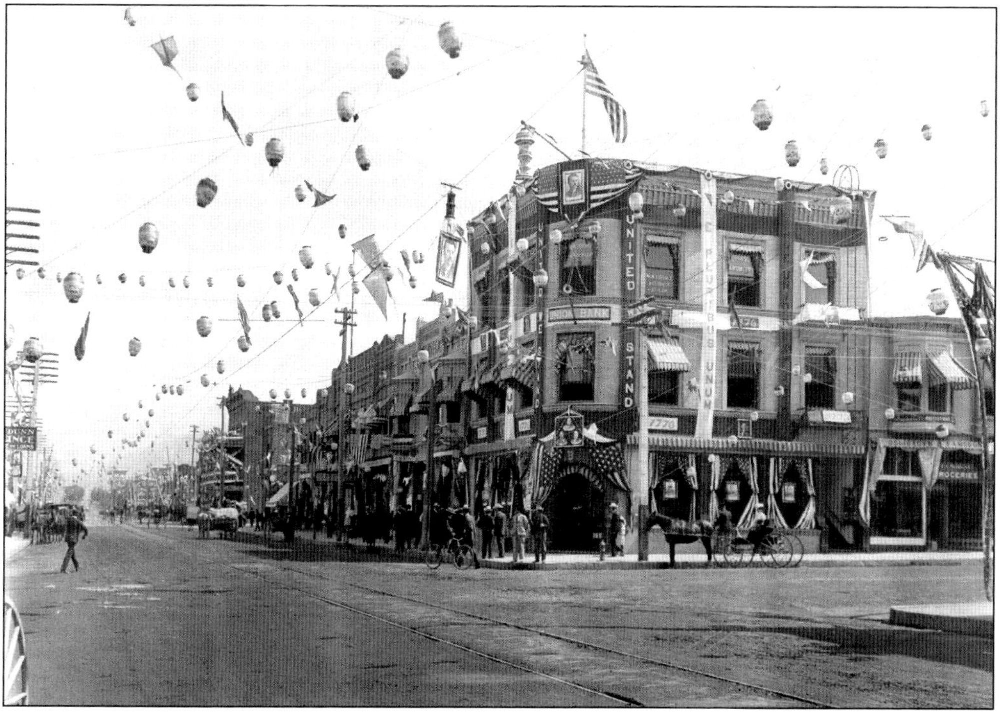

The 1902 photograph above of Orange and State Streets shows how quickly Redlands grew around that time. The image shows the hustle and bustle of the rapidly expanding town, where horse-drawn carriages traveled alongside bicycles and streetcars. New businesses like A.W. Childs & Company Real Estate, the Pioneer Transfer freight transportation service, and Edward E. Roessler's photography studio developed alongside long-standing businesses. Front and center is the Union Bank, which corresponded with international banks by 1903, as the advertisement at right indicates. (Photographer: Elias F. Everitt.)

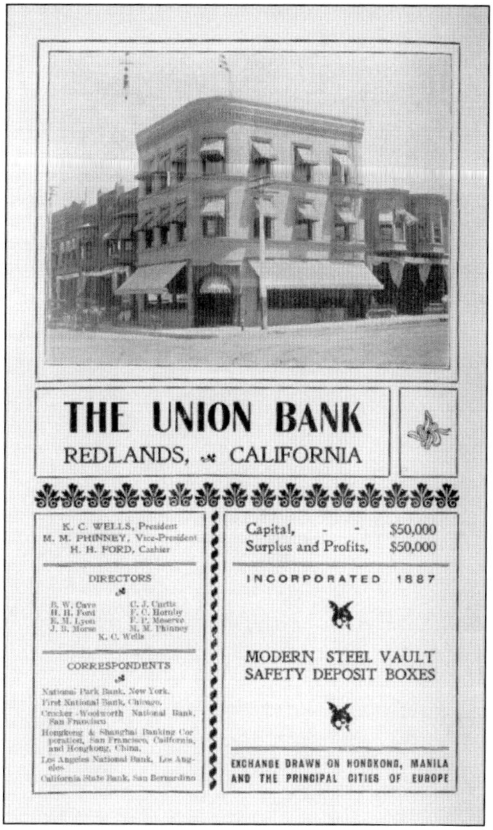

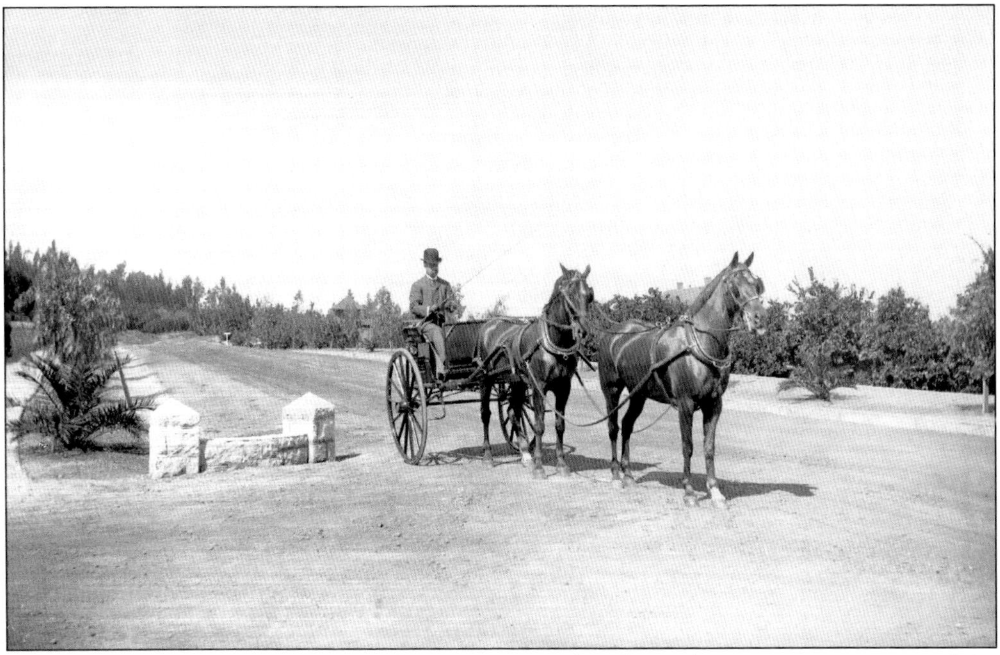

Rapid advancements in technology took transportation from horse-drawn carriages to automobiles very quickly in early 1900s Redlands. Albert C. Burrage's personal buggy (above), pulled by Hackney horses in tandem, was the height of sophistication around 1900 but was nearly obsolete by the time H.W. Kimball drove his 1910 Ford Model T (below) through town. An efficient, affordable, and much cleaner mode of transportation, the Model T redefined how Americans lived, traveled, and connected with the world. (Photographer: Elias F. Everitt.)

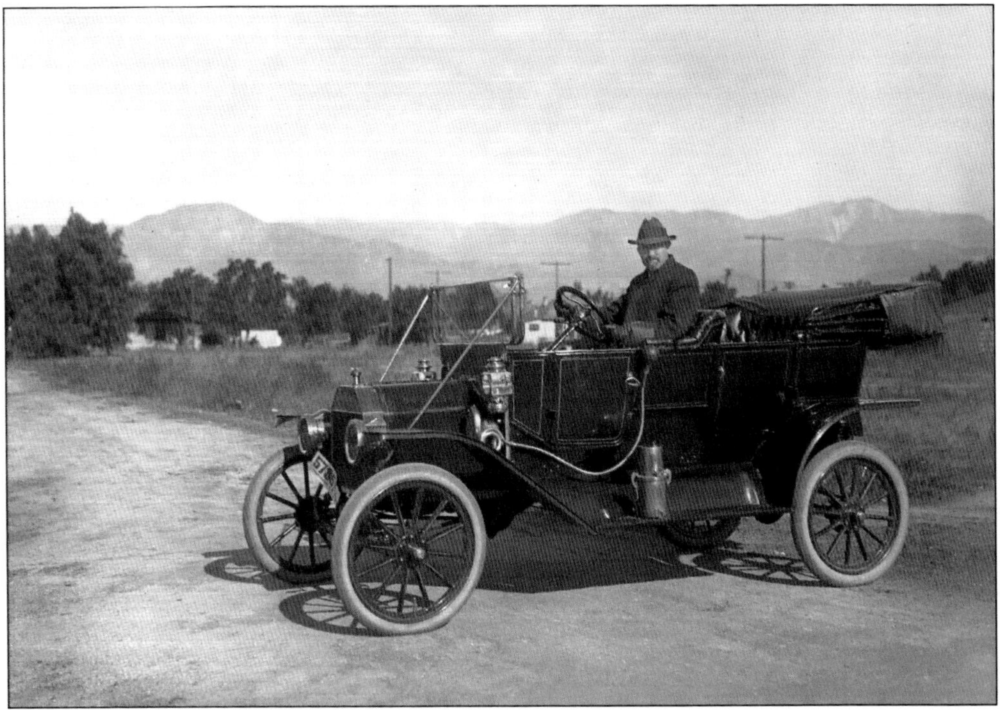

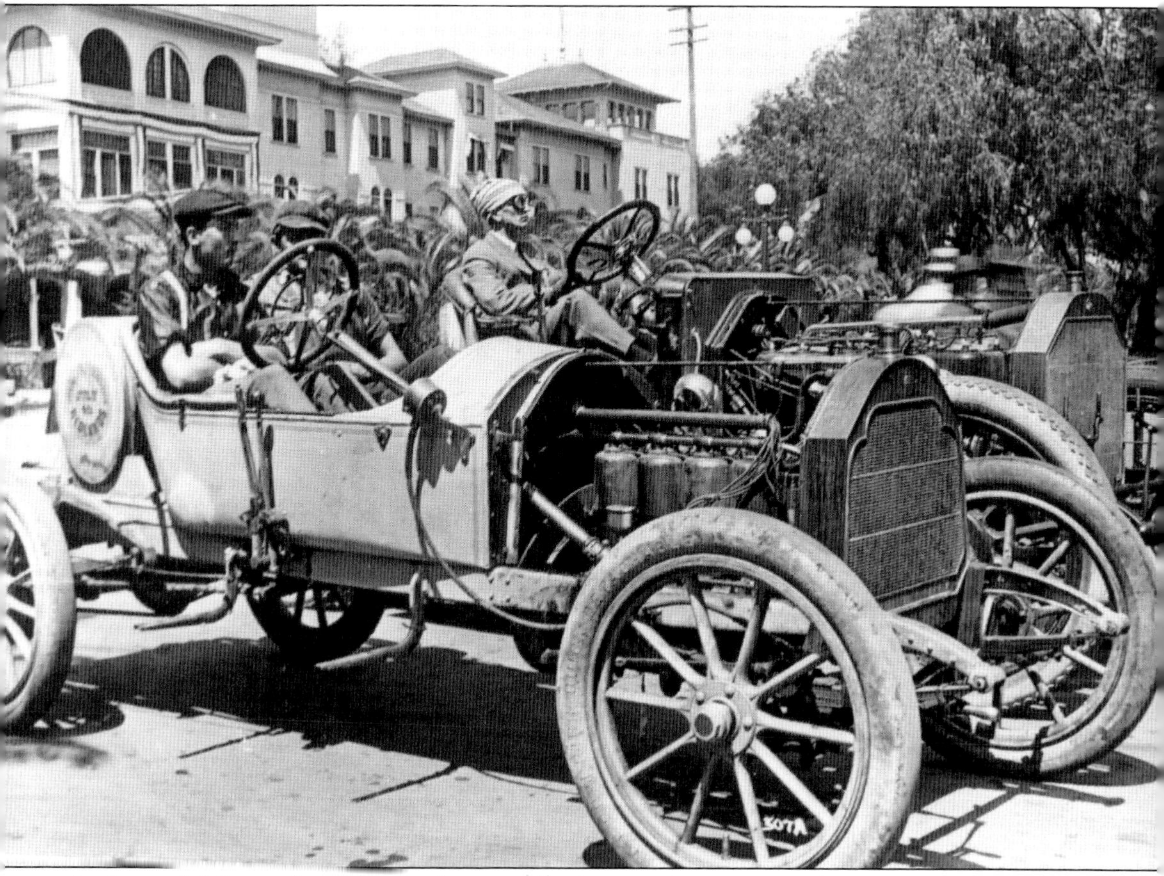

As the availability and popularity of automobiles increased, motorsports became recognized as a legitimate competitive sport. In 1909, the same year the Indianapolis Motor Speedway opened, Redlands organized its own event featuring automobiles and motorcycles. Called the Mile-High Hill Climb, the race began at the Casa Loma Hotel on Orange and Colton Streets, and wound its way to Oak Glen Lodge in the San Bernardino Mountains, at an elevation of just over one mile. The race was a great success, with 15 of the 16 automobiles finishing. As is apparent from this photograph of race car drivers at the Casa Loma Hotel on July 4, 1912, early automobiles offered drivers very little protection. Accounts of the frequency and severity of automobile accidents are easily found in newspaper accounts from this time. (Photographer: Clarence N. Jackson.)

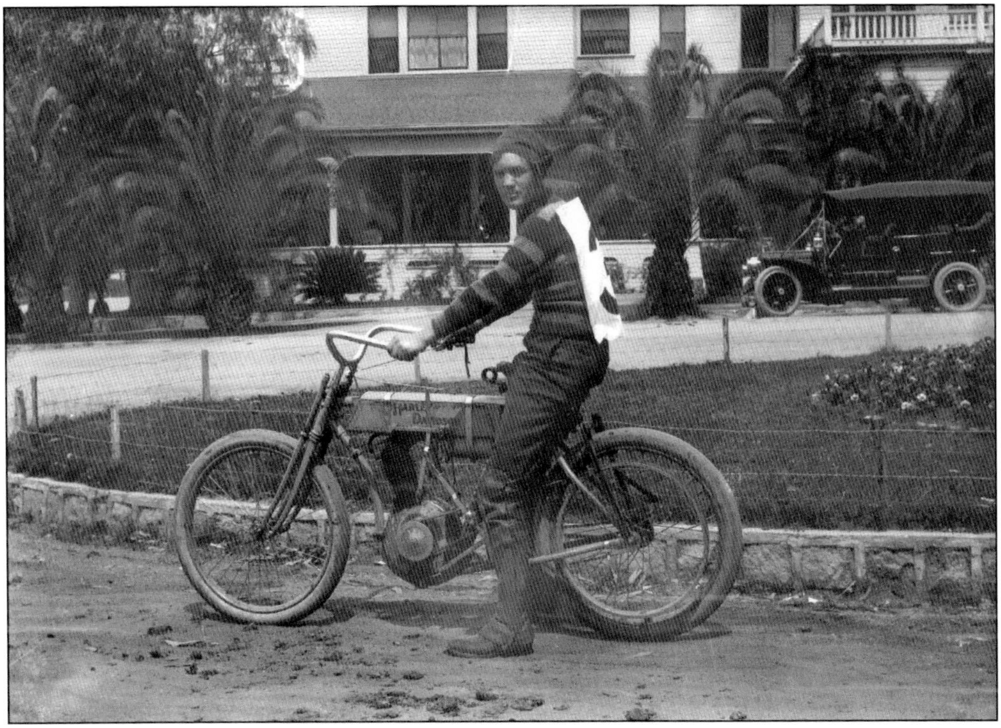

Founded in Milwaukee in 1903, the Harley-Davidson Motor Company found fast success in a society that was enamored with the thrill of speed. Within a decade, Redlanders could purchase motorcycles in town at various dealerships, including Lee Richardson Automobile Co. on Citrus Avenue near Orange Street, where Severn West worked as a repairman. On April 3, 1909, West (above) rode his Harley-Davidson in the first Mile-High Hill Climb. Unlike the automobile portion of the race, the motorcycle competition ended at the Yucaipa post office, with West coming in sixth—last place. In the 1912 advertisement below for Chauncey Clem's Cyclery, the focus is only on Harley-Davidsons, despite the popularity of other motorcycle manufacturers. Early Harley-Davidsons were known as "silent gray fellows" because of their relatively quiet exhaust, a funny notion to anyone familiar with Harley-Davidsons today. (Photographer: Elias F. Everitt.)

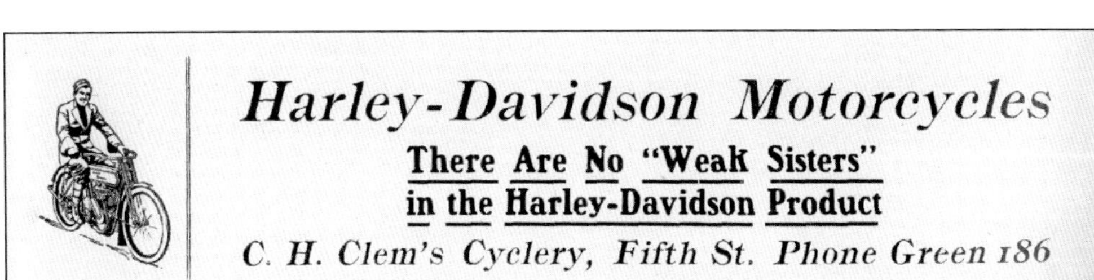

Three

"Humble Cottages and Elegant Residences"

Aptly described as a town of "humble cottages and elegant residences" by the 1895 promotional pamphlet *Souvenir of Redlands, California*, Redlands was home to successful fruit growers and Eastern businessmen who built grand residences, and merchants who built modest homes. From its beginnings, the town's beautiful setting and idyllic climate attracted new residents from across the United States. In 1901 alone, over $950,000 worth of home building and improvements were completed, including 310 homes and a fire station; $9,000 in civic improvements to streets, ditches, and storm water bridges paid for by the town; and over $10,000 in improvements to sidewalks, gutters, and curbs, which residents funded. Redlands was a profitable place to be a builder and vendor of building materials. As reported by the *Redlands Daily Facts* newspaper in March 1902, builders from across the state of California were attracted to Redlands by the abundance of construction projects.

In addition to building, town leaders and residents also invested in beautification projects, creating tree-lined streets, serene parks, and lush gardens. Made possible by the dependable flow of water into the town as a result of the Bear Valley Dam, Redlands became known for the beauty and rarity of its landscaping. Residents hired landscape architects to design intricate gardens with exotic plantings to accompany their citrus grove–flanked homes. Prominent Redlanders, including Jennie Davis and the Smiley brothers, encouraged town and residential beautification developments, a tradition that many still continue in Redlands today.

Professional photographers profited from Redlands' expansion and improvement projects, with the town ordering scenic views and residents commissioning photographs of their homes and gardens. These images were often seen in postcards, stereoviews, promotional pamphlets, and books meant to display the appeal of Redlands as a place to visit and live. Townspeople and tourists could purchase duplicates of these images at drugstores, bookstores, and galleries, and from the photographers themselves. In fact, some of the images in this chapter were also used for those purposes.

NEW ADVERTISEMENT.

PARK VILLA TRACT!!

Corner CYPRESS AVE. & CAJON STREET, REDLANDS.

Pasadena's Only Successful Rival

Destined by its Natural advantages to become the center of magnificent residences.

Streets Graded,
Cement Sidewalks throughout,
Shade trees, Palms and Grevillias,
Domestic Water piped to every Lot.

Improvements Now Being Made!

——Grand view and part of property——

-:-Covered with Fine Orange Trees-:-

Unequalled Opportunity for those desiring to make a home in

THE CHOICEST VALLEY IN THE STATE.

Agents: John P. Fisk, Jr.
Sibley & Daniels.
Easton, Eldridge & Co.

Graded streets, cement sidewalks, shade trees, domestic water, and an orange grove are all features promised to prospective residents of the Park Villa tract in this September 1887 advertisement from *The Citrograph* newspaper. Located on Cypress Avenue and Cajon Street in Redlands, the tract was hailed as a site that was "destined by its natural advantages to become the center of magnificent residences." The Park Villa tract eventually included the homes of Benton Oscar Johnson, an early Redlands merchant, William Graff Moore, the editor of the *Redlands Daily Facts*, and other prominent residents.

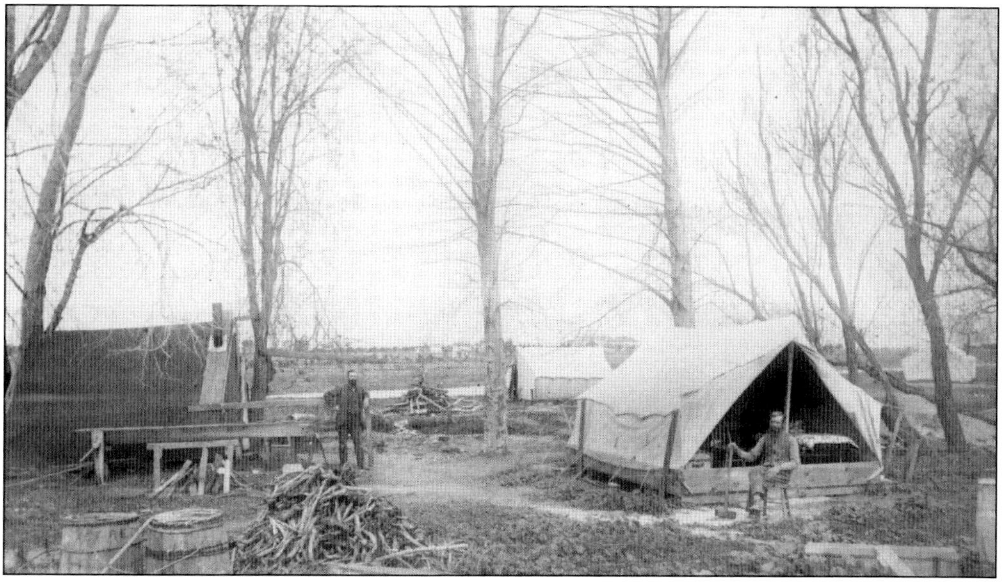

From its infancy, Redlands had a growing population with an immediate need for new businesses and homes. With limited competition, early lumber manufacturers and vendors raised prices, making it difficult for new arrivals to the area. Competition increased as lumber and planing mills were opened, and within a few years, people had many options to choose from, as is apparent from the advertisement at right from the May 23, 1891, issue of *The Citrograph*. The 1887 photograph above of Charles Hammond and Mero Daniels camping on the banks of the zanja, the irrigation canal at Sixth Street, shows how sparsely populated the areas farther away from the Redlands town center were in those early years. (Photographer: Daniel Holt.)

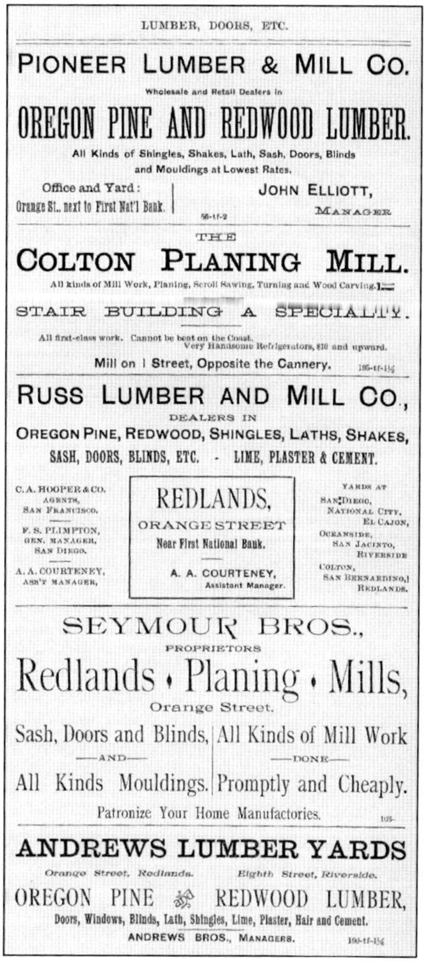

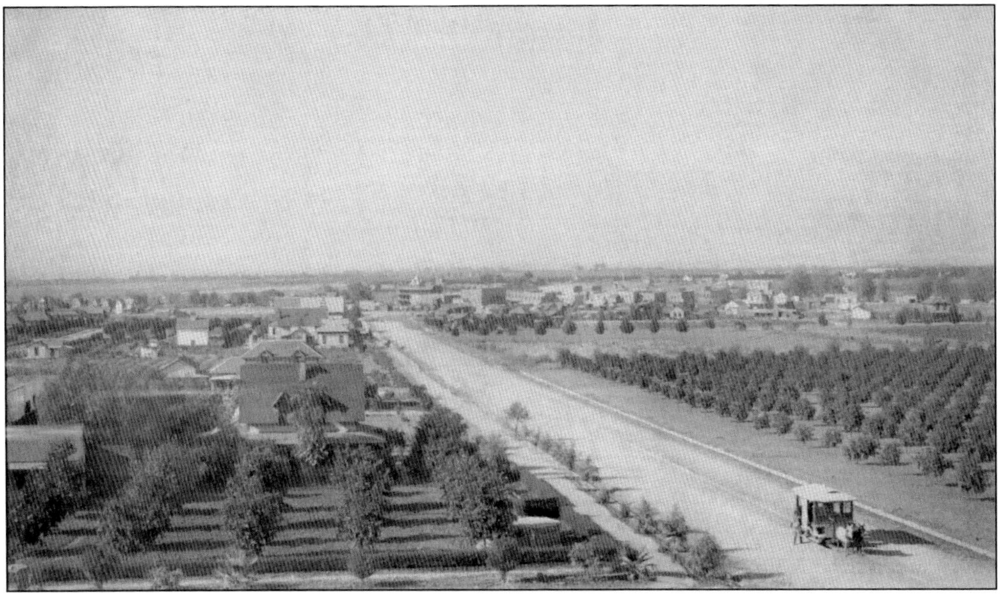

With downtown Redlands in the background, this 1891 photograph of Cajon Street at Fern Avenue is a vivid representation of life in early Redlands, with young orange groves flanked by few homes and open land. The mule-drawn streetcar is indicative of the town's expansion, as residences were built in outlying areas and required transportation to and from the commercial center. (Photographer: Rudolph J. Philippi.)

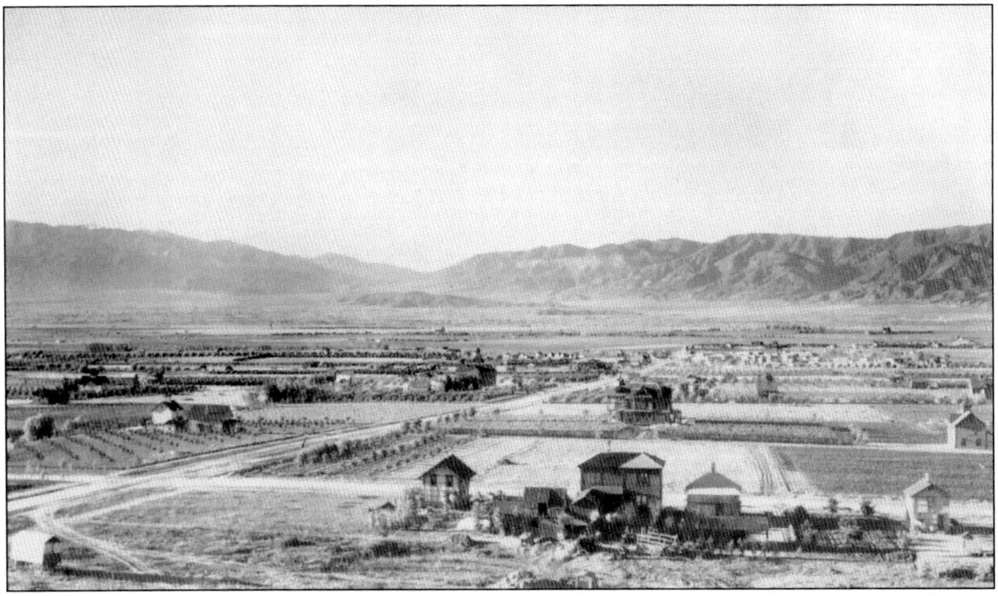

Built on a hill, the home of early Redlands settler and prolific businessman Benton Oscar Johnson offered the ideal vantage point for Rudolph J. Philippi to capture this 1892 panoramic view of the town, with Cajon Pass in the background. After arriving in the San Bernardino Valley in 1884, Johnson worked as a druggist, a merchant, an orange grower, the manager of Redlands Gas Company, and the secretary and treasurer of Bear Valley Irrigation Company. Panoramic views were popular with tourists, making them profitable subjects for professional photographers. (Photographer: Rudolph J. Philippi.)

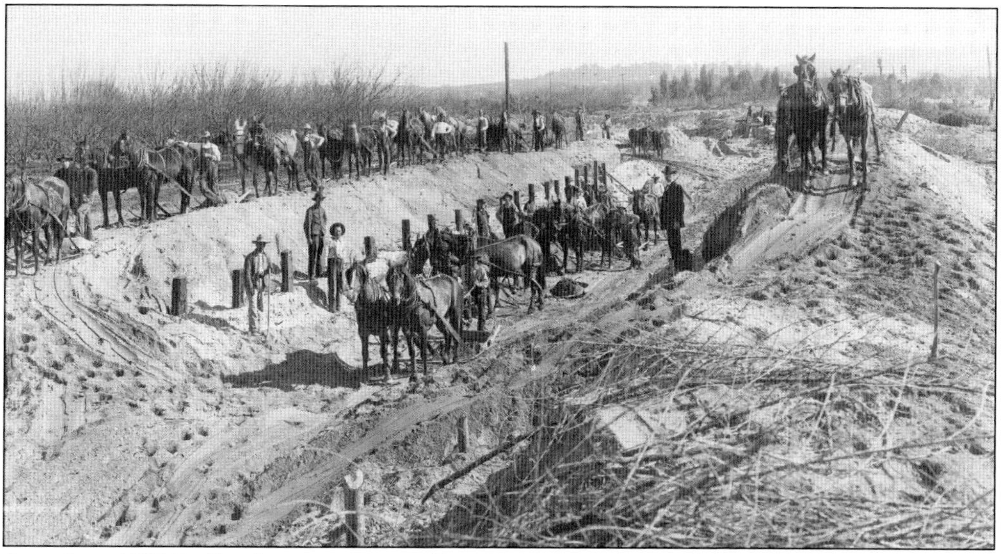

As early as 1887, Redlands streets were under constant construction to accommodate the growing population. This 1908 photograph of the Highway Construction Company shows what massive undertakings these projects were. That year brought many national changes to transportation, including the debut of the Ford Model T, the popularity of which led to a need for the expansion and improvement of streets and highways. (Photographer: Elias F. Everitt.)

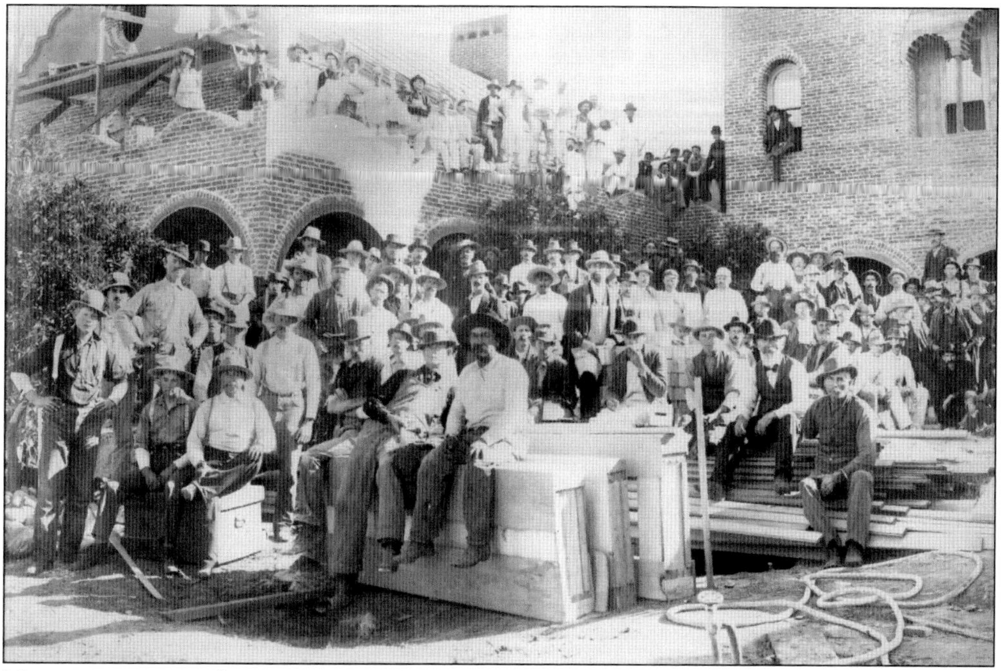

The construction of new commercial and residential buildings kept local real estate agents, architects, contractors, and building supply manufacturers and vendors in business. By 1901, when this image was taken, there were 15 real estate and loan offices and six contractors and builders operating in Redlands. This photograph shows the construction of the mansion of Massachusetts copper baron Albert C. Burrage, which required 127 men working simultaneously with 18 teams of horses and was completed in only four and a half months. (Photographer: Elias F. Everitt.)

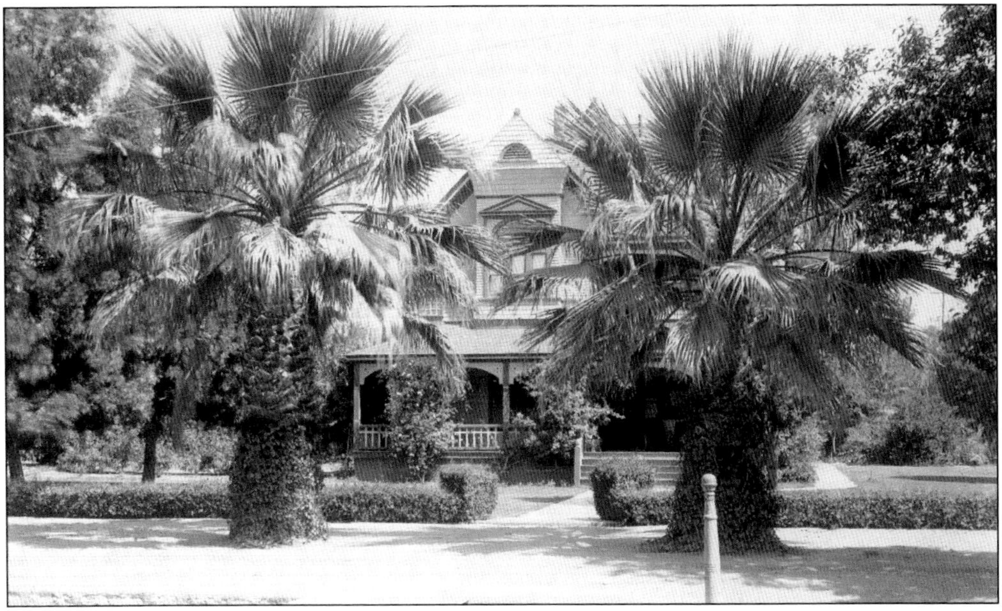

As old as the town itself, the home of Redlands cofounder Edward G. Judson, on West Highland Avenue, is one of 30 homes known to have been built in 1888 that still stand in Redlands. Built by Jerome Seymour of the Seymour brothers' Redlands Planing Mill, the Victorian Stick–style home was remodeled in 1911, around the same time Chase Thorn took this photograph. (Photographer: Chase Thorn.)

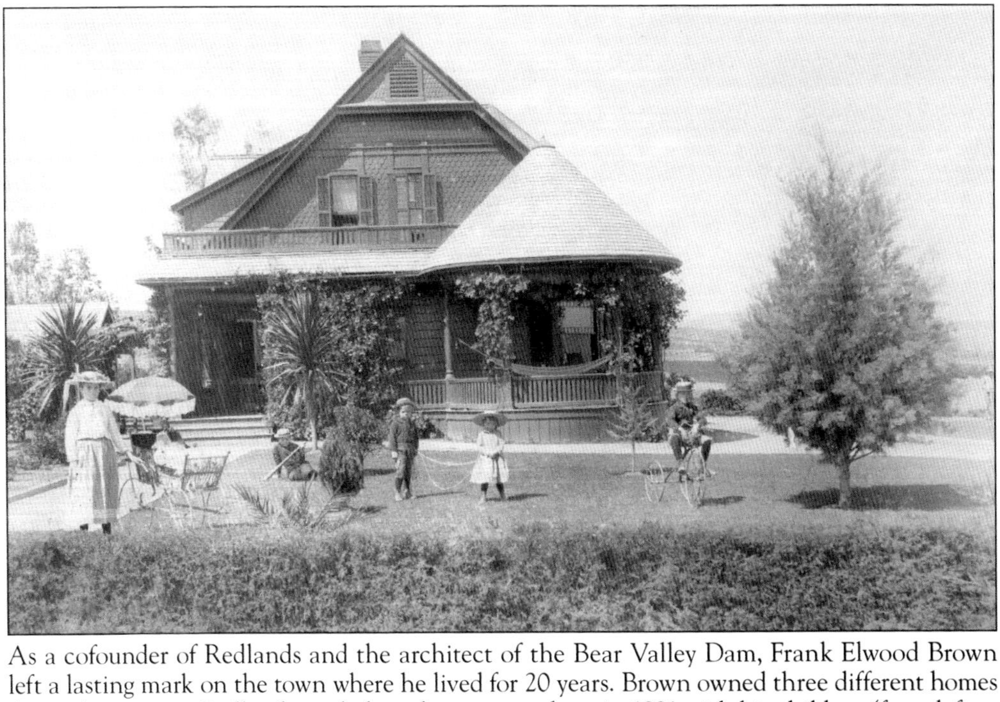

As a cofounder of Redlands and the architect of the Bear Valley Dam, Frank Elwood Brown left a lasting mark on the town where he lived for 20 years. Brown owned three different homes during his time in Redlands, including the one seen here in 1891 with his children (from left to right) Emeline, Paul, Reuben, Edward, Alessandra, and Elwood. Built between 1890 and 1891, the property cost $7,500 to develop. (Photographer: Rudolph J. Philippi.)

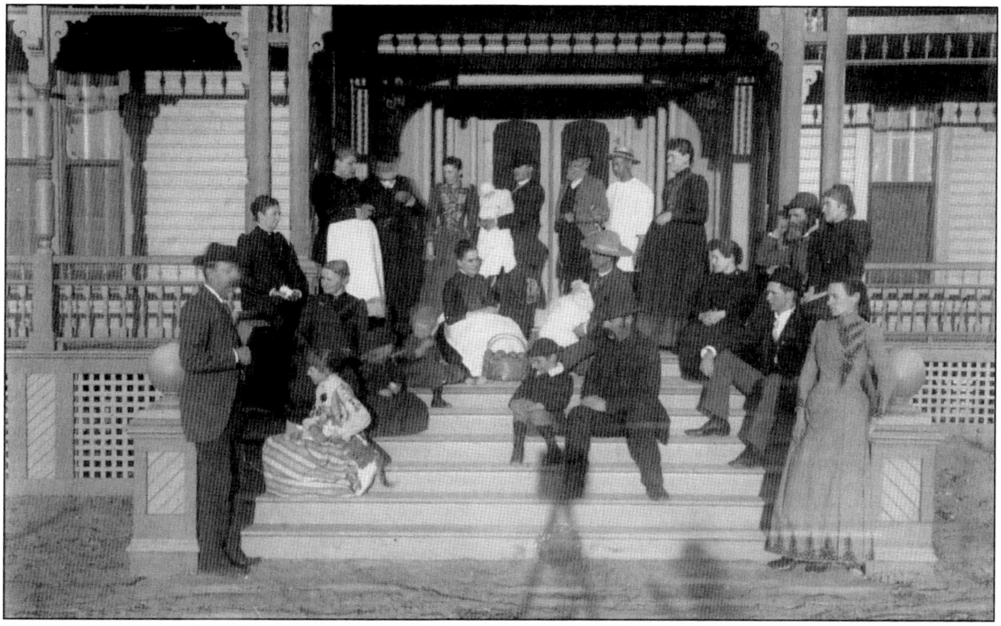

By way of his shadow (bottom right), Rudolph J. Philippi inadvertently included himself in this photograph of a group at the James S. Edwards residence. Taken on Christmas Day 1891, such a casual snapshot of a group of people who appear to be preparing for a photograph is rare for a professional in this time period. The three-story Edwards home had 10 bedrooms, an elevator, a water-pumping system, a laundry room, and a room for the family cook. (Photographer: Rudolph J. Philippi.)

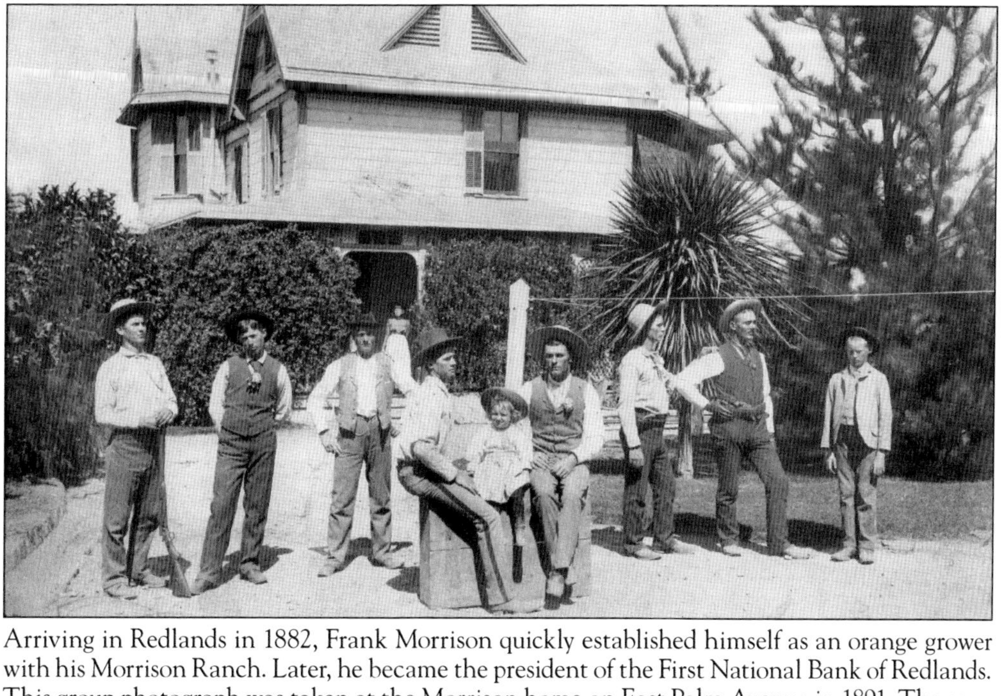

Arriving in Redlands in 1882, Frank Morrison quickly established himself as an orange grower with his Morrison Ranch. Later, he became the president of the First National Bank of Redlands. This group photograph was taken at the Morrison home on East Palm Avenue in 1891. The man seated on the left of the box is Jay Page, who went on to become the foreman of Morrison Ranch. (Photographer: Rudolph J. Philippi.)

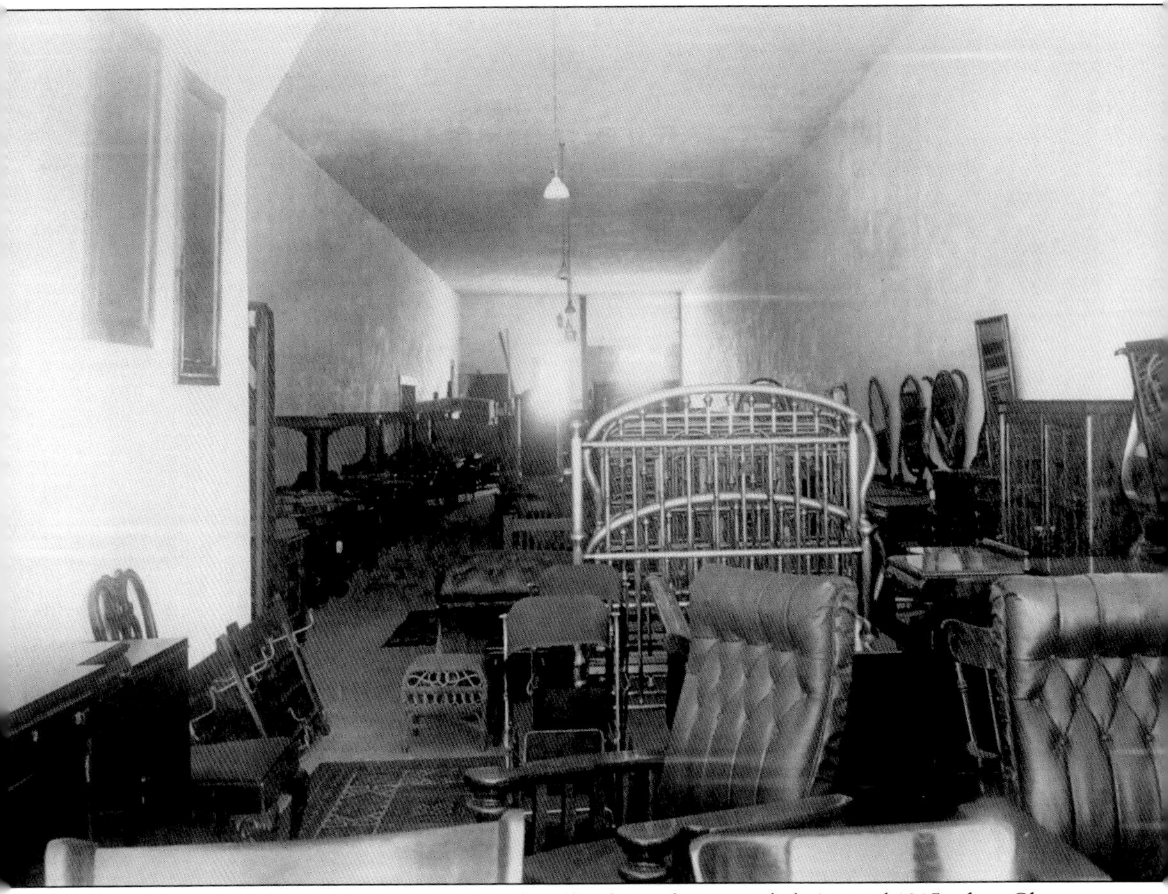

New homes required new furnishings, and Redlands vendors provided. Around 1915, when Clarence N. Jackson photographed the interior of this furniture store, there were seven furniture stores to choose from, including Redlands Furniture and Carpet Company. Located in the center of town on State Street, Redlands Furniture and Carpet Company advertised themselves as having the best quality and the lowest prices in town. (Photographer: Clarence N. Jackson.)

The Victorian era (about 1830 to 1901) was a time of opulence and ornamentation in home decor. Fanciful wallpaper, fringed curtains, and animal-skin rugs decorated Victorian homes like that of Dr. Robert T. Allan, on the southwest corner of Highland Avenue and San Jacinto Street. Photographed here in the mid-1890s, the Allan home was a typical Victorian residence. (Photographer: Frank C. Fryett.)

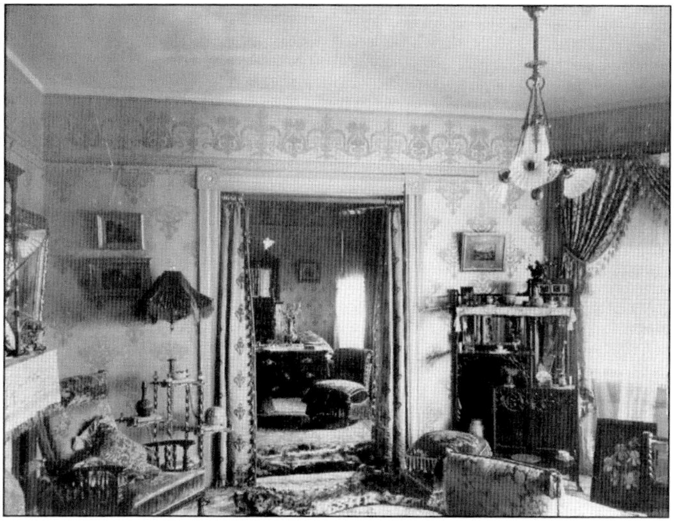

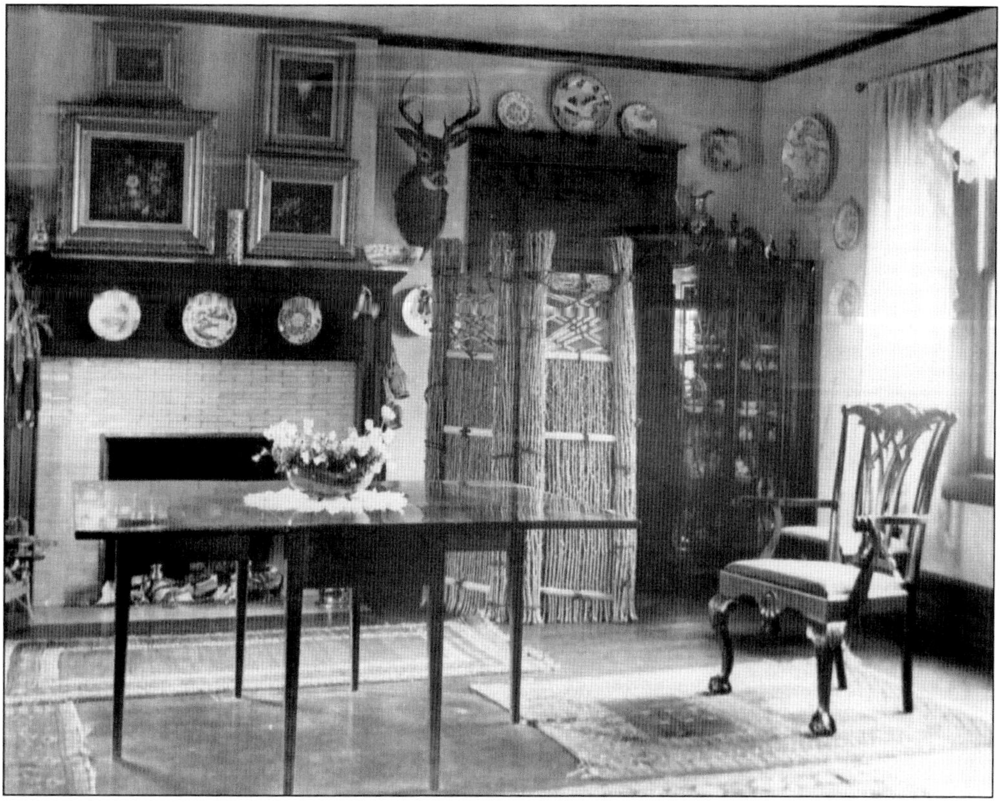

Known as La Belle Epoch, or "the beautiful era," in Europe, the Edwardian period (about 1901 to 1910) moved away from the pomp of the Victorian era. As seen in this photograph of the Sewall home on Summit Avenue from about 1901, the splendor of the image above was replaced with lighter, airier fabrics, colors, and more subdued furniture. Photographing personal residences proved to be profitable for professional photographers, some of whom advertised residences and parties as their specialty. (Photographer: Elias F. Everitt.)

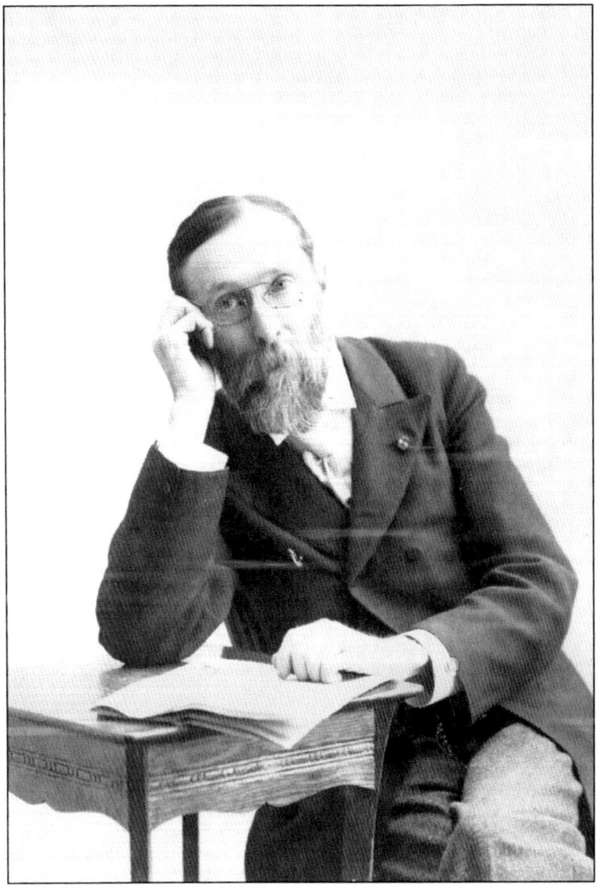

Like so many people at the time, William Graff Moore arrived in Redlands as a result of health problems in June 1895. Deciding to stay after an improvement in his health, Moore purchased the *Redlands Daily Facts* newspaper in August of that year. The portrait at left, by the photographic studio of Grace E. Laney and Charles C. Melvin, appeared in the *Illustrated Redlands* booklet, published in 1897 by the *Redlands Daily Facts*. His home (below), on Cajon Street near Fern Avenue, was photographed a year after his 1899 death with his widow, Elmira, in the foreground possibly wearing all black. Victorian etiquette required women to dress in mourning for at least two years, while men wore it for at least one year. As an elderly woman, Mrs. Moore would likely have followed this tradition. (Photographers: left, Grace E. Laney and Charles C. Melvin; below, Elias F. Everitt.)

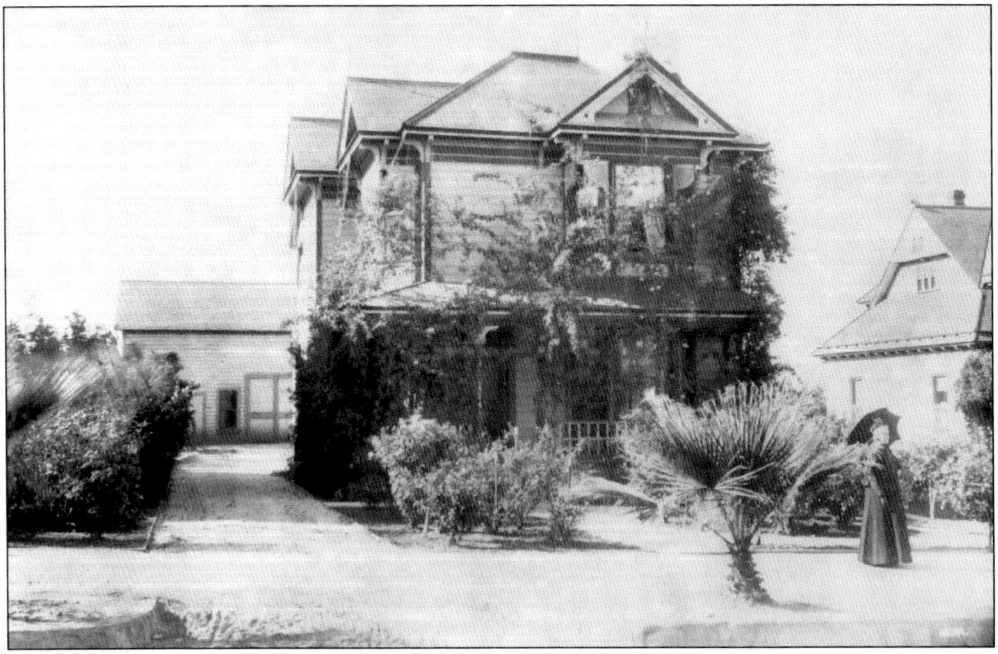

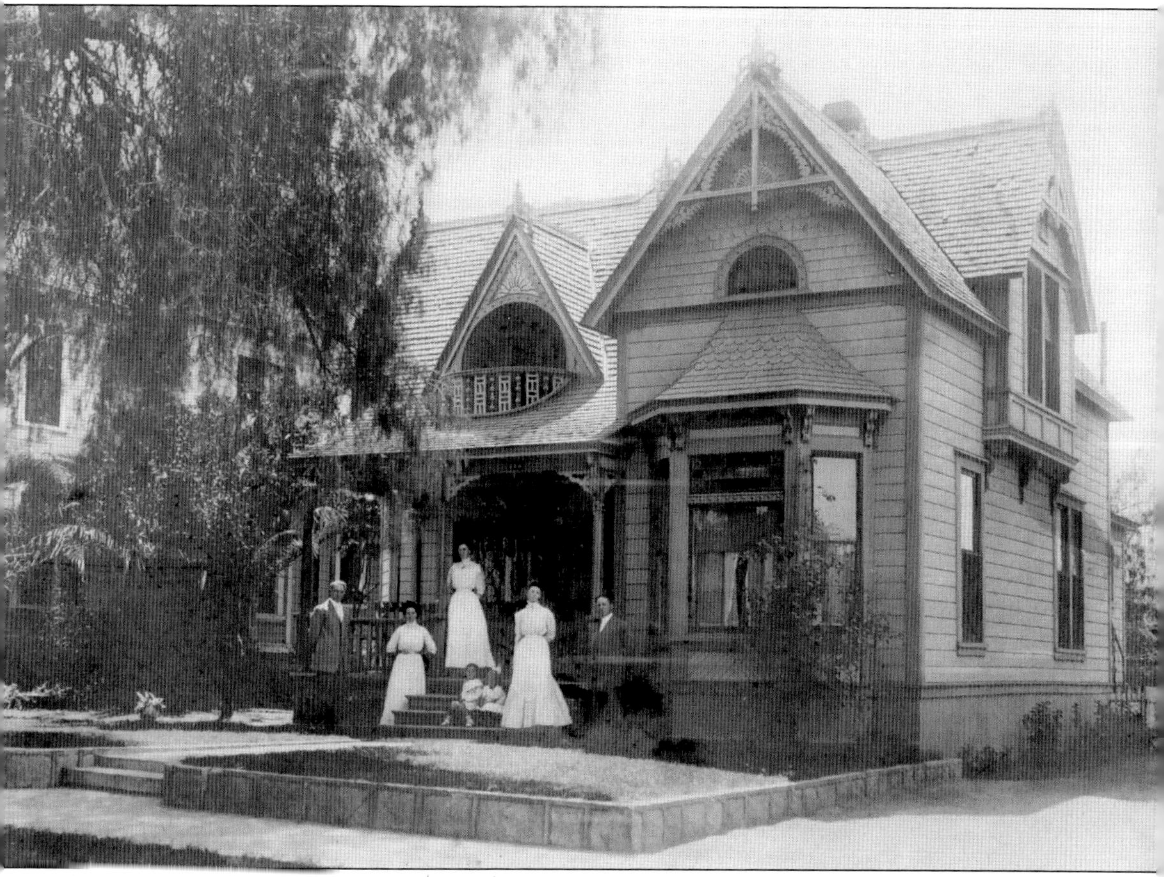

A quintessential Queen Anne–style residence, the home of Chauncey Adams stood on Eureka Street and Fern Avenue. Queen Anne architecture was popular in the United States in the last 20 years of the 1800s and is characterized by many design elements seen in this c. 1900 photograph, including the carved wood panels over the windows, the bay window, the multi-gabled roof, the second-story gable with the recessed porch, the fish-scale shingles, and the horizontal siding. The architectural style was most common in residences, many of which still stand in Redlands. (Photographer: Elias F. Everitt.)

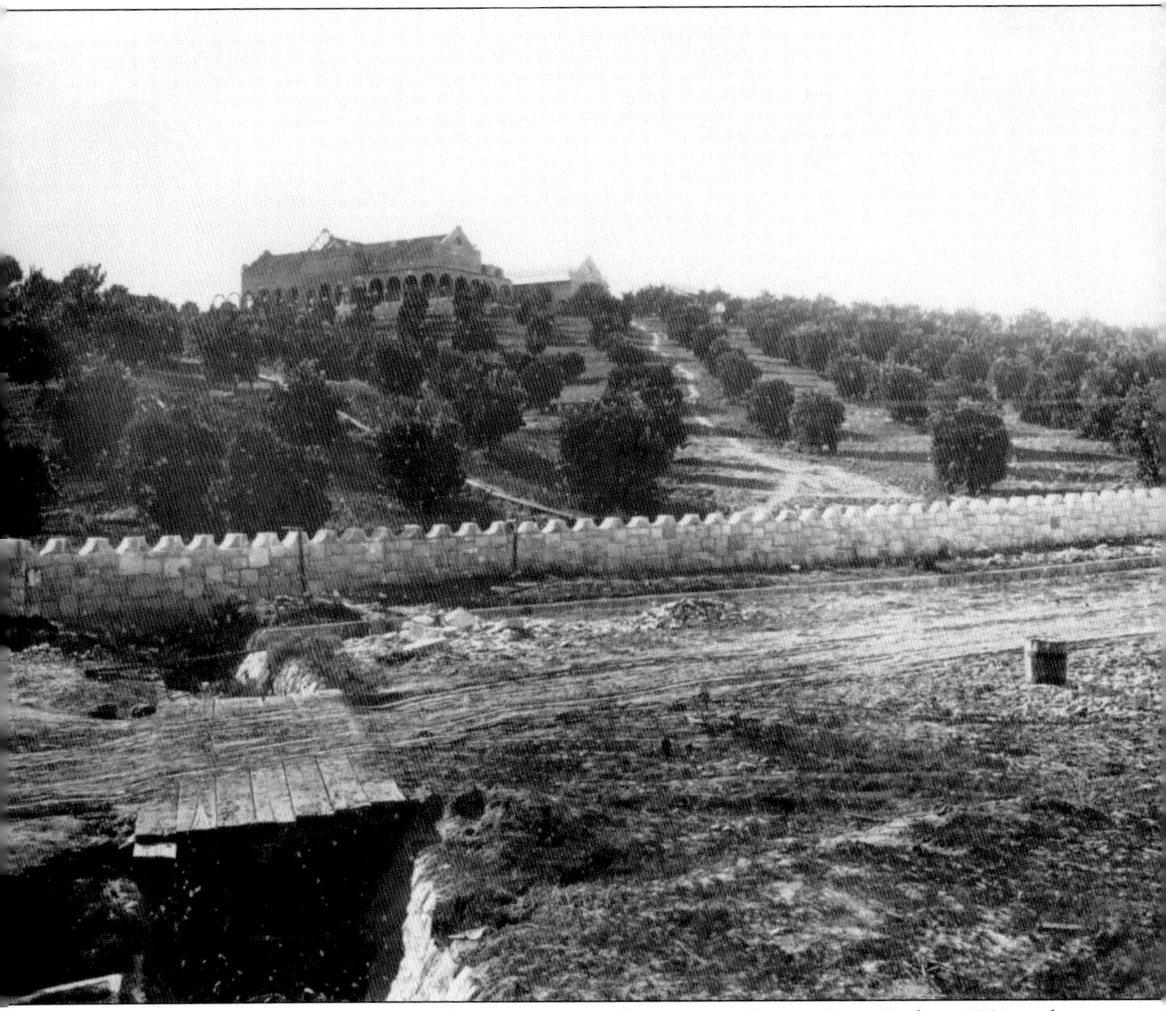

Construction of the Burrage family winter retreat began near Cañon Crest Park in 1901 and was documented by photographer Elias F. Everitt. These photographs provide a look into early 1900s home building and have been useful for historical architecture analysis of the period. With the mansion still under construction in the background, this image includes a yet-to-be-paved Crescent Avenue and a ditch that may have been utilized as part of the home's drainage system. The home and scalloped wall seen here still stand today. (Photographer: Elias F. Everitt.)

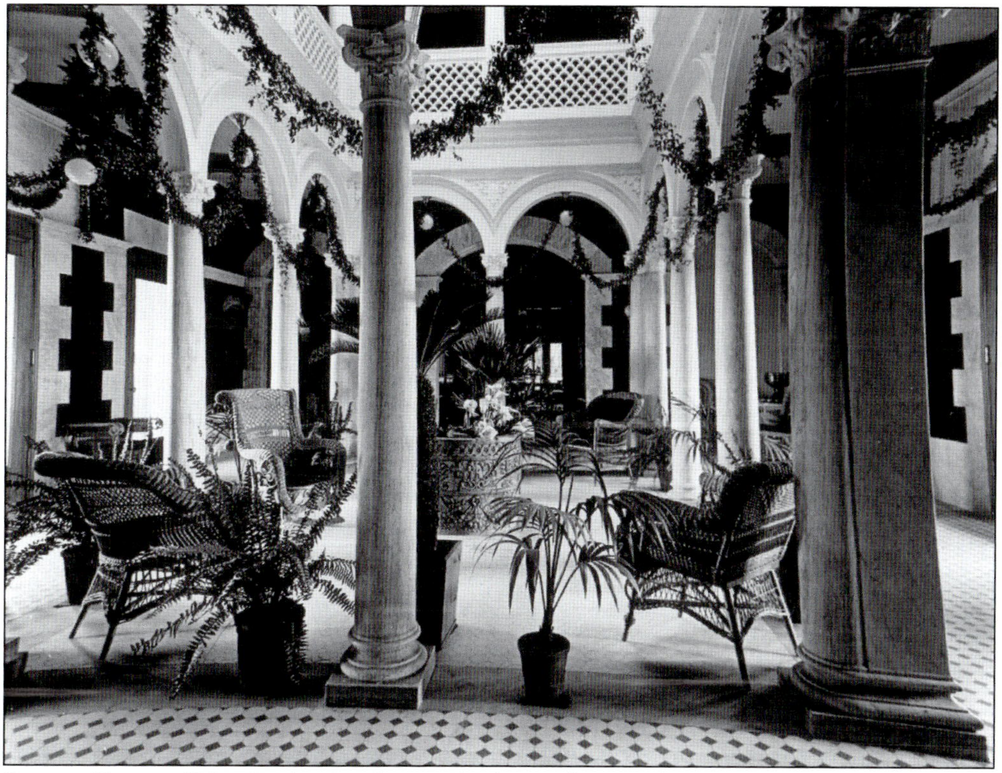

Designed by noted New England architect Charles Brigham in the popular Mission Revival style, the Burrage mansion cost $100,000 to complete in 1901, more than any other building in town at the time. Using local businesses, the property included a large H-shaped, enclosed swimming pool, a carriage house, a guest house, and even a polo field. In March 1902, the *Redlands Daily Facts* published a detailed account of the home, including a description of the lavish furnishings seen here in the entry hall. (Photographer: Elias F. Everitt.)

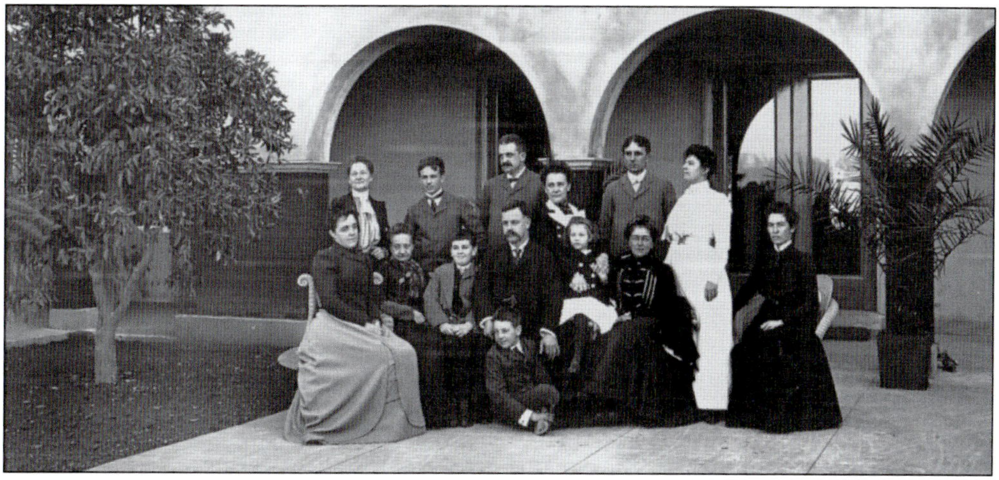

Though the Burrage family only wintered in Redlands for six years, their annual excursions were an event unto themselves. Accounts of the family arriving in style on a train with their servants were widely reported. This family portrait was captured by Elias F. Everitt during their first visit, in 1901. (Photographer: Elias F. Everitt.)

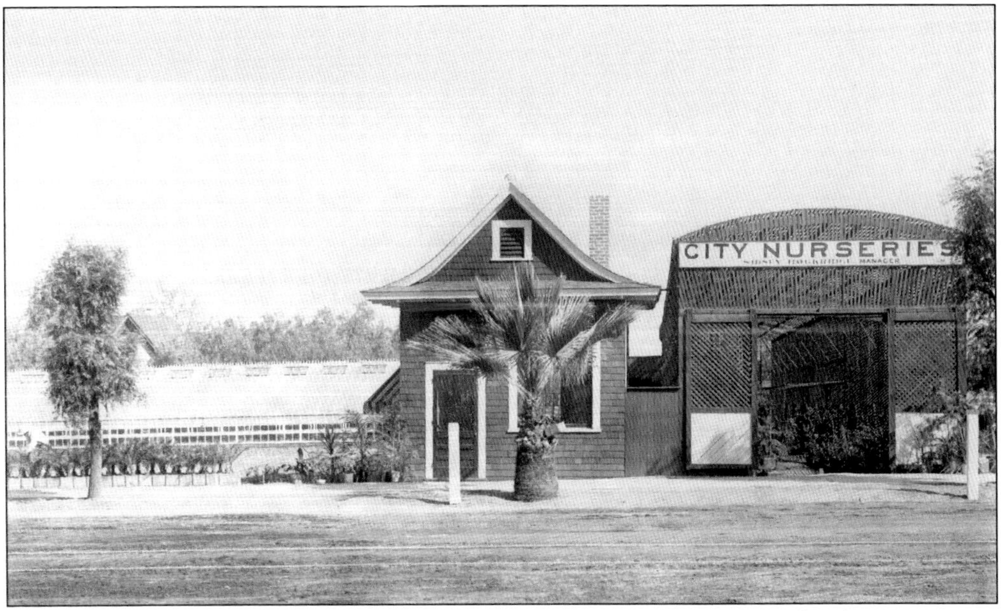

CITY NURSERIES

OFFICE AND GREENHOUSES
E. CYPRESS AVE., COR. FOURTH ST.

SIDNEY HOCKRIDGE, Manager.

Ornamental Shrubbery
Decorative Plants
Landscape Gardening
Cut Flowers

INTERIOR DECORATIONS

Our facilities for having on hand at all times a large assortment of Flowering and Decorative Plants, Ferns, Etc., enables us to do splendid and effective work at moderate charges.

LANDSCAPE

We employ trained and experienced men for this branch, and can assure those, who may favor us with commissions, that the quality of Plants, Trees, Etc furnished, as well as the variety according to the circumstances, will be of the best.

VISITORS

Visitors are always welcome at our establishment, which will be found to be the best equipped in Southern California.

Beginning his career in Redlands as a gardener at the Smiley estate in 1897, Sidney Hockridge went on to manage City Nurseries (above), on Cypress Avenue and Fourth Street, from 1902 until 1912. In that year, he opened Hockridge Nurseries, where he imported plants from around the globe and supplied them to Redlands residences large and small. In addition to his local customers, Hockridge also worked with the Huntington Estate in San Marino and with the Los Angeles park system. Photographer Chase Thorn worked in Redlands from around 1904 to 1915 and photographed City Nurseries while it was still managed by Hockridge. (Photographer: Chase Thorn.)

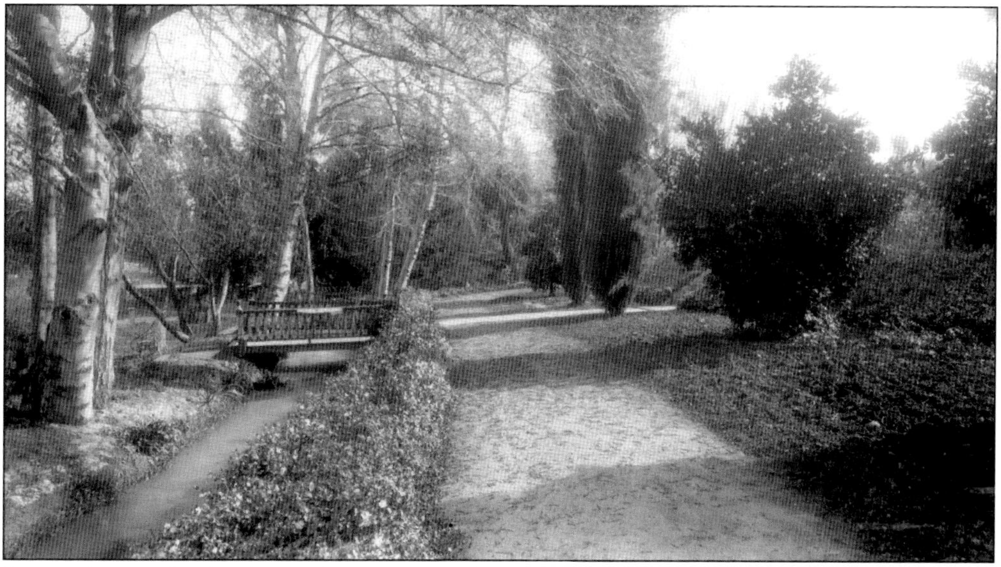

Situated near the banks of the zanja, the Brookside Avenue home of longtime Redlands resident Jennie Davis was surrounded by beautifully tended grounds. Regarded as a leader in city beautification, Davis was the president of the Redlands Horticultural and Improvement Society. She also designed a Japanese garden on her property where she entertained family and friends. This c. 1900 photograph was used in the promotional book *Souvenir of Redlands, California* in 1901. (Photographer: Elias F. Everitt.)

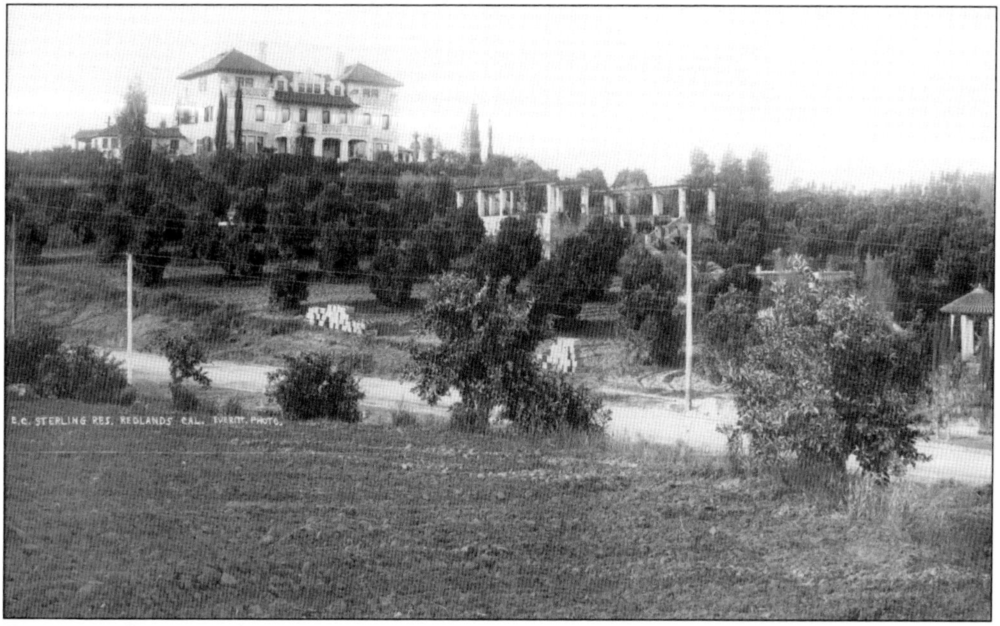

Constructed in 1902, the Sterling estate was known for its Italian-style gardens, which were the ideal subject for postcards and other promotional material. Characterized by lily ponds, wide lawns, and palm trees, Italian-style gardens became popular in California in the early 1900s. Known as La Casada, the estate was owned by Edward Canfield Sterling, an orange grower. From the stacks of crates near the orange trees, it looks as if the photograph was taken during the harvest. (Photographer: Elias F. Everitt.)

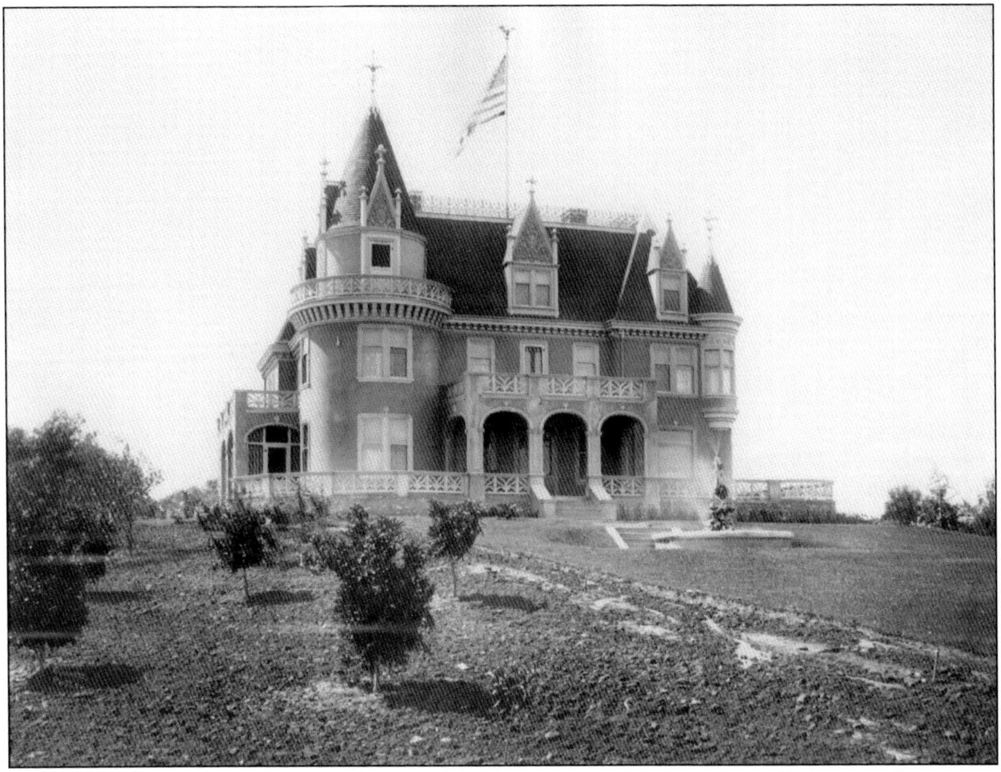

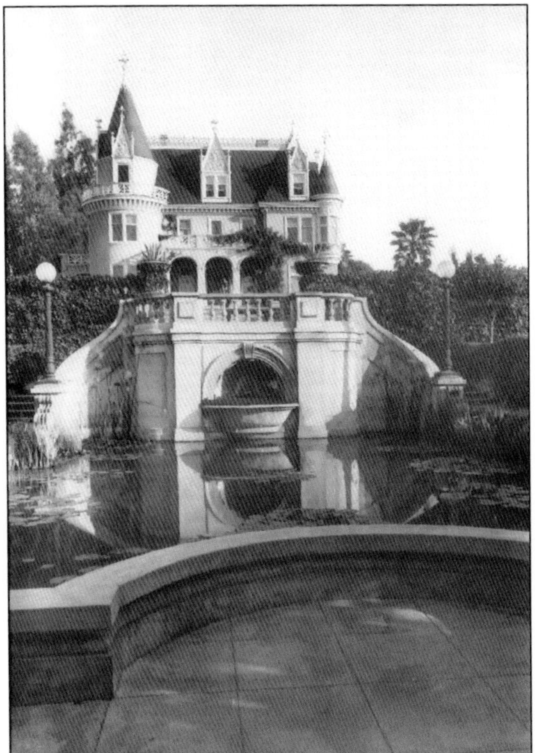

Built on Prospect Hill in 1897, the Kimberly Crest mansion was constructed by local contractors Davis and Daniel Donald in the French chateau architectural style. Originally the home of Cornelia Ann Hill, the home was purchased in 1905 by John and Helen Kimberly and remained in the family for 75 years. This Elias F. Everitt photograph, taken around 1900, shows the limited landscaping and young orange trees on the property at the time. (Photographer: Elias F. Everitt.)

After purchasing the home, the Kimberly family hired the architectural firm of Parkinson & Bergstrom to design Italian-style gardens throughout the grounds. Completed in 1909, the gardens replaced orange groves with curving staircases, cascading water, fountains, and structures that were reminiscent of Roman ruins. This 1916 view of the large fountain is still a popular subject for photographers and artists. (Photographer: Elias F. Everitt.)

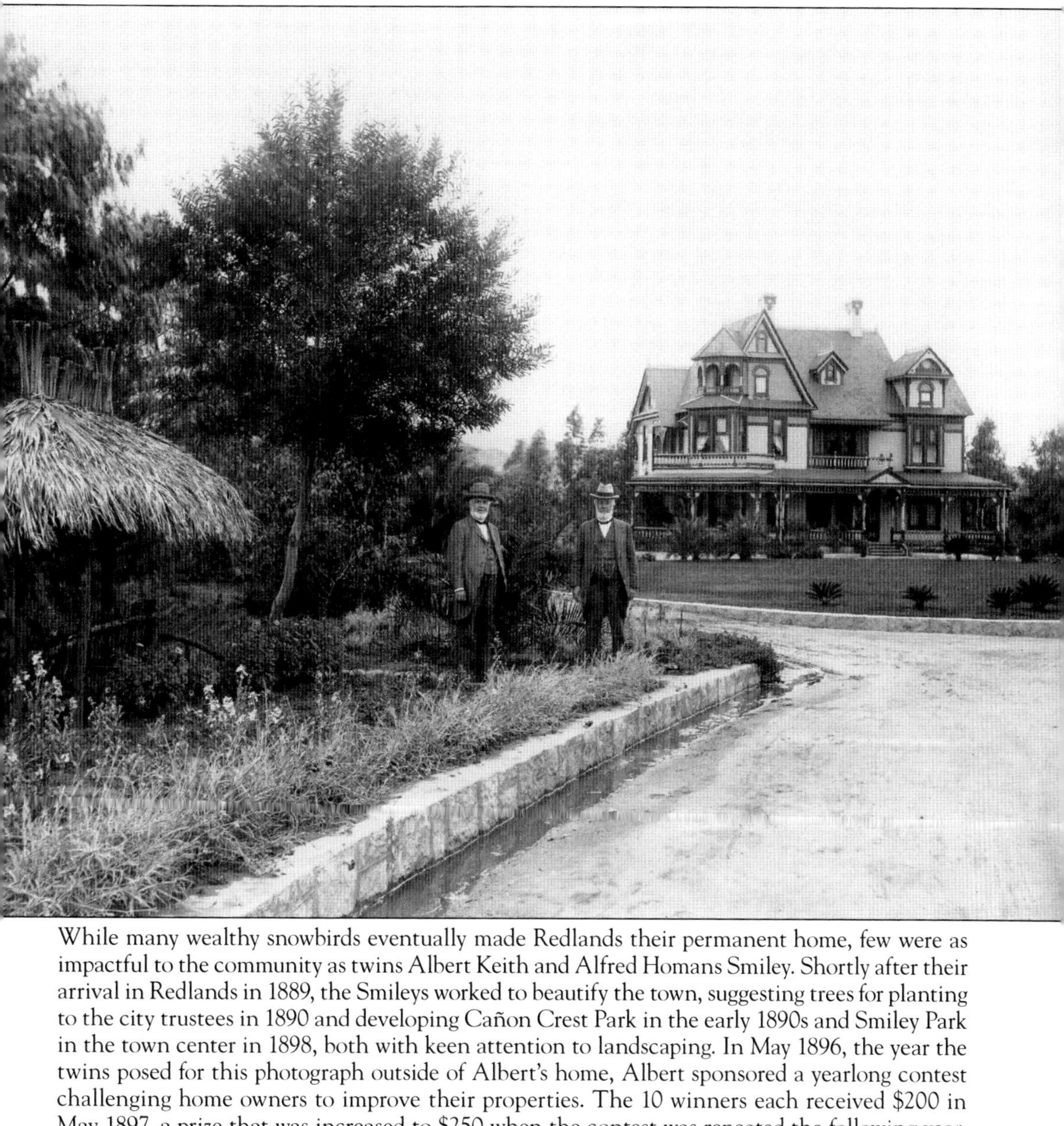

While many wealthy snowbirds eventually made Redlands their permanent home, few were as impactful to the community as twins Albert Keith and Alfred Homans Smiley. Shortly after their arrival in Redlands in 1889, the Smileys worked to beautify the town, suggesting trees for planting to the city trustees in 1890 and developing Cañon Crest Park in the early 1890s and Smiley Park in the town center in 1898, both with keen attention to landscaping. In May 1896, the year the twins posed for this photograph outside of Albert's home, Albert sponsored a yearlong contest challenging home owners to improve their properties. The 10 winners each received $200 in May 1897, a prize that was increased to $250 when the contest was repeated the following year. (Photographer: Rogers & Herndon.)

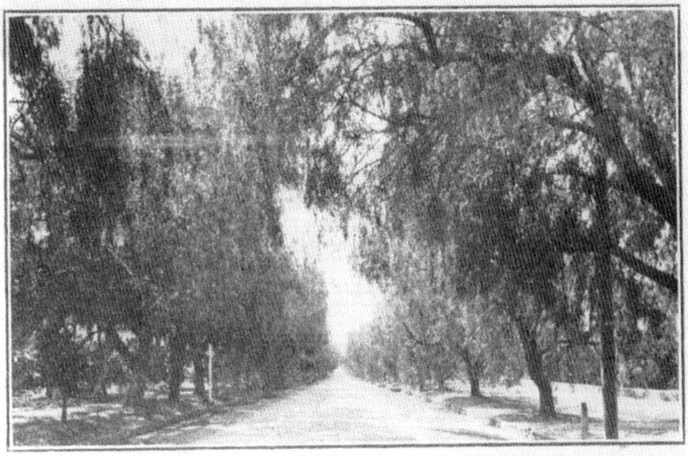

Pepper Trees Along Paved Boulevard

REDLANDS HAS

Best climate the year around.
Most beautiful scenery in California.
Abundance of pure, cold water.
Three hundred days of sunshine every year.
The finest citrus and deciduous orchards.
Wonderful agricultural opportunities.
Industrial advantages and openings.
Exceptional transportation facilities.
Paved roads and highways in all directions.
Beautiful home sites.
The finest modern schools.
Strong, friendly churches.
Large fraternal orders with clubs and homes.
Large beautiful parks, with playgrounds.
Free automobile camp with free gas and other conveniences.
Electric light and power, also domestic gas service.
Street cars, auto lines and taxi service.
Paved streets, sanitary sewers, fire department.
Every thing to make life healthful, happy and worth while.

Read the whole story, it is worth while.

The 1919 booster brochure *Redlands, California* ended with this image of a street lined with pepper trees above a list of what "Redlands Has." Among the advertised virtues of the town were "beautiful home sites," electricity, power, and gas, and "paved streets, sanitary sewers, and a fire department." In short, Redlands had all the modern conveniences people wanted. These promotional works included professional photographs to catch the attention of tourists and potential home buyers. Who would not want to live in a place with the "best climate" and "most beautiful scenery in California"?

Four

"An Up-to-Date School"

Redlands believed in education and supported it from grammar school through college. Schools from the communities of Redlands, Lugonia, and Crafton fed into Redlands Union High School as early as 1891. Its first graduating class, in 1894, had only 12 students, but the student body grew rapidly, necessitating successive remodels. The 1903–1904 school year was particularly messy, with a huge expansion going on next to classrooms. The constant building of schools in Redlands earned this chapter the title "An Up-to-Date School," taken from the high school annual of 1906. By the fall of 1906, the name of the school changed to Redlands High School, reflecting the consolidation of earlier school districts. In addition to academics, high school spirit appeared through sports, whether by participating in or attending the games. This gave rise to many different school yells. The 1902 Redlands Union High School (RUHS) cheer was particularly creative: "Hobble Gobble! Razzle Dazzle! Zip! Boom! Bah! R.U.H.S. Rah! Rah! Rah!"

Once finished with high school, Redlands alumni often went on to college, reflecting the quality of education provided by the high school. Many of the 12 graduates in the first class of 1894 pursued higher education, with three earning bachelor's degrees from Stanford and one from the University of California, Berkeley. In addition, one student went on for a PhD at Harvard and another went on for a medical degree at the University of California, Berkeley. Subsequent classes added graduates of the University of Southern California and Pomona College, in Claremont, along with numerous Midwestern and East Coast colleges and universities. The University of Redlands opened to students in the fall of 1909, allowing local students to attend a college in their own town.

School annuals from Redlands High School provide a wealth of information about students and their lives, including postgraduate information such as name changes for women, college educations, occupations, and where they later lived. Senior photographs in these annuals also helped to keep professional photographers in business, and their advertisements in these books help date them in Redlands.

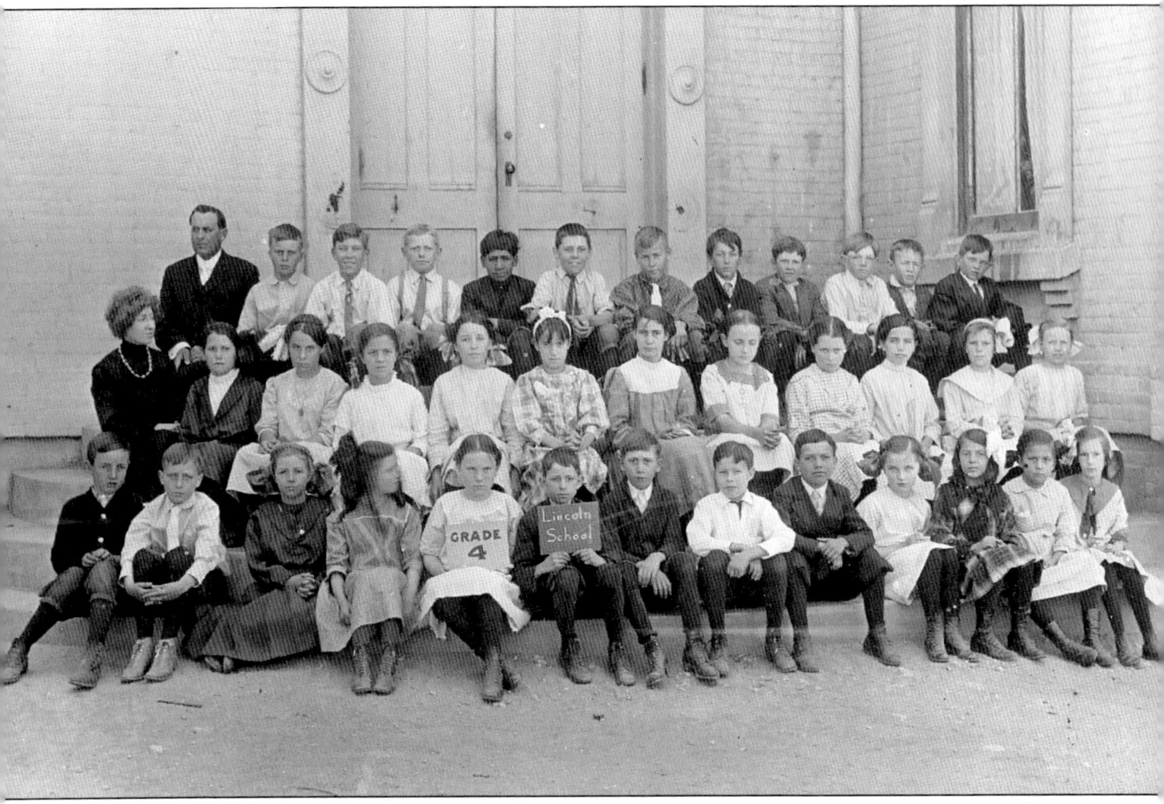

Redlands had no middle school until about 1919, so pre–high school education took place in grammar schools such as Lincoln School, which was on West Colton Avenue between Lawton and Texas Streets. This image was dated between 1912 and 1917 through knowledge of when the photographer worked in Redlands. (Photographer: Clarence N. Jackson.)

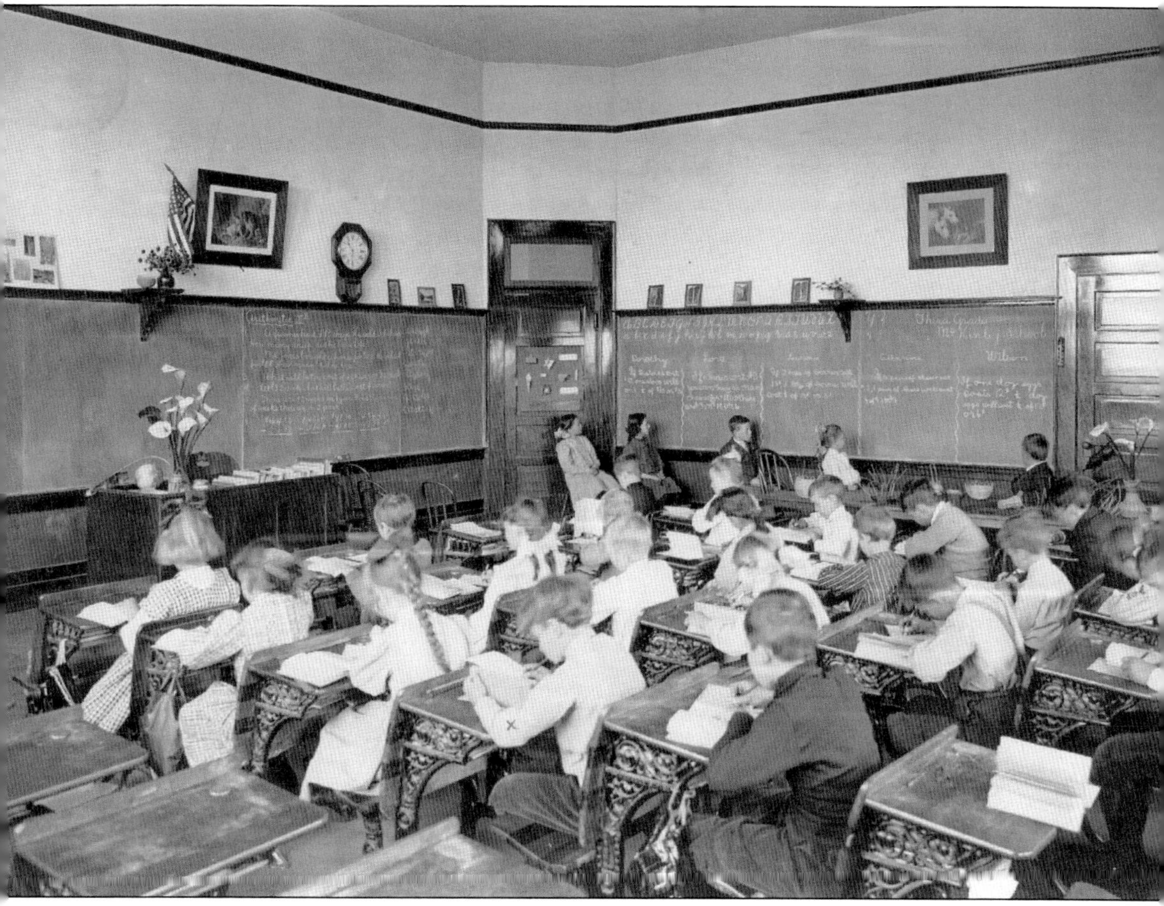

McKinley School opened in 1903 at Center Street and Olive Avenue. It was likely named in honor of Pres. William McKinley, who had visited Redlands in 1901, shortly before his assassination. Answers to arithmetic problems cover the board, including Dorothy's, on the far left, which states, "If 2 stoves cost $10, one stove will cost ½ of $10 or $5." Edward Wilmot, marked with an "x" in this photograph, was born in 1900, dating this third-grade classroom to about 1908. (Photographer: Elias F. Everitt.)

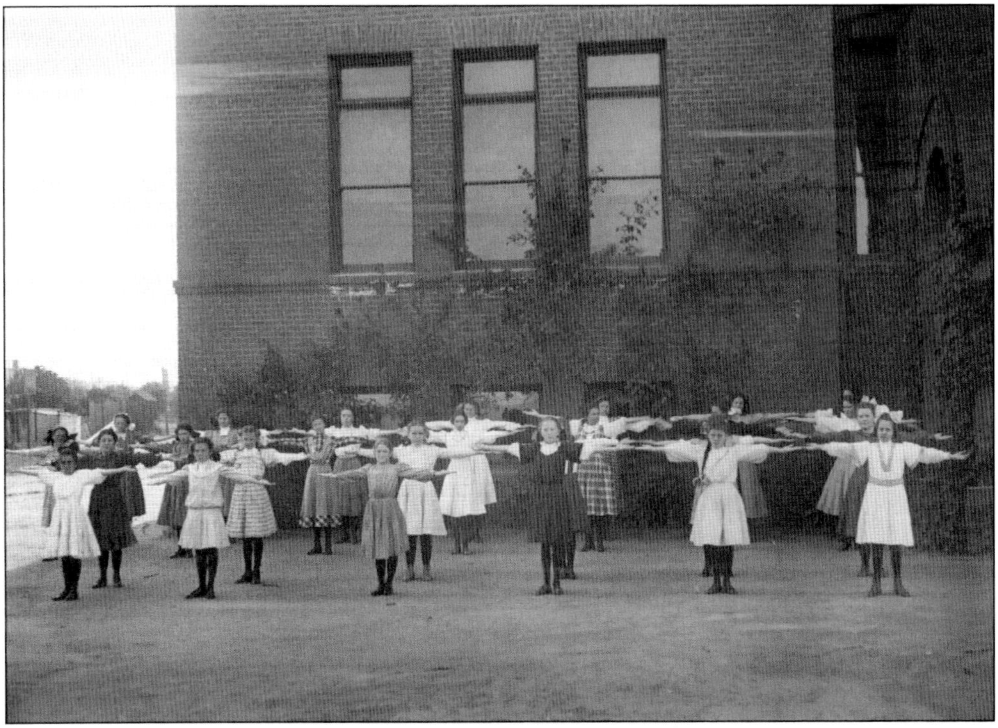

Here, the outside of McKinley School dwarfs the rows of girls doing calisthenics, a popular form of exercise around 1905, when this photograph was taken. There were no gym suits here; instead, girls wore dark stockings, short dresses to suit their younger age, and lots of pigtails and bows. (Photographer: Elias F. Everitt.)

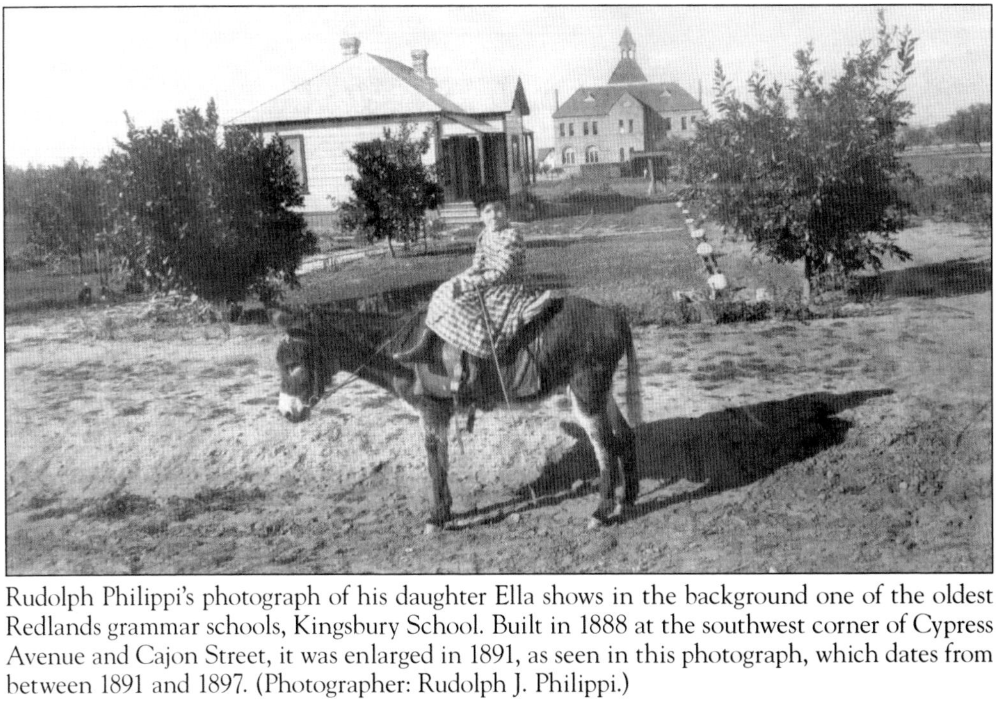

Rudolph Philippi's photograph of his daughter Ella shows in the background one of the oldest Redlands grammar schools, Kingsbury School. Built in 1888 at the southwest corner of Cypress Avenue and Cajon Street, it was enlarged in 1891, as seen in this photograph, which dates from between 1891 and 1897. (Photographer: Rudolph J. Philippi.)

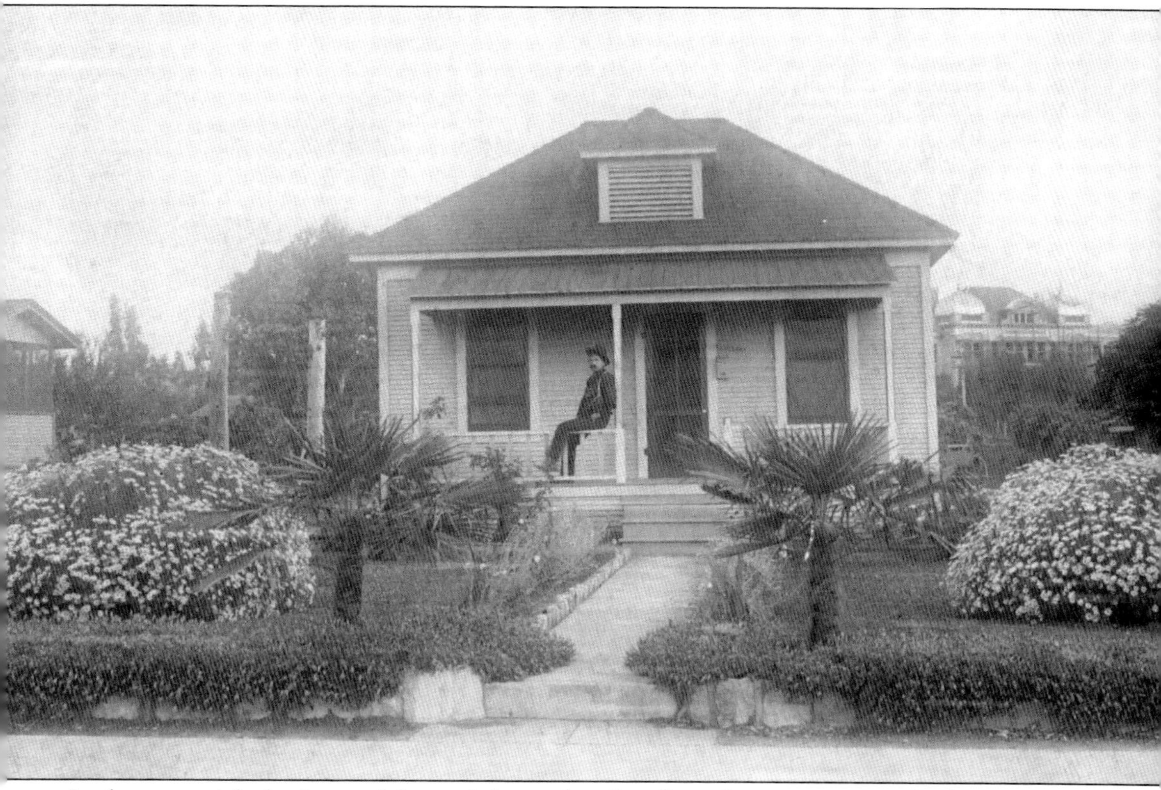

In the upper right background, beyond the modest East State Street cottage in the foreground, Redlands Union High School was undergoing its massive 1904 reconstruction. Scaffolding surrounds the structure and domes have appeared. The 1904 annual stated that students "could study to the music of the hammers and falling bricks." (Photographer: Elias F. Everitt.)

To the High School

Our compliments and best wishes to the High School in general; and to the Senior Class in particular. May you always be as successful in life, as you have been in R. H. S.

Chas. O. Barnett

The Photo Shop

In 1912, probably his first year in Redlands, professional photographer Charles Barnett had already realized the importance of high school photographs to his business, placing this advertisement in the annual. "RHS" refers to Redlands High School, where he became a well-known figure for over 10 years photographing seniors, faculty, clubs, sporting events, and theatricals.

Compliments of

The

Shuford Studio

Time is fleeing; our school days will soon be over. Now is the time to have a Photo taken to remind you of the PAST in years to come.

We allow a special discount to school students

Shuford Studio

Thomas Shuford's advertisement in the Redlands High School annual of 1914 played on nostalgia to get parents and students to have photographs taken. Then as now, images of graduating seniors provided needed income for professional photographers.

Gertrude Willows, an 1899 Redlands Union High School graduate, came to the United States from England in 1892 at about 12 years of age. She acquired US citizenship in 1898. She then obtained a bachelor of arts degree from Pomona College in Claremont, followed by a master of arts degree at the University of California, Berkeley. Ultimately, she became a high school teacher in Claremont. (Photographers: Grace E. Laney and Charles C. Melvin.)

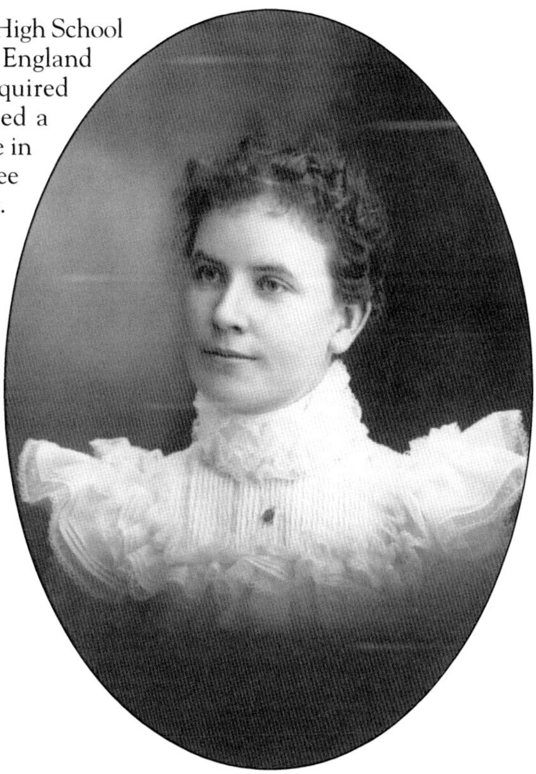

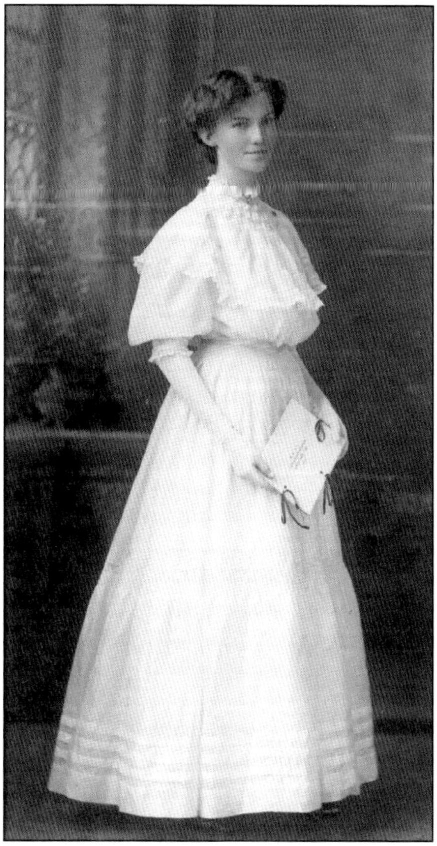

Alice Horton's portrait was taken for her 1906 graduation from Redlands Union High School. The high school annual of 1906 stated that she planned to attend the Los Angeles State Normal School, which later became the University of California, Los Angeles. By 1915, Horton was the vice principal of Barton School on Nevada Street in Redlands. (Photographer: William C. Butman.)

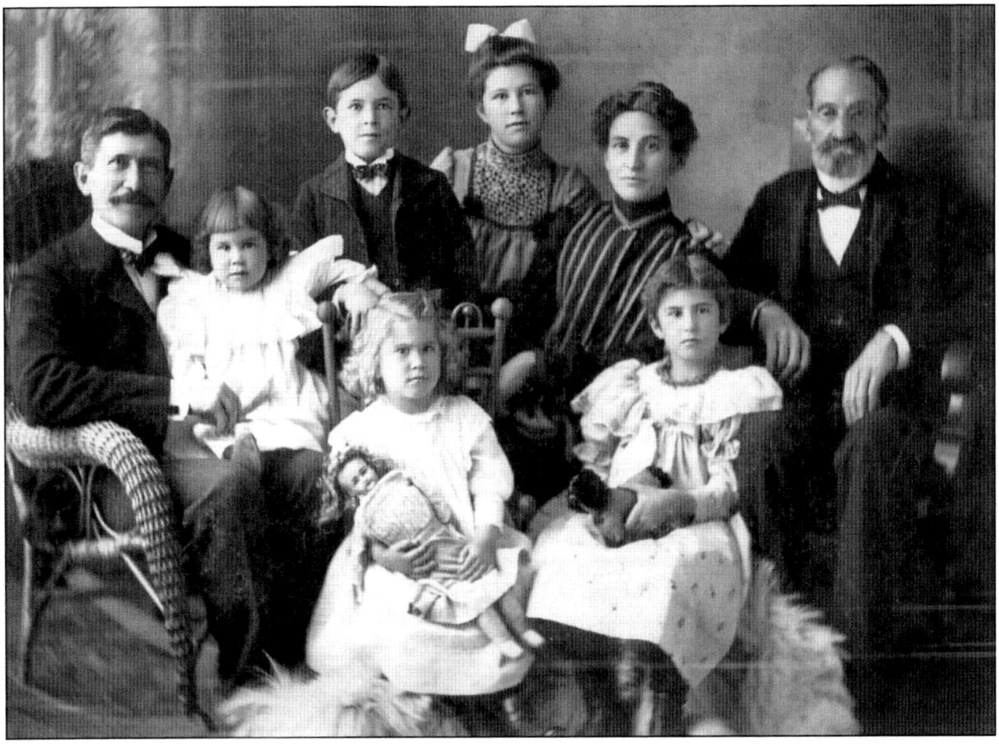

Three generations of the Avery family appear in this December 1902 photograph. Lewis B. Avery (far left) served as principal of Redlands Union High School from 1895 through 1908. Well-liked by the students, he was described in the 1906 annual as "a Principal who is also an adviser, helper, and friend." Three-year-old Priscilla Avery holds the very large doll. (Photographer: Edward E. Roessler.)

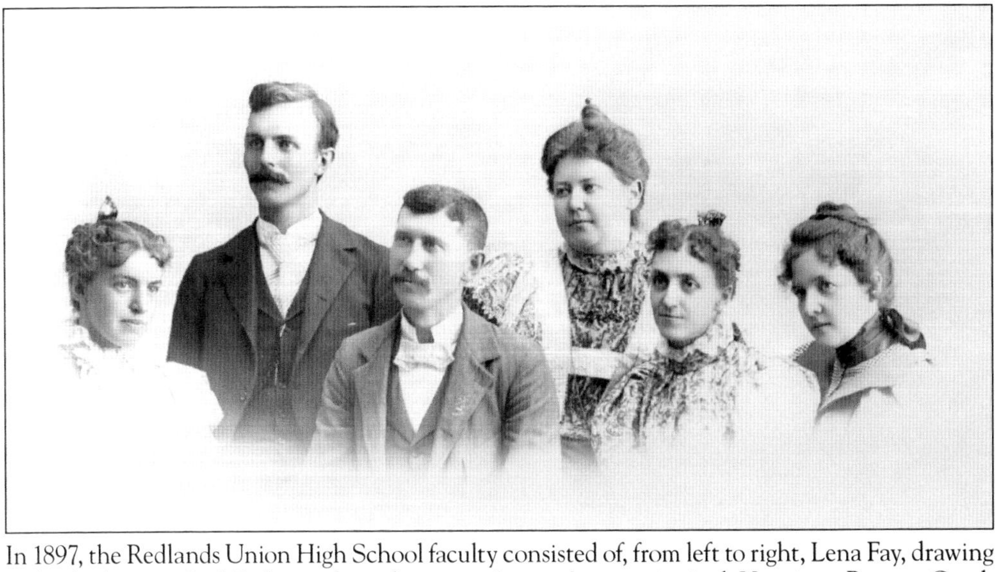

In 1897, the Redlands Union High School faculty consisted of, from left to right, Lena Fay, drawing and calisthenics; Carl Richmond, mathematics; Lewis Avery, principal; Henrietta Brewer, Greek and history; Katherine Fall, Latin and US history; and Georgia Reed, who was possibly a literature teacher. (Photographers: Grace E. Laney and Charles C. Melvin.)

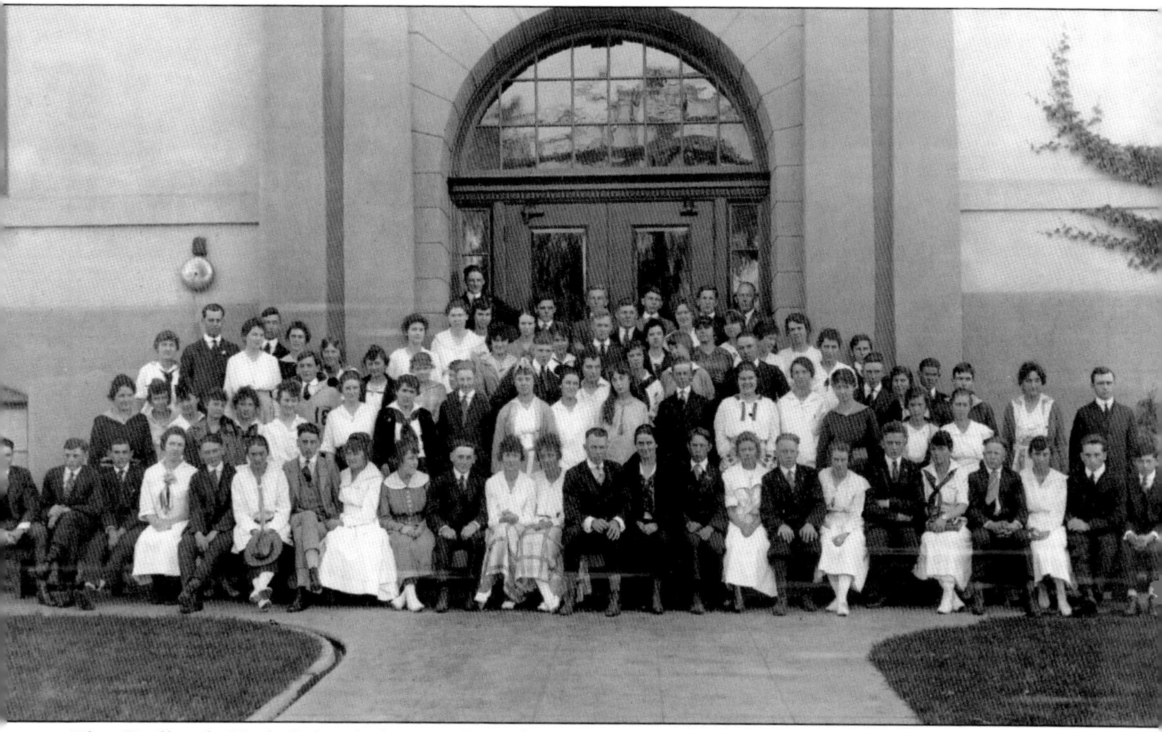

This Redlands High School class graduated in 1918, in the midst of World War I. At the time of graduation, 12 members of its class had already joined the military. Their principal, Henry G. Clement, wrote a poignant note in their annual stating that "no class ever left this high school when we felt so concerned over what might await them." (Photographer: Guy L. Fairbanks.)

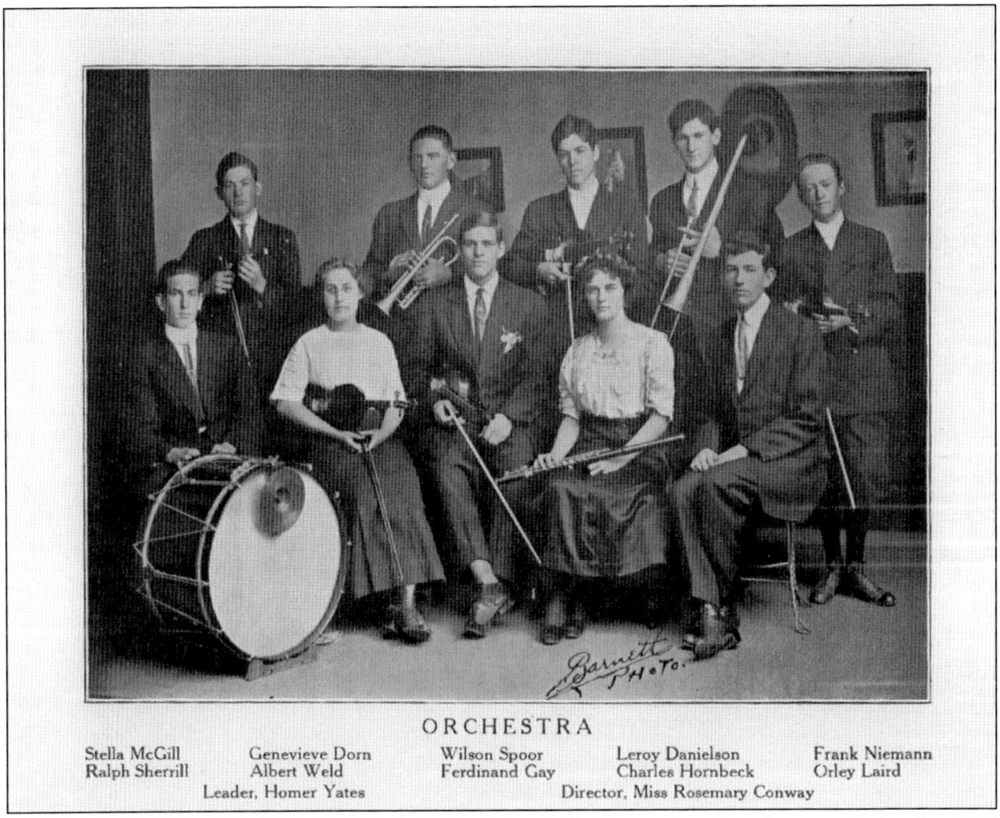

Charles Barnett captured the Redlands High School Orchestra for this photograph in the 1912 annual. Frank Niemann, second from left in the back row, holding a trumpet, went on to be a professional musician, including working with an opera house in Elsinore. Wilson Spoor, seated behind the drum at far left, became a druggist and took over his father's pharmacy in Redlands. (Photographer: Charles O. Barnett.)

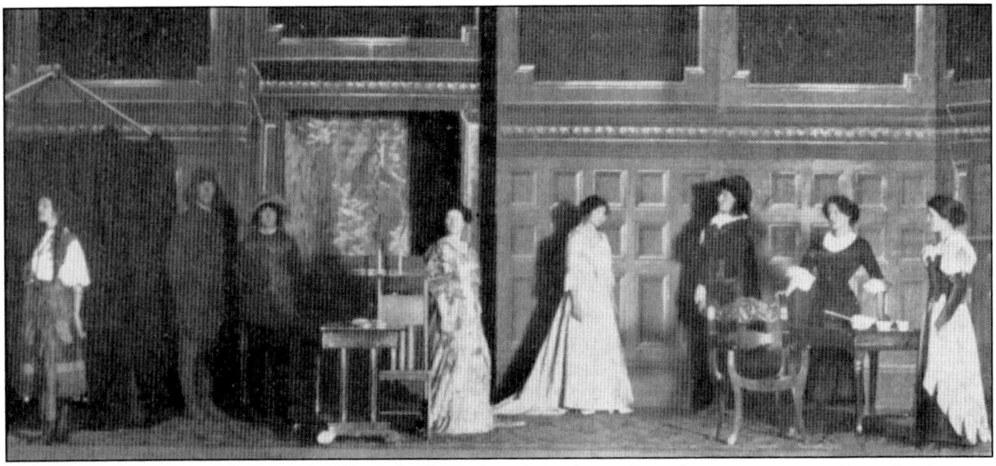

Professional photographers not only took class photographs and graduation pictures but also images of high school drama productions. The Redlands High School senior class of 1912 produced the play *The Road to Yesterday*, which began in 1903 but reverted to 1603, resulting in the older-looking costumes and the ornate backdrop and props. (Photographer: Charles O. Barnett.)

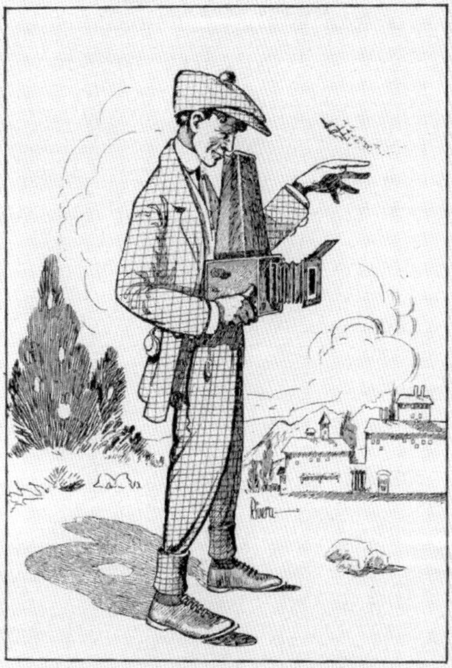

Seeing The Game Through A Press Camera.

Compliments
of
Your Photographer

CHAS. O. BARNETT

"The Photo Shop"

One of the ever-present sections of the high school annual related to sports. Professional photographer Charles Barnett became well known at high school games, prompting this line drawing in the 1913 annual by Rolando Rivera, who later became a professional artist. Rivera was the son of longtime Redlands constable Jose Rivera. Fannie E. Barnett, Barnett's wife, eventually became a partner in his photographic business.

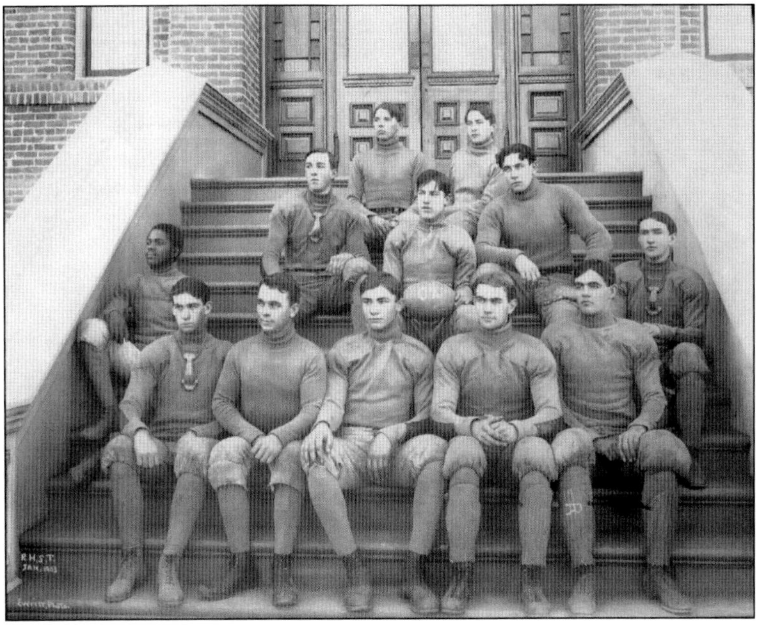

Early football, as played by these Redlands Union High School students in 1902, was a violent sport. Their skimpy protective gear included padded pants, jerseys with some shoulder padding, shin guards like those worn by the two boys at lower right, and occasional use of nose guards, as seen around the neck of the young man at lower left. (Photographer: Elias F. Everitt.)

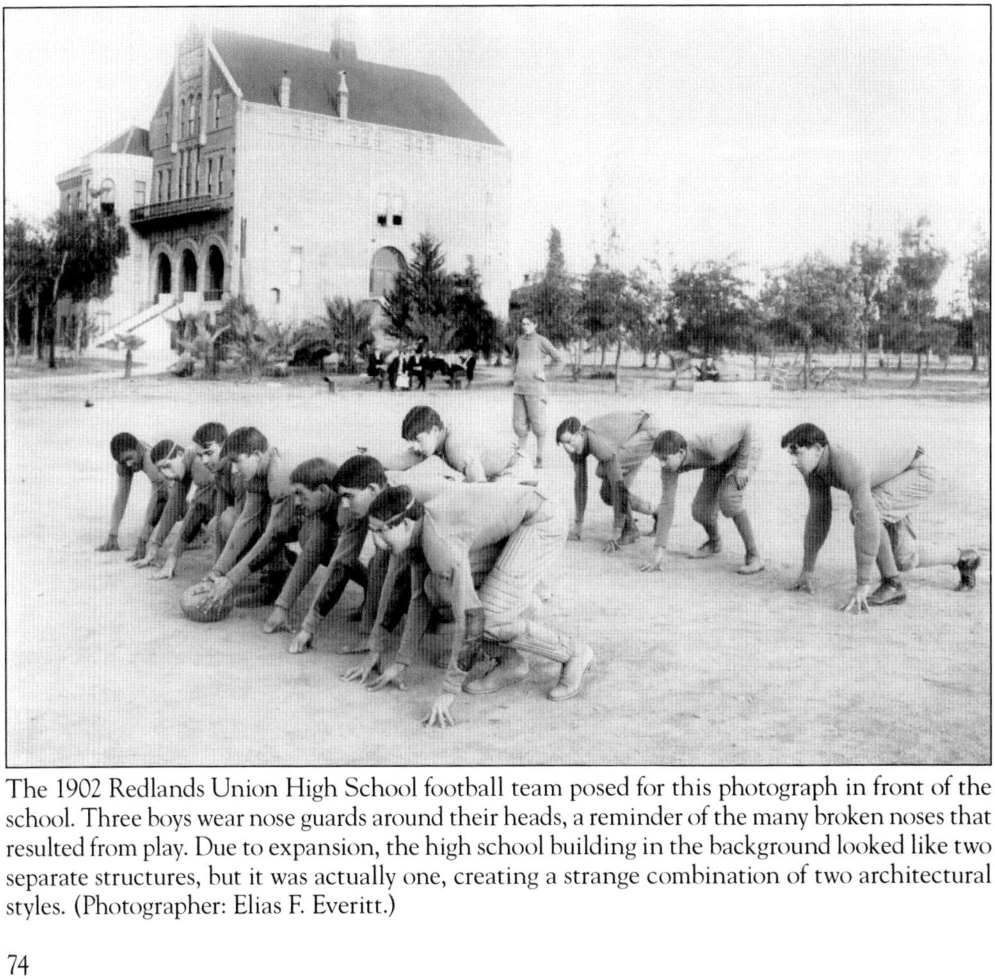

The 1902 Redlands Union High School football team posed for this photograph in front of the school. Three boys wear nose guards around their heads, a reminder of the many broken noses that resulted from play. Due to expansion, the high school building in the background looked like two separate structures, but it was actually one, creating a strange combination of two architectural styles. (Photographer: Elias F. Everitt.)

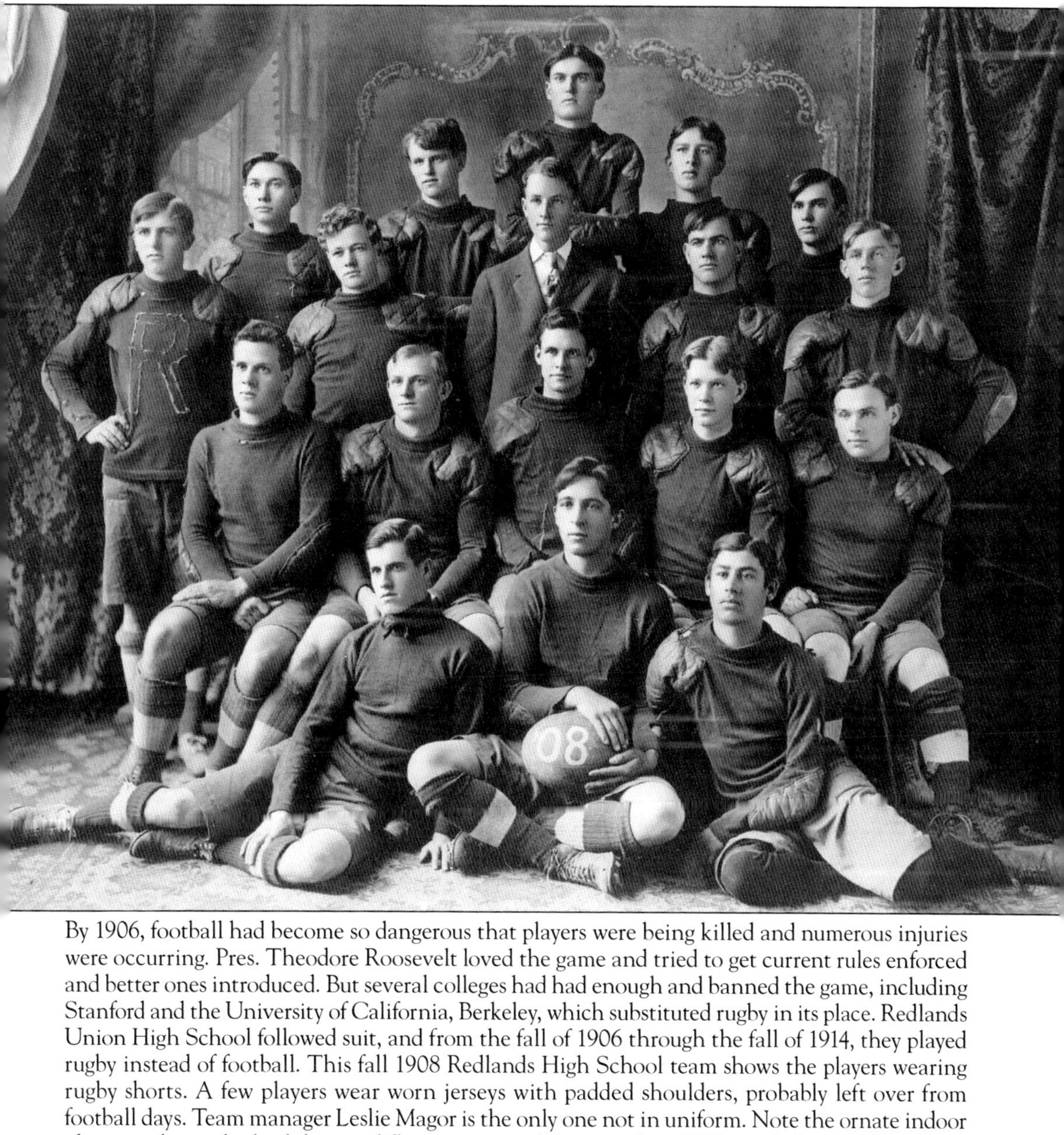

By 1906, football had become so dangerous that players were being killed and numerous injuries were occurring. Pres. Theodore Roosevelt loved the game and tried to get current rules enforced and better ones introduced. But several colleges had had enough and banned the game, including Stanford and the University of California, Berkeley, which substituted rugby in its place. Redlands Union High School followed suit, and from the fall of 1906 through the fall of 1914, they played rugby instead of football. This fall 1908 Redlands High School team shows the players wearing rugby shorts. A few players wear worn jerseys with padded shoulders, probably left over from football days. Team manager Leslie Magor is the only one not in uniform. Note the ornate indoor photography studio backdrop and floor covering. (Photographer: William C. Butman.)

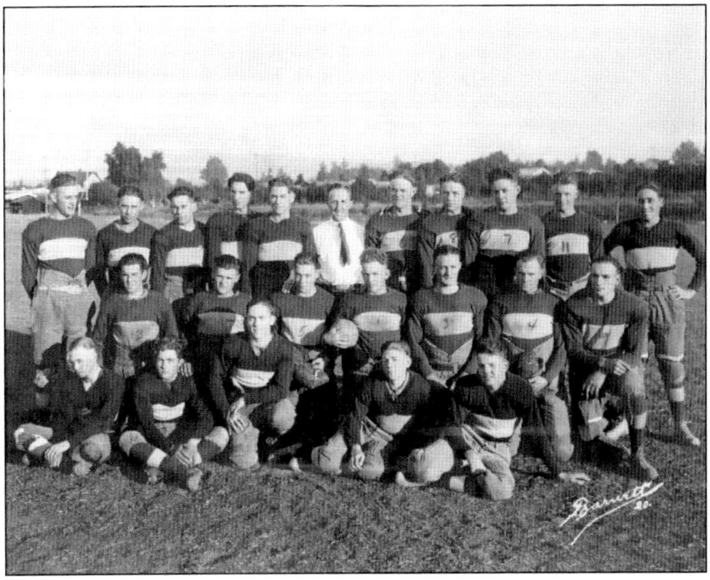

By 1915, California colleges found that Midwestern and East Coast schools were returning to football, or had never banned it, and that safer rules and play had been instituted. The University of California, Berkeley, made the change back, apparently prompting Redlands High School to also return to football. This 1920 Redlands team included four seniors who went on to play football at the University of Redlands the following year. (Photographer: Charles O. Barnett.)

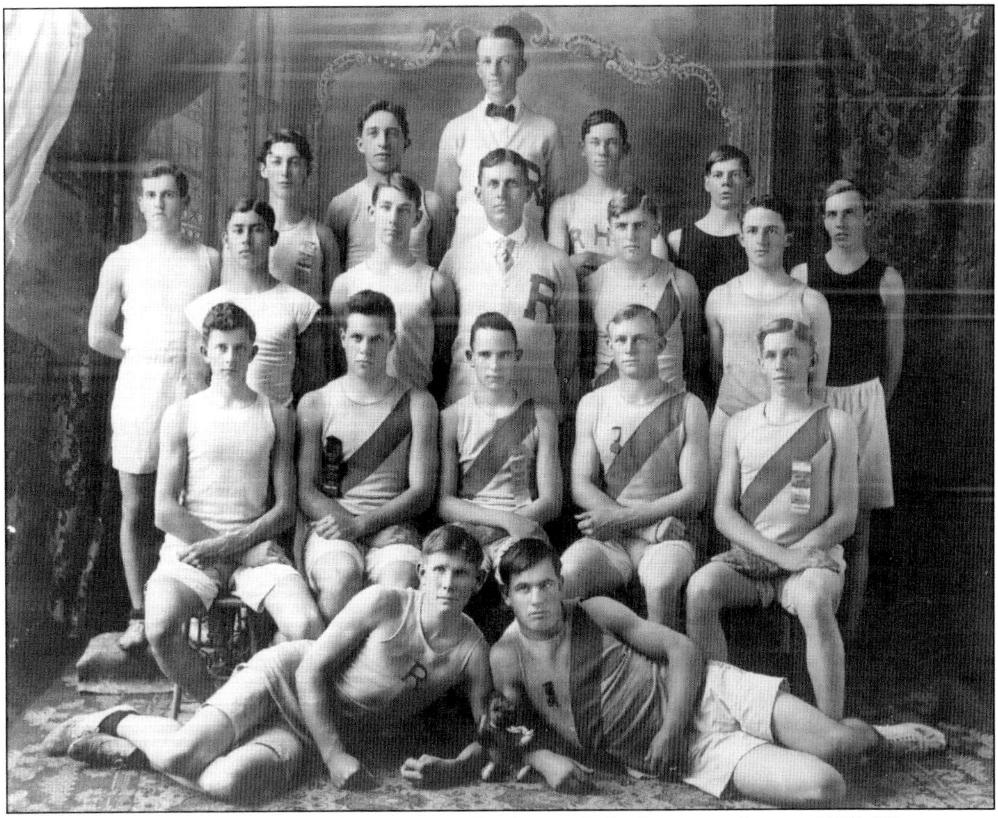

This Redlands High School track team won the Citrus Belt championship in 1909. Three team members received first-place medals: Ervin Best in the 220-yard dash, at 23.2 seconds; R. Bonnell for the high jump, at 5 feet 7.5 inches; and Harry Ford in the shot put, at 40 feet 10.5 inches. (Photographer: William C. Butman.)

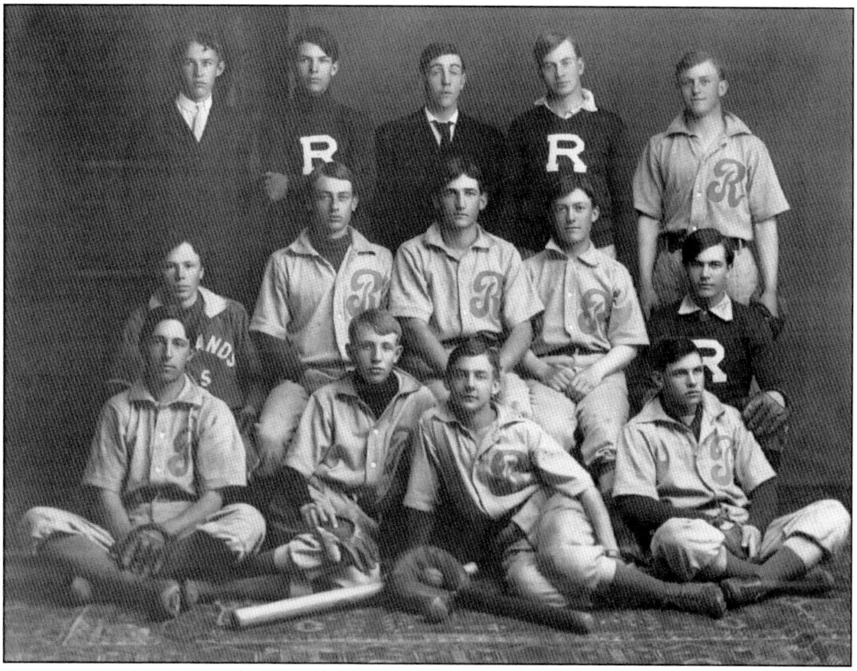

Baseball was an early sport at Redlands High School, and game write-ups and photographs were printed in annuals. The image above shows the 1907 team, with their coach at center rear. According to the 1907 annual, baseball was increasing in popularity and there was more competition for the 1907 team positions than in earlier years. Below is the Redlands High School baseball team just two years later, in 1909, with new uniforms. Note that the photographer, William Butman, was using the same elaborate studio backdrop and rug as in the 1909 track team photo on the opposite page. (Photographers: above, Thomas R. Shuford; below, William C. Butman.)

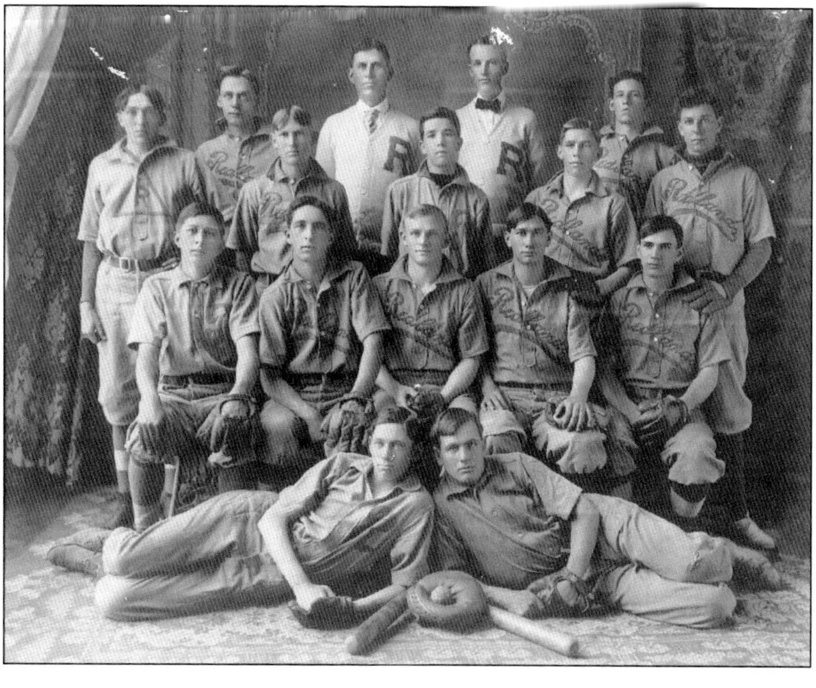

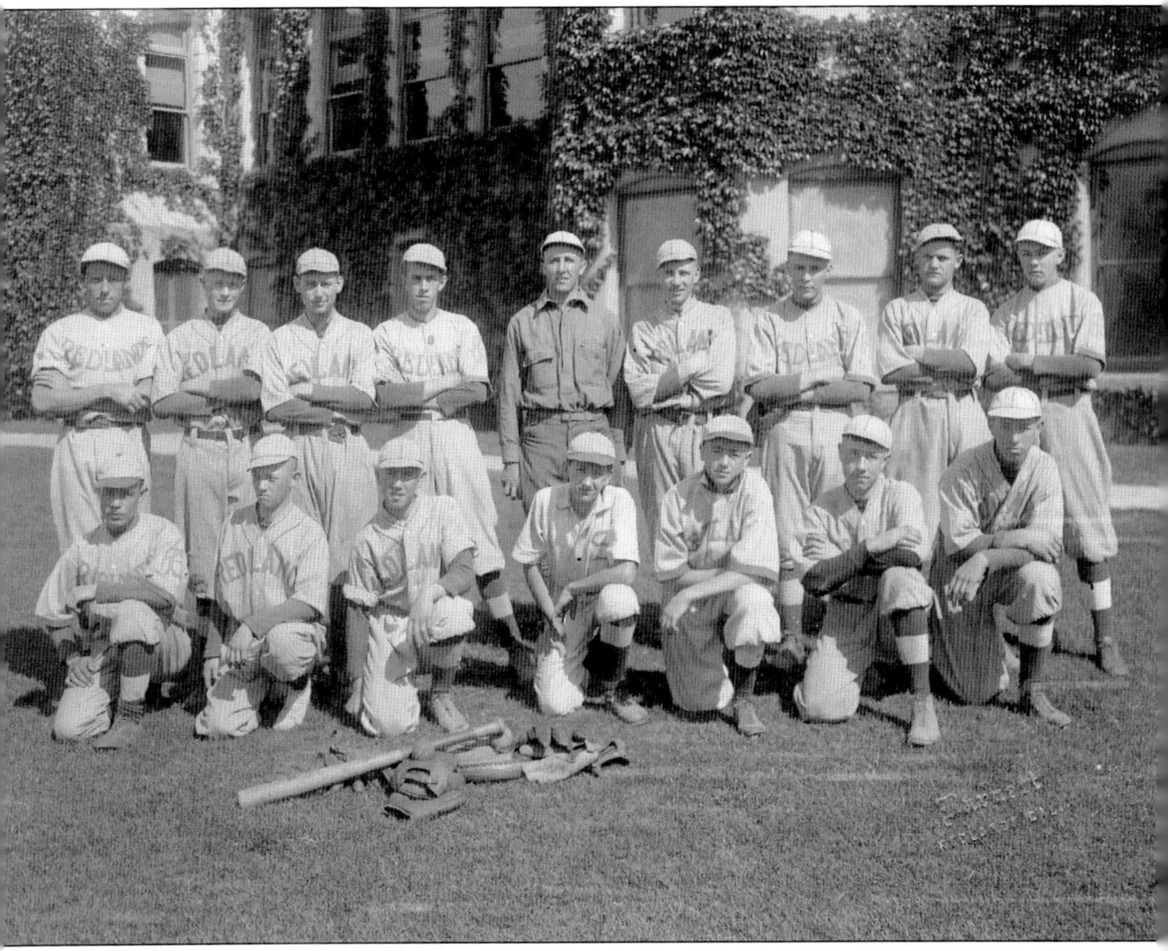

The 1919 Redlands High School baseball team posed for this photograph outside the main school building. That season, athletics competed with the devastating worldwide influenza epidemic of 1918. In fact, the 1918 football season was delayed after all the team members got the flu, pushing the last game of the season to February instead of before Christmas. This overlapped with early basketball practices, causing some scheduling problems. (Photographer: Charles O. Barnett.)

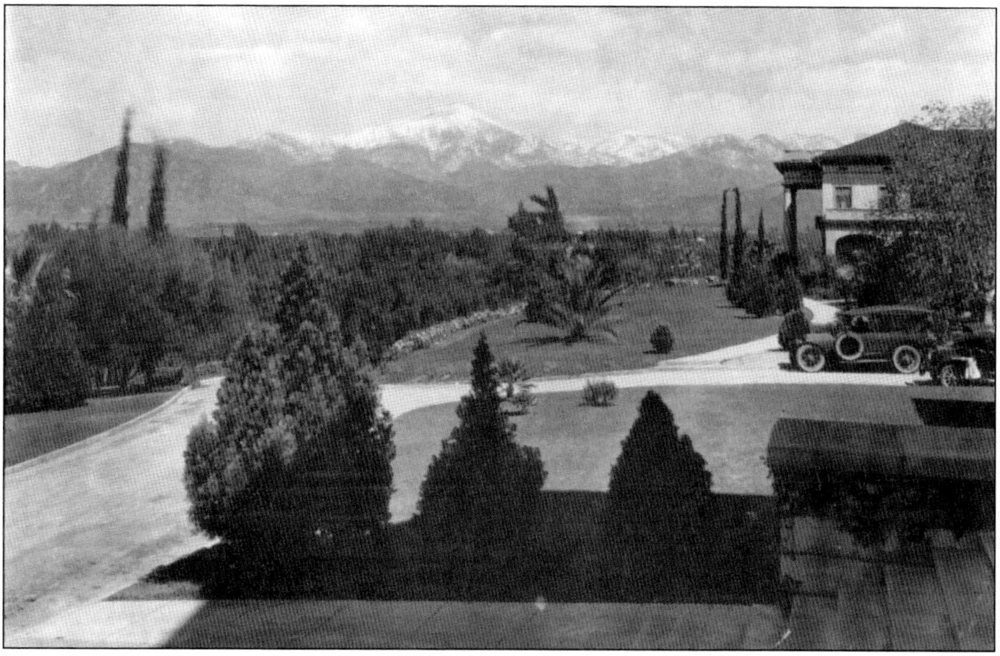

The University of Redlands opened to students in fall 1909 and was only 11 years old when this photograph was taken in March 1920. To the right is the president's mansion, which was later moved a short distance to the east—no small task for a building that size. It eventually became the Alumni House. (Photographer: Elias F. Everitt.)

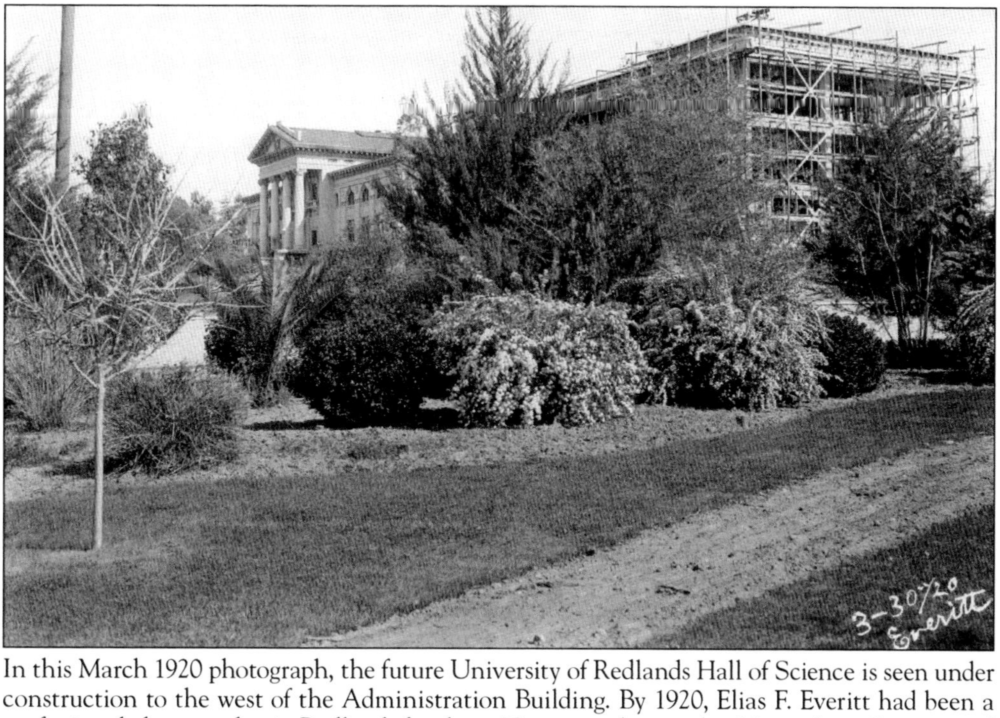

In this March 1920 photograph, the future University of Redlands Hall of Science is seen under construction to the west of the Administration Building. By 1920, Elias F. Everitt had been a professional photographer in Redlands for about 23 years and was in his 80s, yet he still continued to work. (Photographer: Elias F. Everitt.)

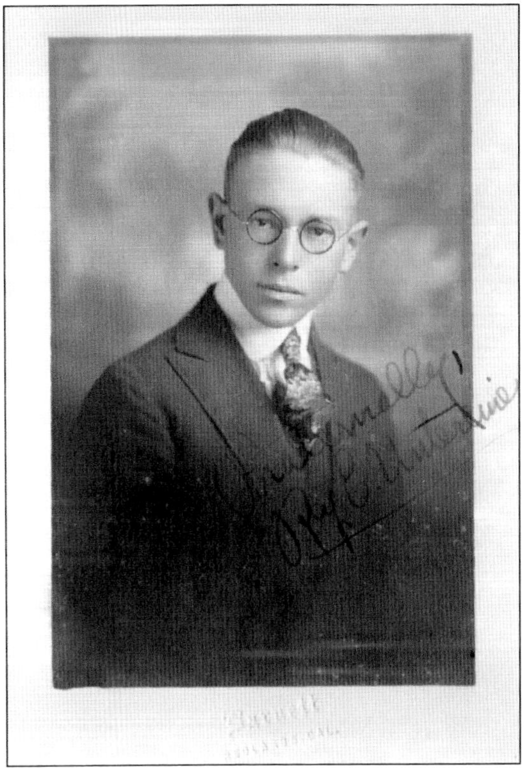

Raymond Untereiner, a graduate of Redlands High School (1916) and the University of Redlands (1920), went on to be a professor at the California Institute of Technology in Pasadena. He signed this 1920 photograph "Fraternally yours," in reference to his membership in the Kappa Sigma Sigma fraternity at the university, which is now one of the oldest on campus. He served on the university's board of trustees in 1964–1965. (Photographer: Charles O. Barnett.)

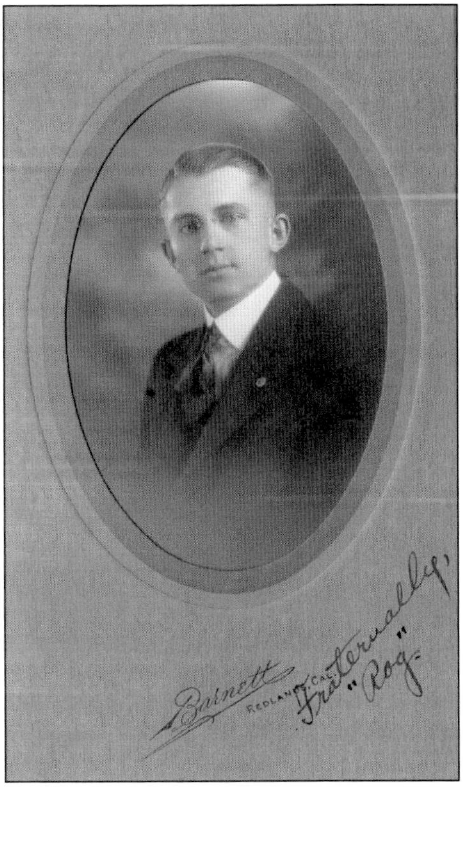

This 1920 photograph shows another Kappa Sigma Sigma brother, Roger Truesdail, who also graduated from Redlands High School (1917) and the University of Redlands (1921). He never lost his passion for the university, serving on the board of trustees from 1935 to 1974 while working as a chemist and opening his own laboratory in the Los Angeles area. (Photographer: Charles O. Barnett.)

Five

"Amusements"

The period from 1880 to 1920 saw vast changes in entertainment sources, from a do-it-yourself attitude to an increase in being entertained by others. Redlands eagerly followed the national trends. If one wanted to hear music in the 1880s and 1890s, most people either played and sang it themselves, usually around a home piano, or listened to locally performed amateur music with occasional visiting professionals. Making music was very important to people such as Fred Gernich, a Redlands resident working in the San Bernardino Mountains, who wrote to his sister in December 1891, "I miss music ever so much, I would just like to sit down and hear you play and sing over some of the songs with you and Millie." Access to professional music expanded after 1900 through phonographs sold in town stores.

Live theater also provided entertainment, with many of the performances again being produced by locals. The first theater in Redlands was the 500-seat Wilson's Opera House, which opened in 1887 upstairs in the Wilson & Berry block in Lugonia. A January 1888 production of *Uncle Tom's Cabin* included three bloodhounds, two trained donkeys, and over 25 performers. Redlands soon needed more performance space, and another opera house opened in March 1891 upstairs in the Academy of Music block on the northeast corner of Orange Street and Citrus Avenue. It could hold 1,000 people. Finally, in 1904, the 1,200-seat Wyatt Opera House opened on the northwest corner of Orange Street and Colton Avenue. The upstart motion picture theaters eventually pushed most opera houses out of operation, including in Redlands. Movies tended to be less expensive than live theater and changed rapidly from week to week.

Professional photographers kept busy taking pictures of plays for publicity, events that were considered historical and that could be sold to locals and tourists, and chamber of commerce opportunities to publicize the town. By 1900, these same professional photographers entered into the business of selling cameras to amateurs and developing their film, creating the piles of home photographs many families have today.

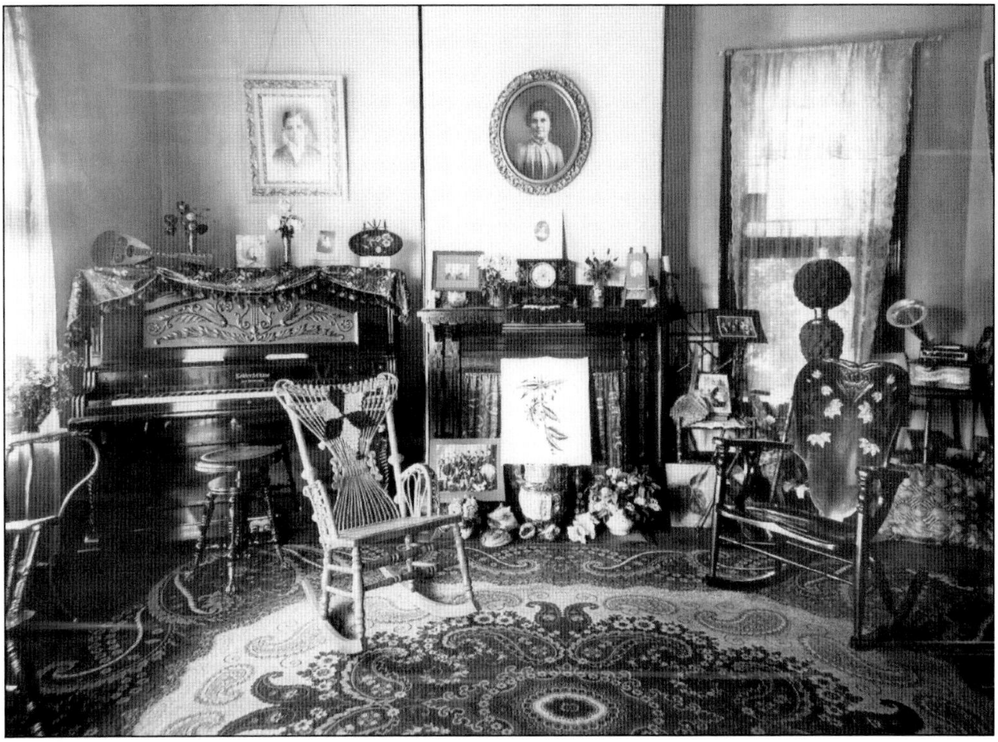

By 1900, the Gowland family home in Redlands had a music area that included a piano, a mandolin, and, in the right corner, a small early phonograph called a Graphophone. This photograph, although taken by an unknown photographer, is included to show how common photographs were in homes of this era. Note the photograph of a band on the floor in front of the fireplace and the portrait photographs scattered about, many with photographers' imprints. (Unknown photographer.)

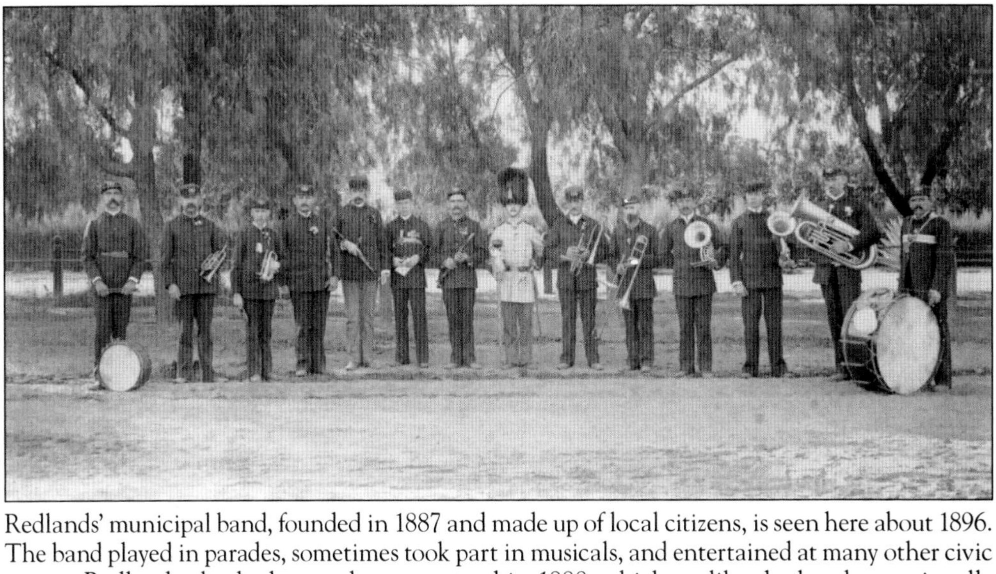

Redlands' municipal band, founded in 1887 and made up of local citizens, is seen here about 1896. The band played in parades, sometimes took part in musicals, and entertained at many other civic events. Redlands also had an orchestra, started in 1888, which, unlike the band, occasionally allowed women to perform. (Photographer: Frank C. Fryett.)

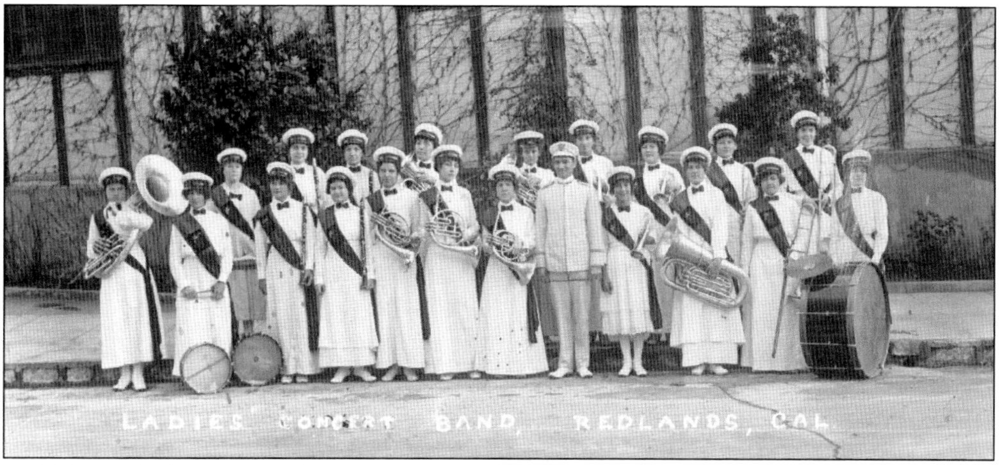

By 1916, the Ladies Concert Band existed in Redlands, allowing a musical outlet for women who wished to perform in a band. Many municipal bands remained all male until World War II, when a lack of available men broke the gender barrier. Here, band members wear matching caps, sashes, and bow ties. Their bandleader, Mr. Ball, stands near the center of the first row. (Photographer: Clarence N. Jackson.)

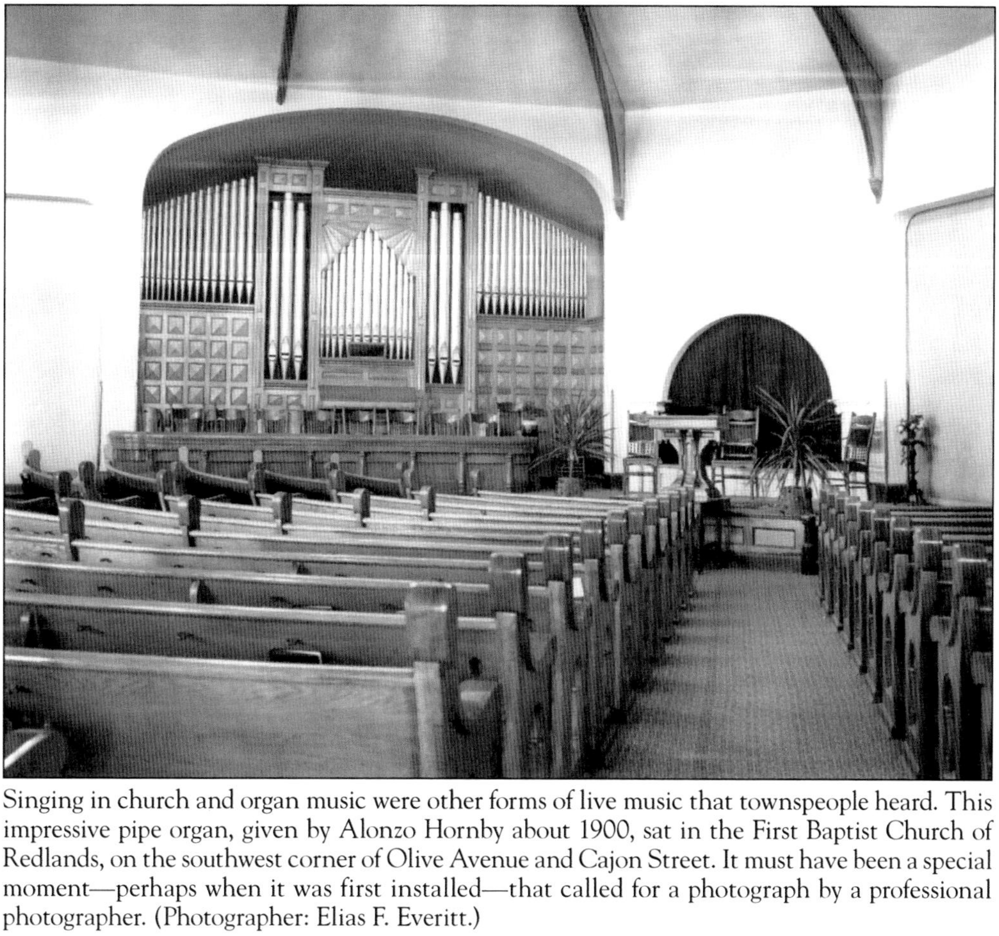

Singing in church and organ music were other forms of live music that townspeople heard. This impressive pipe organ, given by Alonzo Hornby about 1900, sat in the First Baptist Church of Redlands, on the southwest corner of Olive Avenue and Cajon Street. It must have been a special moment—perhaps when it was first installed—that called for a photograph by a professional photographer. (Photographer: Elias F. Everitt.)

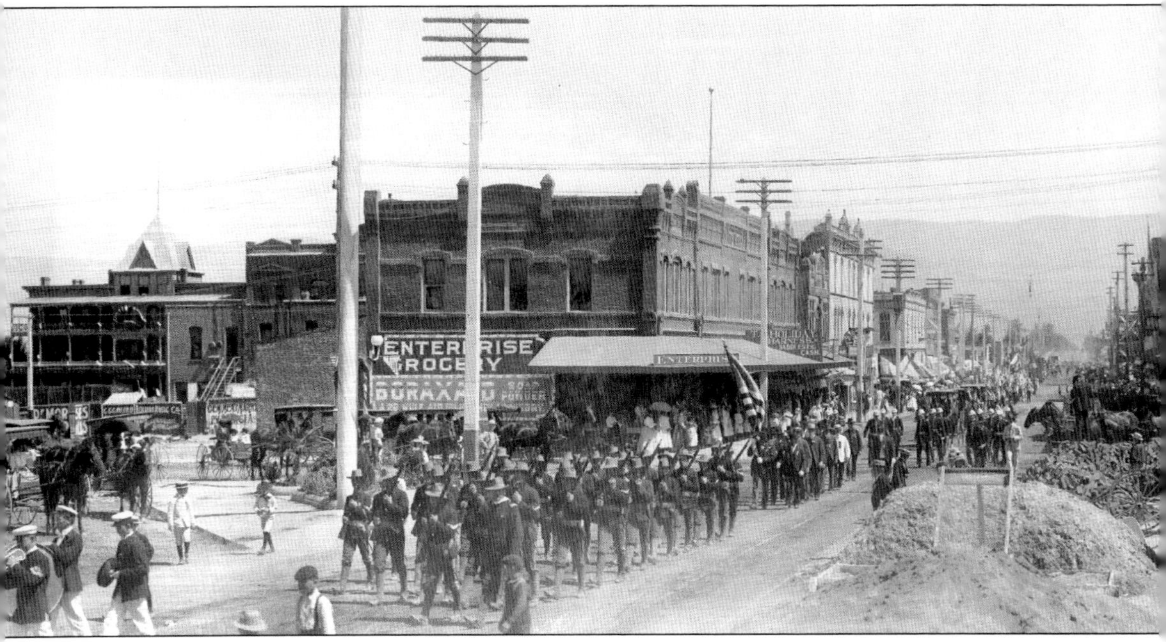

Parades have been and still are important to Redlands life. Here, the 1899 Fourth of July parade marches south onto Cajon Street just past Citrus Avenue. The Redlands City Band (far left) preceded the local California National Guard unit, Company G of the 7th California Infantry, 1st Brigade. Company G returned in October 1898 from San Francisco, which was as far as it got after being called up for the Spanish-American War. Following the band, with the American flag waving, marched members of Bear Valley Post No. 162 of the Grand Army of the Republic, a local Union veterans' organization of the Civil War. The men with the fancy helmets came from the local Redlands Knights of Pythias, a fraternal organization. What appears to be rubble on the right would actually become the Fisher Building, on the southeast corner of Citrus Avenue and Cajon Street. Photographs of parades must have been profitable for professional photographers such as Everitt. Another photographer with his camera stands atop the rubble at right to capture the event. (Photographer: Elias F. Everitt.)

1776. 1899.

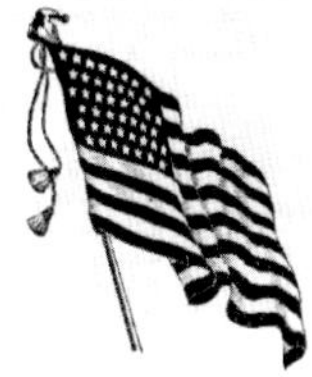

REDLANDS WILL CELEBRATE

— THE —

Glorious Fourth of July, 1899,

With a Complete Program of

Patriotic Observances,
Games, Sports,
And Fireworks,

Making the Most Elaborate Celebration of the Day Ever Held in San Bernardino County.

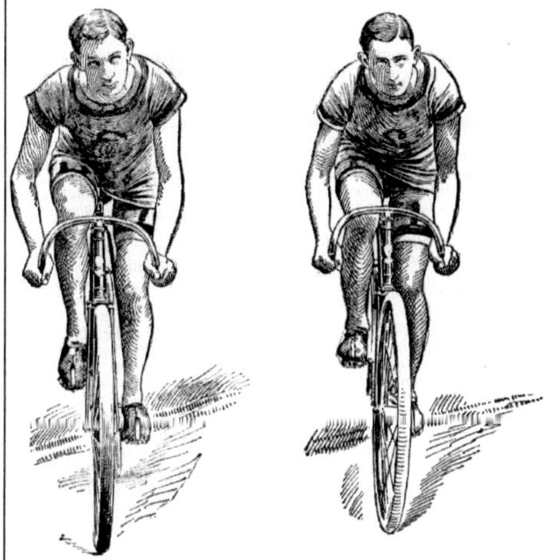

THE DAY WILL OPEN WITH A

GRAND PARADE,

Comprising all the

Uniformed Orders, Civic Bodies and Social Organizations of the City.

Parade will start promptly at 9:00 a. m., and will be followed by open air exercises at the Triangle. The orator of the day will be

HON. WILL A. HARRIS,

Of Los Angeles, well known as a brilliant and eloquent speaker. The afternoon will be devoted to Sports, Races, games, etc. In the evening will be given the

FINEST DISPLAY OF FIREWORKS

Ever seen in Redlands. One thousand dollars worth of magnificent Fireworks will be exploded on this occasion, under the direction of an expert. There will be more than a hundred brilliant Four-Pound Rockets, Showers of Pearls, Mottoes, all the Ordinary Pieces, a Splendid Portrait in Flame of Admiral Dewey, the exhibition to conclude with a representation of the far-famed

BATTLESHIP OREGON.

After the fireworks a Grand Ball will be held at the Academy of Music. Special rates on all railroads. Everybody welcome.

For full particulars see Program published elsewhere.

As listed in this newspaper announcement, the same Fourth of July, in 1899, contained many other events besides the parade. Speeches, sporting events, including bicycle races, and a grand fireworks display all occupied the townspeople. A representation of the face of Adm. George Dewey, the hero of the Spanish-American War, and the battleship *Oregon* were both set off. The expensive fireworks cost over $20,000 in today's money.

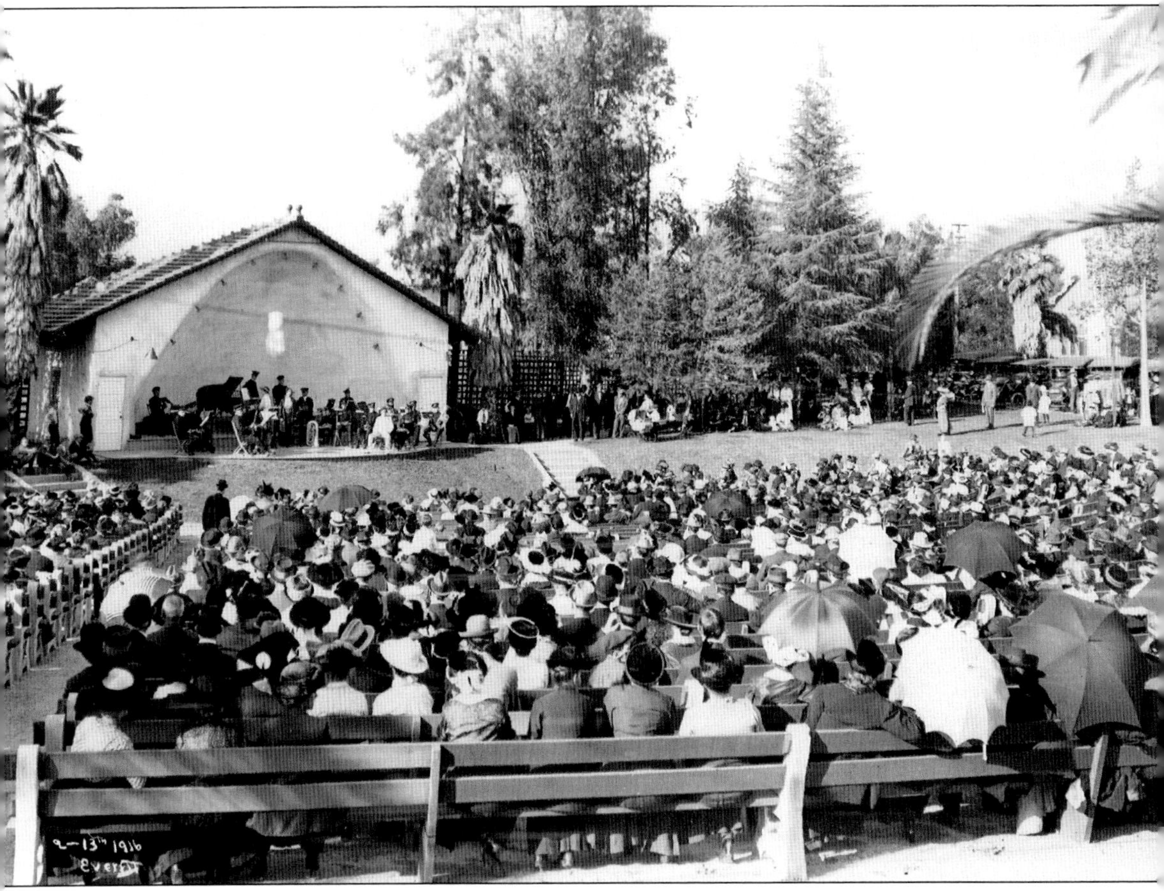

This Sunday afternoon concert at the Redlands Amphitheater in 1916 appears to be in hot summer weather, as women hold umbrellas to shield themselves from the sun. However, it was actually on February 13, with a temperature at 81 degrees. The Redlands Municipal Band performed with Miss Barkelew on piano and Miss Strauss and Mr. Kendall singing. The Redlands Bowl now occupies the former site of this amphitheater, between Eureka and Grant Streets. More than one professional photographer was busy that day, as John Mee was taking motion pictures of this performance for chamber of commerce publicity. A splendid array of women's hats and automobiles are seen in the image. (Photographer: Elias F. Everitt.)

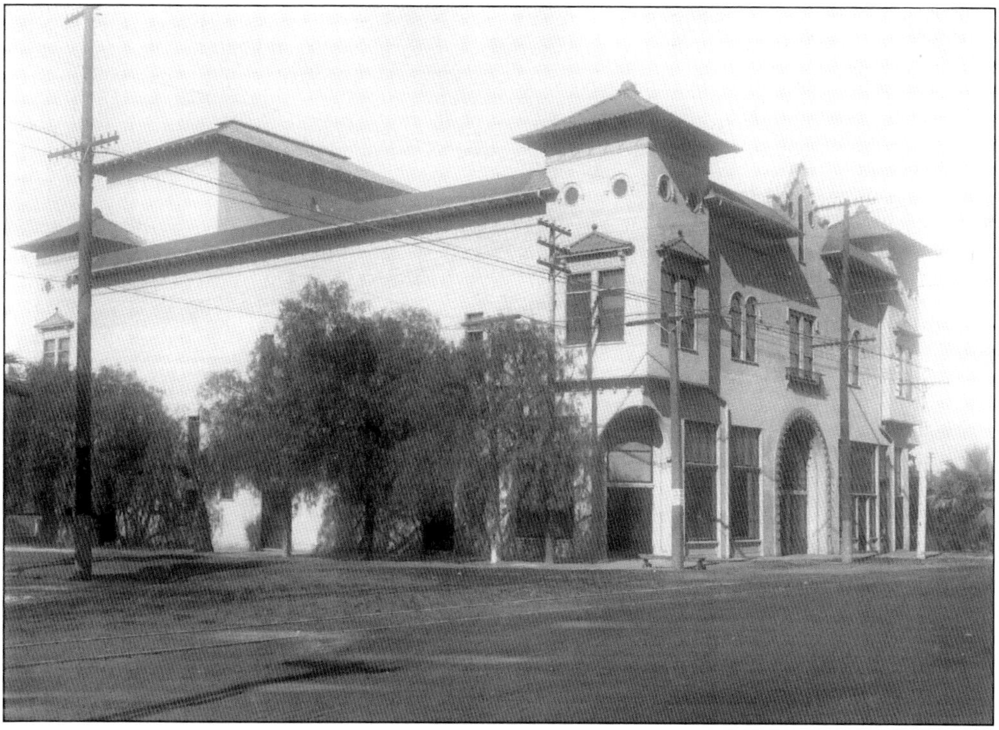

The Wyatt Opera House stood across from the large Casa Loma Hotel on the northwest corner of Orange Street and Colton Avenue. It was also on the town streetcar line, which eventually included a double track in front to load and unload passengers for the theater. After opening in December 1904, it was used for town benefits, professional shows, and graduations. Thankfully, no fires hit the building before it was demolished in 1929, when an inspection showed it to be a firetrap. (Photographer: Elias F. Everitt.)

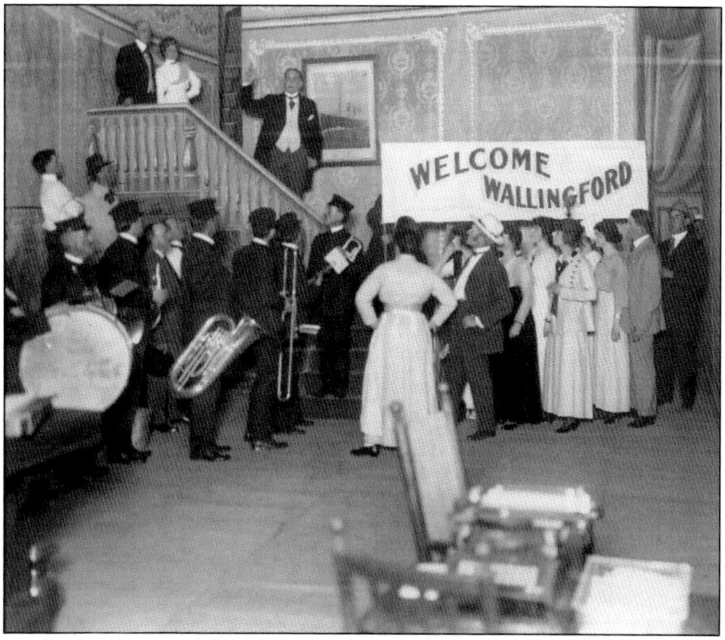

In March 1915, the comedy *Get Rich Quick Wallingford* was performed at the Wyatt Opera House by the Elks Club, with a mostly local amateur cast. This George M. Cohan play, adapted from stories by G.R. Chester, portrayed Wallingford as a scam artist who fell in love with a good woman who redeemed him from his sinful ways. The cast, including the Redlands Municipal Band, is seen here. (Photographer: Charles O. Barnett.)

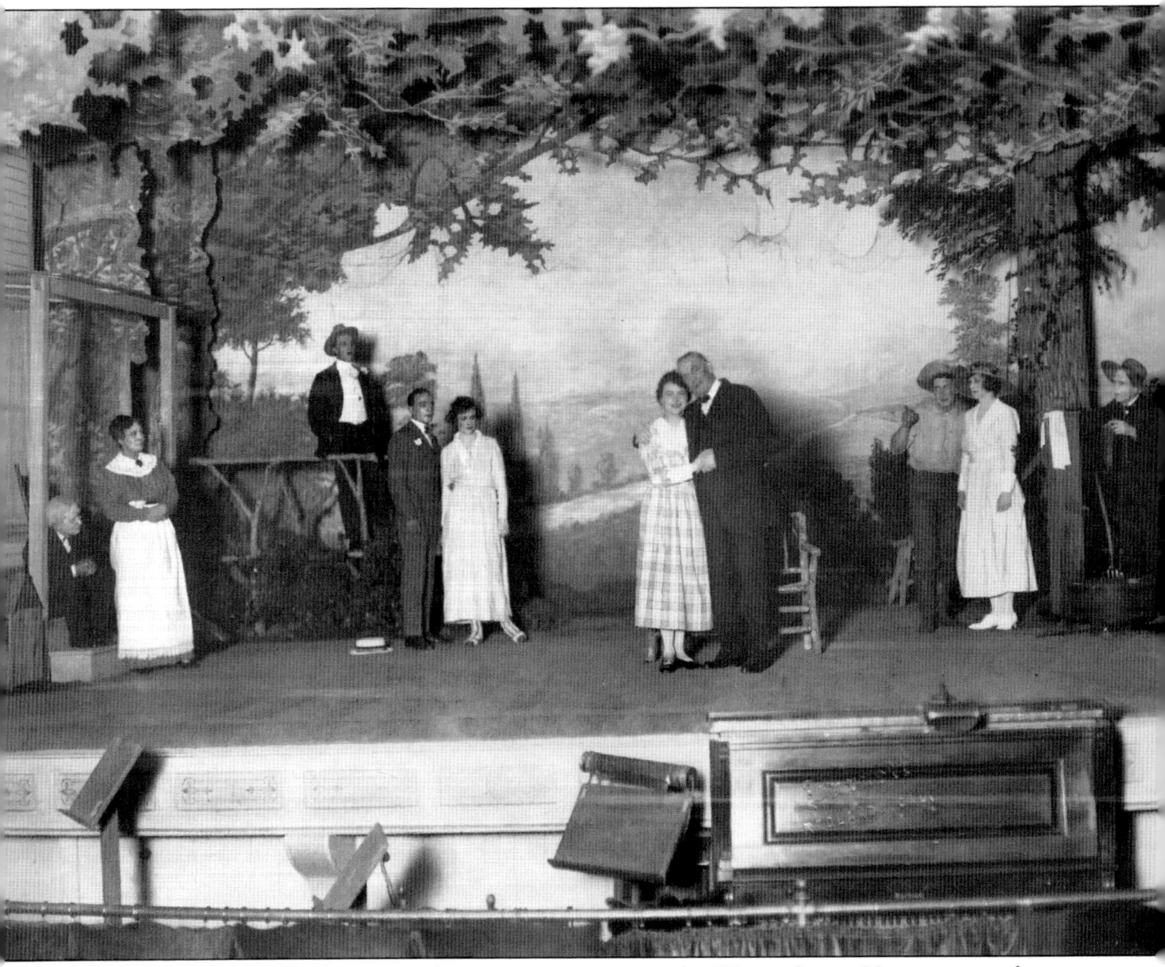

This publicity still of actors and actresses on stage at the Wyatt Opera House comes from an undated photograph. Knowing that the photographer, Charles Barnett, worked in Redlands from 1912 to 1923 places this image within that date range. The set decorations are the star here, as the massive overhanging forest above the stage creates a three-dimensional look. The piano and orchestra pit allowed for live music to accompany events. (Photographer: Charles O. Barnett.)

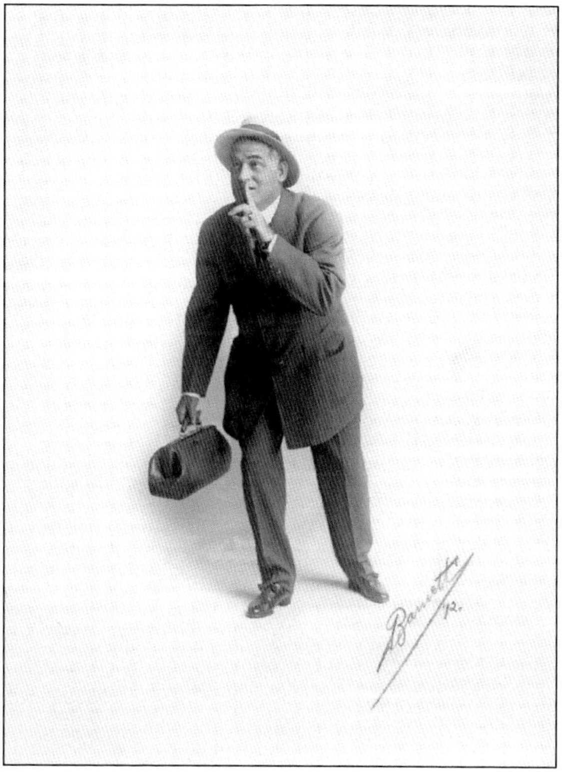

Hal O. Smith, likely an amateur actor, but much sought-after for local theatricals, often performed at the Wyatt Opera House, as seen in these publicity stills by Charles Barnett, who worked in Redlands from about 1912 to 1923. No play names appear with the images, but Barnett included the date of 1912 on one. (Photographer: Charles O. Barnett.)

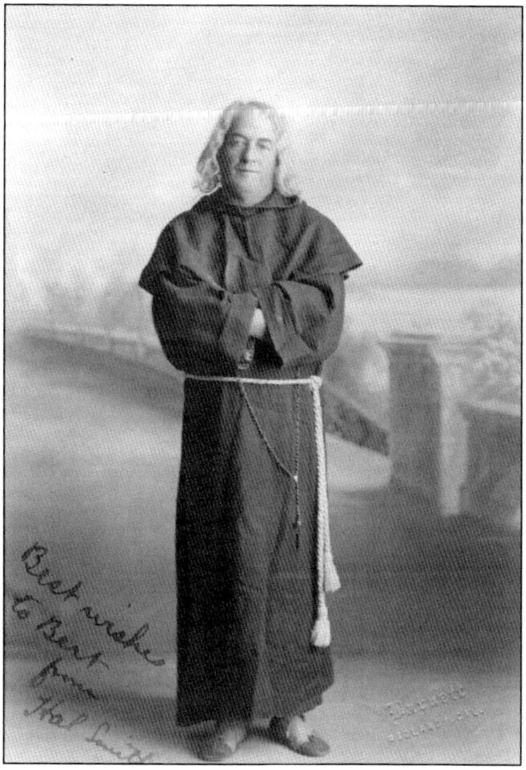

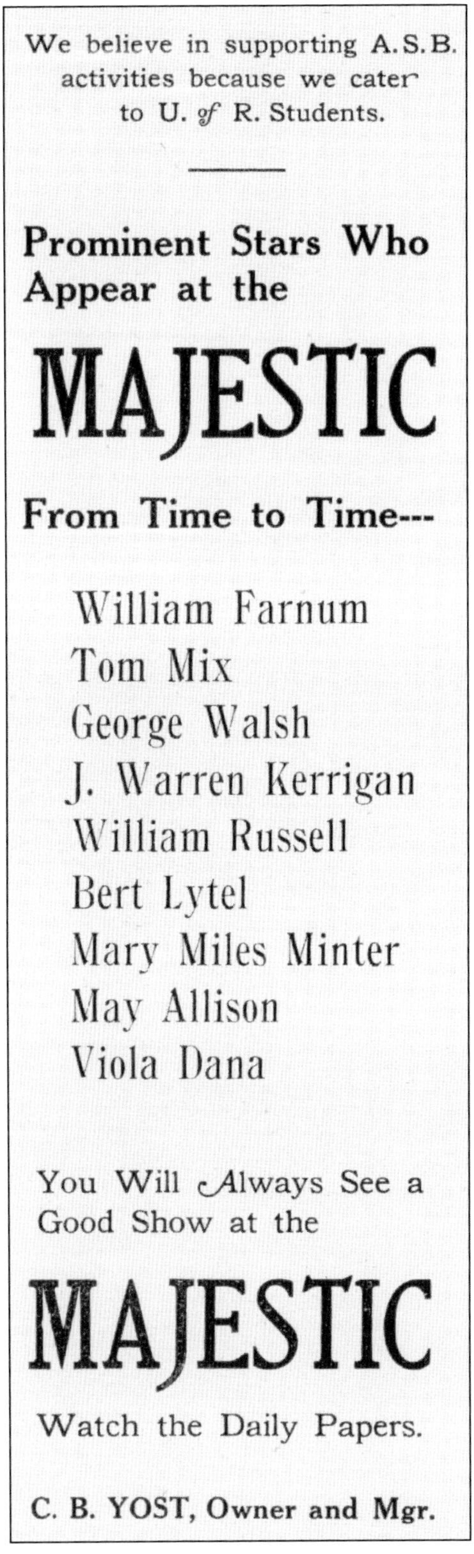

We believe in supporting A. S. B. activities because we cater to U. of R. Students.

Prominent Stars Who Appear at the

MAJESTIC

From Time to Time---

William Farnum
Tom Mix
George Walsh
J. Warren Kerrigan
William Russell
Bert Lytel
Mary Miles Minter
May Allison
Viola Dana

You Will Always See a Good Show at the

MAJESTIC

Watch the Daily Papers.

C. B. YOST, Owner and Mgr.

Despite being in black and white with no sound, movies quickly gained in popularity. Redlands had at least three movie theaters by 1911. The Majestic, at 502 Orange Street, had been open for nine years when it placed this advertisement in the University of Redlands annual in 1920. The title of this chapter, "Amusements," actually comes from a section in several local newspapers that described upcoming movies.

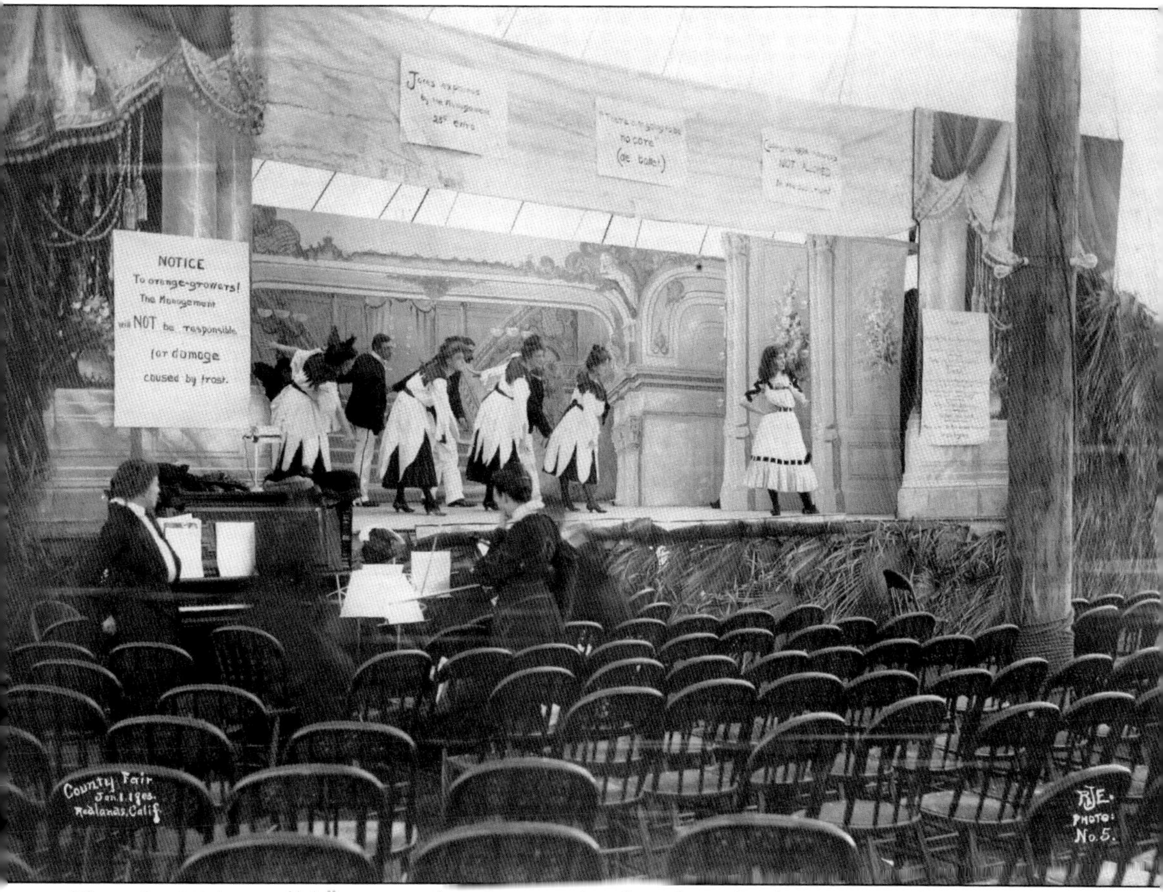

The title of "County Fair" seen on this photograph referred to a fundraising event held at Jennie Davis's property on Brookside Avenue on January 1, 1903. The citizens of Redlands staged this as a fake, comic county fair to raise money for The Settlement, a local charity for low-income tuberculosis patients. It was wildly successful and the descriptions of how they raised money, including this vaudeville performance, made for entertaining reading in the *Redlands Daily Facts*. An entrance fee got one in, but that just started the costs. A lunch room, a Japanese tea garden, an ice cream stand, and an Italian garden all charged for food, the vaudeville shows cost more, and numerous other tents contained other ways of spending money, including viewing a live coyote that had just recently been found. Thousands of people attended, causing traffic problems, which were partially eased by transporting participants from farther away at Citrus Avenue and Orange Street. The event raised over $30,000 in today's dollars. (Photographer: Raymond J. Everitt.)

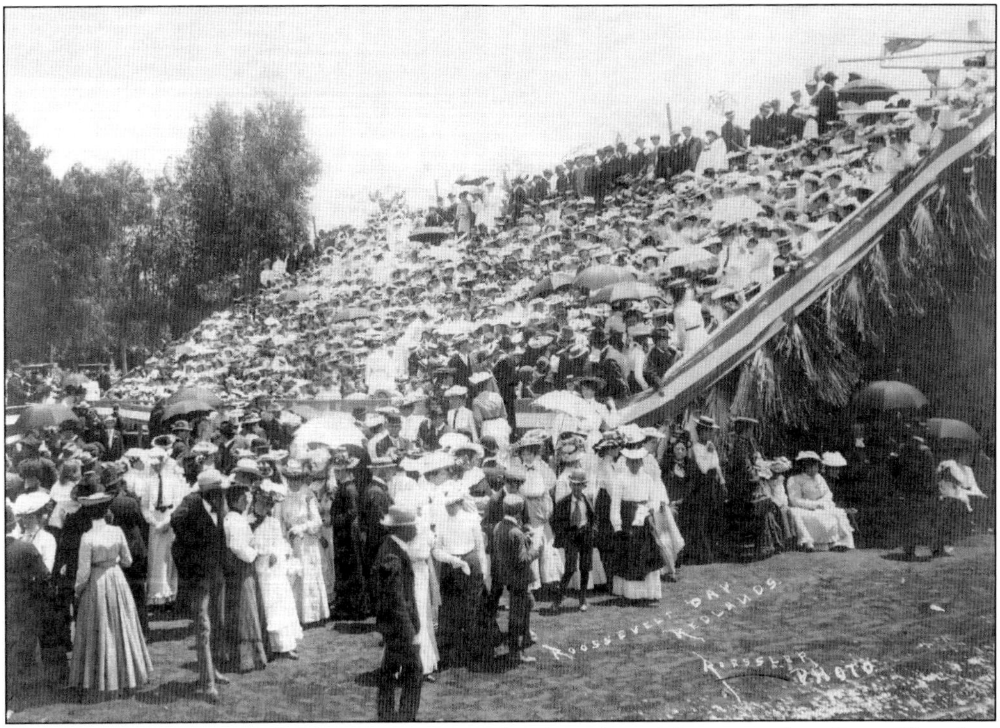

Entertainment also included listening to speeches by political figures such as Pres. Theodore Roosevelt, who visited Redlands on May 7, 1903. A very large crowd assembled in bleachers near the Casa Loma Hotel, on the northeast corner of Colton Avenue and Orange Street, to hear him. Although it was only May, the 80-degree day caused an abundance of shade umbrellas. At least 1,400 schoolchildren sang "The Star-Spangled Banner" to President Roosevelt before his speech. (Photographer: Edward E. Roessler.)

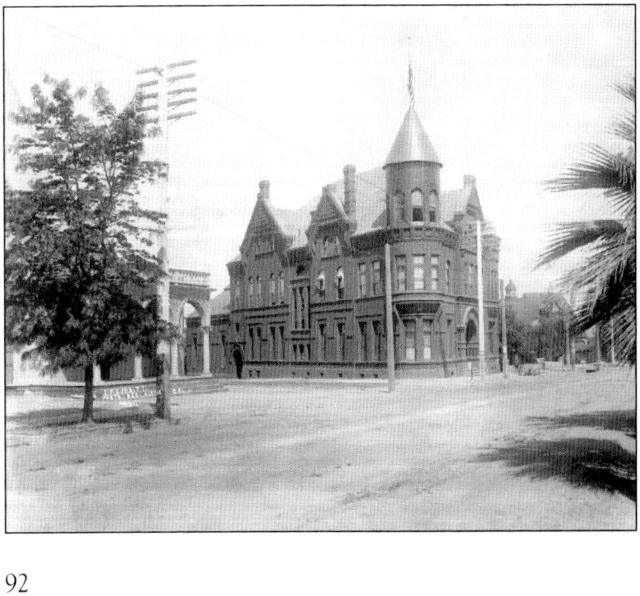

Reading as a pastime could be edifying and morally uplifting, but it was also a form of amusement. Redlands was very proud of its new YMCA building, which opened in 1894 on the corner of Cajon and Vine Streets. It housed the first public library in town in a single room downstairs, located where the four windows to the left of the rounded front corner are seen. Alfred H. Smiley deserves credit for encouraging the town to organize the Redlands Public Library Association in 1893 and to create this first library. (Photographer: Elias F. Everitt.)

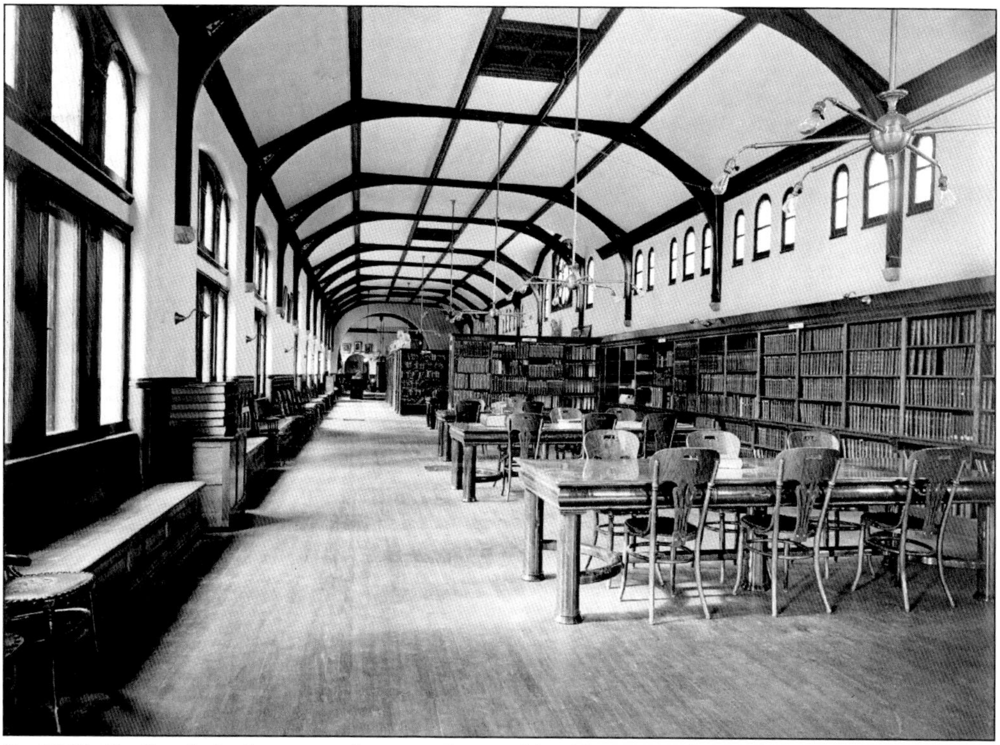

By 1898, Redlands had its own freestanding public library, with the land and the building donated by Albert K. Smiley, the twin brother of Alfred H. Smiley. Due to public demand and increasing population, the building kept growing. The image above shows an impressive vista of books occupying the new east wing in 1907, which was also built with funding from Albert K. Smiley. The photograph below shows the reference room. Today, a visit to the A.K. Smiley Public Library, the home of the images used in this book, reveals many of these same chairs still in use. (Photographer: Elias F. Everitt.)

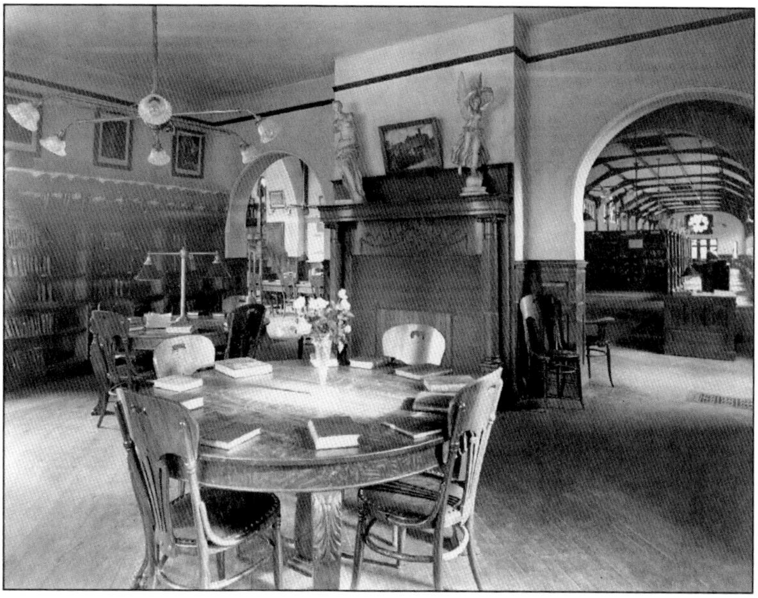

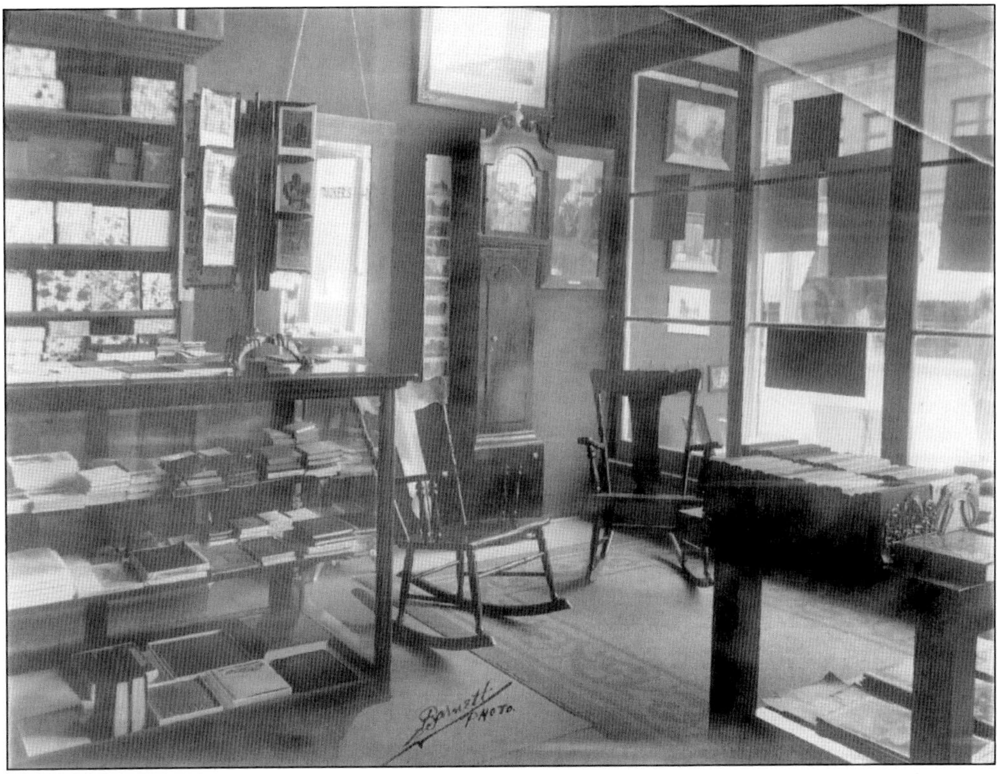

The 1897 *Illustrated Redlands* stated that "books, periodicals of high grade, and all that is elevating in the literary field, is eagerly sought for when fresh from the press." Bookstores and newsstands appeared early in Redlands' history to fill the townspeople's demands. The Tucker Book and Stationery Company, seen here about 1912 at 13 West State Street, served Redlands from 1904 to about 1929. (Photographer: Charles O. Barnett.)

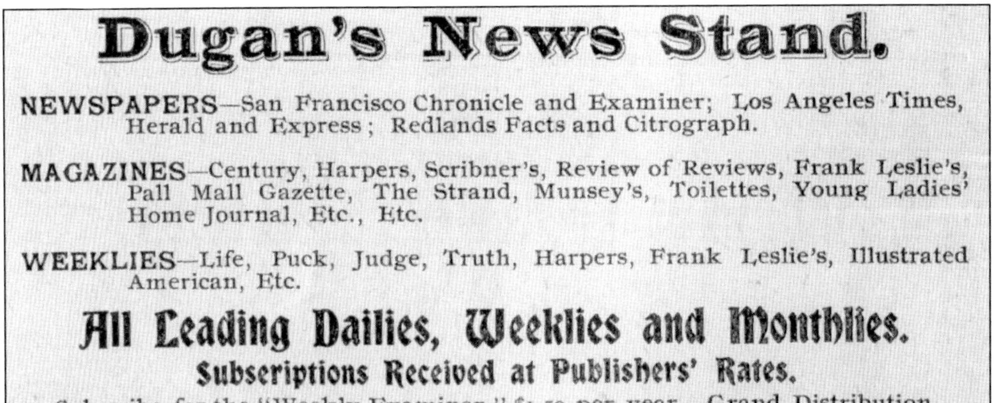

Dugan's News Stand.

NEWSPAPERS—San Francisco Chronicle and Examiner; Los Angeles Times, Herald and Express; Redlands Facts and Citrograph.

MAGAZINES—Century, Harpers, Scribner's, Review of Reviews, Frank Leslie's, Pall Mall Gazette, The Strand, Munsey's, Toilettes, Young Ladies' Home Journal, Etc., Etc.

WEEKLIES—Life, Puck, Judge, Truth, Harpers, Frank Leslie's, Illustrated American, Etc.

All Leading Dailies, Weeklies and Monthlies.

Subscriptions Received at Publishers' Rates.

Subscribe for the "Weekly Examiner," $1.50 per year. Grand Distribution.

Otis Block, ORANGE STREET.

In 1896, locals and visitors could stay in touch with the nation and the world through newspapers and magazines for sale at Dugan's News Stand. Redlands may have been small, but it was not out of touch. Dugan's News Stand started in 1887 on Orange Street in downtown Redlands and lasted until at least 1902.

This massive pile of books represents some of the more than 5,000 books collected in Redlands during a national book drive held on March 18–25, 1918, for sailors and soldiers during World War I. Requested books included Westerns, works by Kipling, Baedeker's travel guides, poetry, biographies, and humor. The War Service of the American Library Association ran the campaign to collect two million books nationwide from private individuals. These would go to the libraries in large Army camps, on ships at sea, and overseas in Europe. Books provided soldiers and sailors with recreation and improved morale in addition to increasing their education level within the military and for future jobs. Citizens of Redlands brought the books to the A.K. Smiley Public Library and the *Redlands Daily Facts* office, and, on Saturday, March 23, Boy Scouts went to private homes and picked up books if a person called ahead. As the sign in the photograph says, "They signal 'Send Books,' " and Redlands responded generously. (Photographer: Guy L. Fairbanks.)

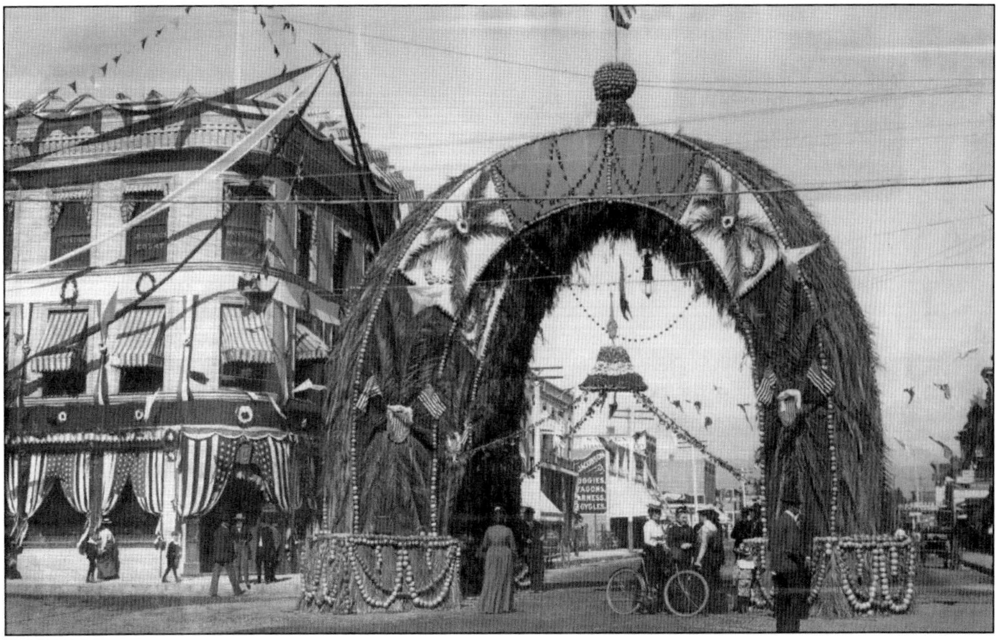

The cover photograph for this book, of President McKinley's visit on May 8, 1901, can also be used to note the importance of bicycles for sport and transportation. In the 1890s, when safer bicycles appeared, they represented an exciting new form of recreation. Redlands eagerly took part and had a cycling club and a racetrack by the 1890s. Even women participated, as represented by the woman with her bicycle under the arch. (Photographer: Elias F. Everitt.)

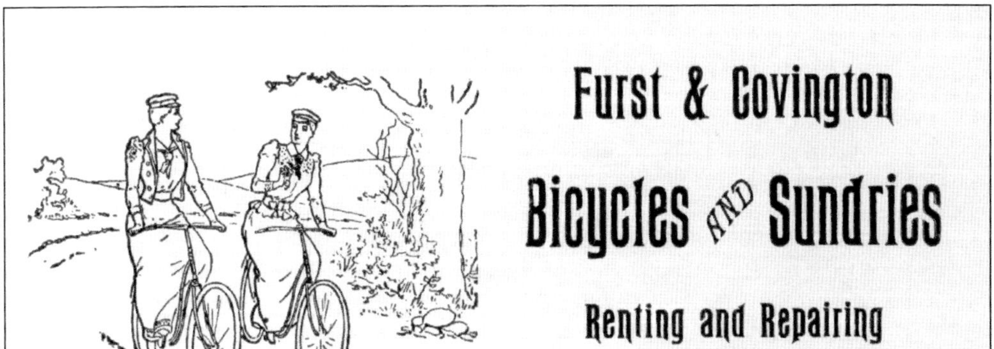

Soon, businesses in Redlands carried not only bicycles but also sundries, the accessories needed for enthusiasts. In this 1900 advertisement in the city directory, Furst & Covington also offered the rental and repair of bicycles and even "wheel lessons." Note the rather cumbersome clothing worn by the women in this advertisement.

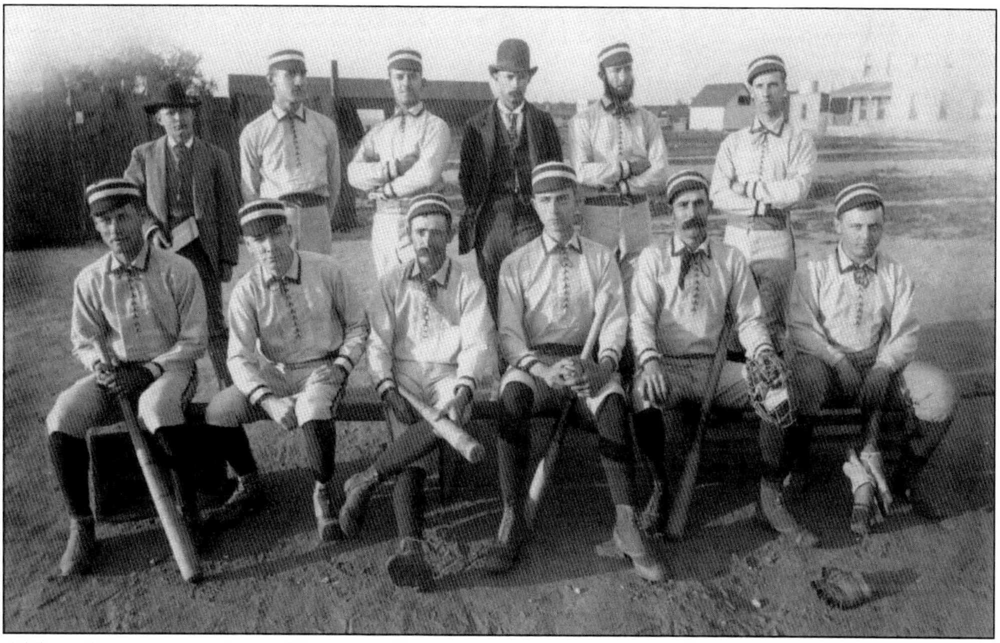

Although townspeople could eventually watch high school football and basketball games, one of the earliest spectator sports in town was baseball. These serious baseball players from Redlands are wearing expensive matching suits of the latest style. According to an advertisement of 1889, one outfit probably cost several hundred dollars in today's money. (Photographer Daniel Holt.)

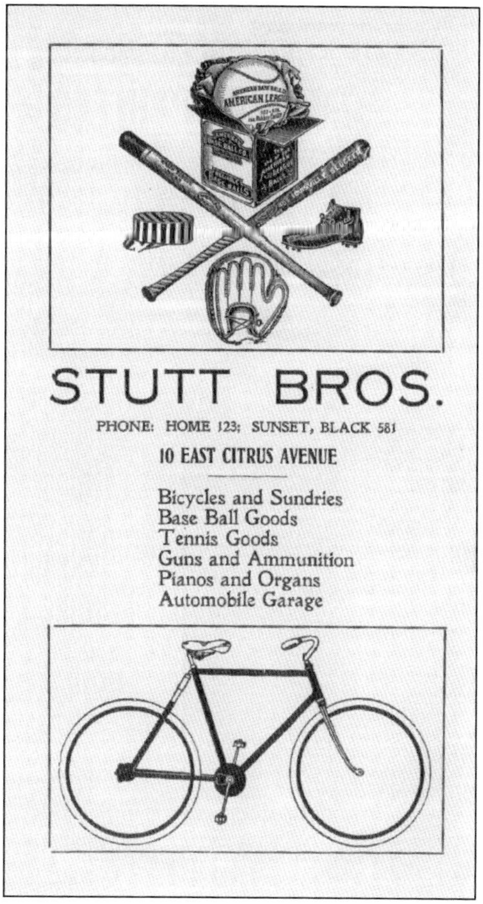

Redlands merchants eagerly supplied baseball equipment to those who wanted to play. This 1905 Stutt Brothers advertisement from the city directory promotes supplies for baseball, bicycling, and tennis, as well as the ever-present piano. Changes in transportation and communication were starting to appear in Redlands, as noted with the "automobile garage" available and the telephone numbers for contact.

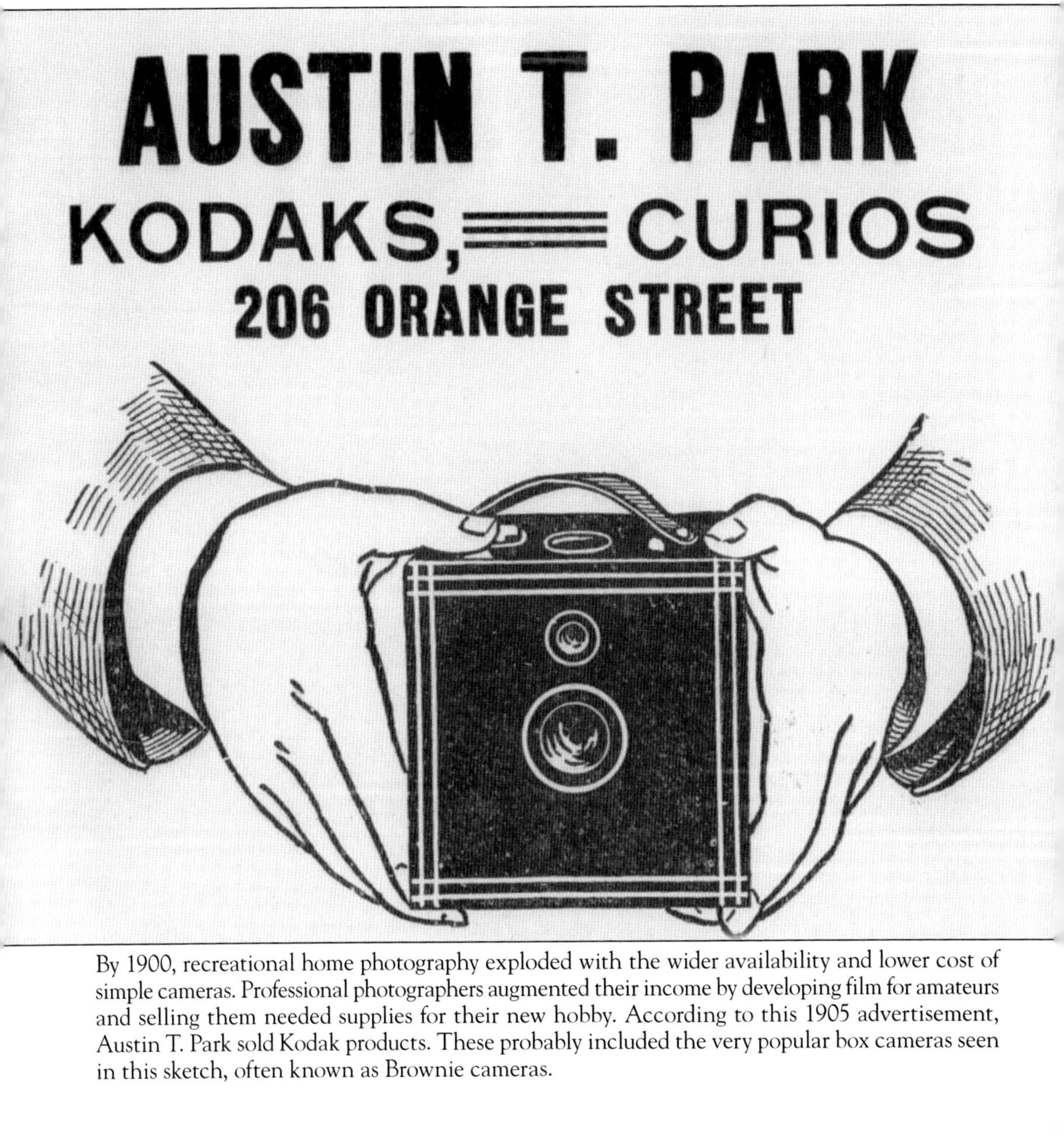

By 1900, recreational home photography exploded with the wider availability and lower cost of simple cameras. Professional photographers augmented their income by developing film for amateurs and selling them needed supplies for their new hobby. According to this 1905 advertisement, Austin T. Park sold Kodak products. These probably included the very popular box cameras seen in this sketch, often known as Brownie cameras.

Six

"Beautiful in Situation and Surroundings"

As citrus groves were planted, railroads came to town, and the population increased, another phenomenon developed in Redlands: tourism. The title of this chapter, "Beautiful in Situation and Surroundings," from the *Redlands Daily Facts* in October 1887, described the scenery around Redlands. With dry air, clear skies, and warm temperatures most of the year, Redlands attracted those who suffered from ailments such as tuberculosis. An 1891 directory bragged, "Many persons have been cured of pulmonary and throat complaints, asthma and rheumatism, by the pure invigorating atmosphere."

The San Bernardino Mountains, with peaks reaching over 10,000 feet, sit very close to Redlands to the north and east. Mountain resorts attracted those escaping hot summers. The vast majority of tourists streamed into Redlands from the early 1890s into the 1920s to see the gorgeous, exotic, and refreshing Cañon Crest Park, created by Alfred and Albert Smiley, and the smaller Prospect Hill Park, developed by the England family. The parks were phenomenally successful and free to the public, attracting thousands of tourists each year on Southern Pacific and Atchison, Topeka & Santa Fe railroad day trips out of Los Angeles.

Professional photographers played a large role in bringing visitors to Redlands through the photographs they took of the parks and mountains. These were sold directly to tourists, to railroad companies to advertise scenic tours, and to postcard companies. As automobiles became more popular, many visitors wanted to drive through Cañon Crest Park, but the short time required—mere minutes—did not allow tourists to see the carefully planned short segments of garden. The Smileys did not allow automobiles in the park for many years to encourage slower travel. Livery stables, hotels, restaurants, drugstores, and other merchants also gained from the tourist visits.

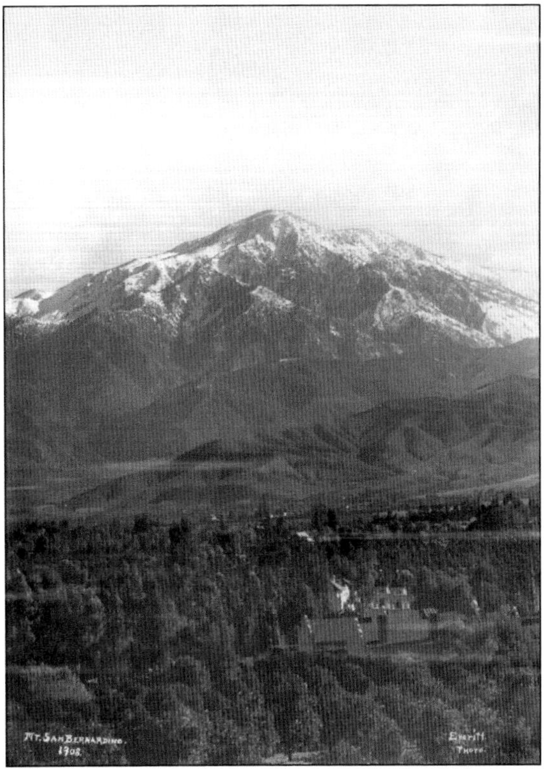

Redlands sits in a spectacular location with mountains to the north and east. In this 1908 view, snowy Mount San Bernardino rises above the valley, with the roof of the large Burrage mansion, built in 1901, showing through the citrus groves in the foreground. (Photographer: Elias F. Everitt.)

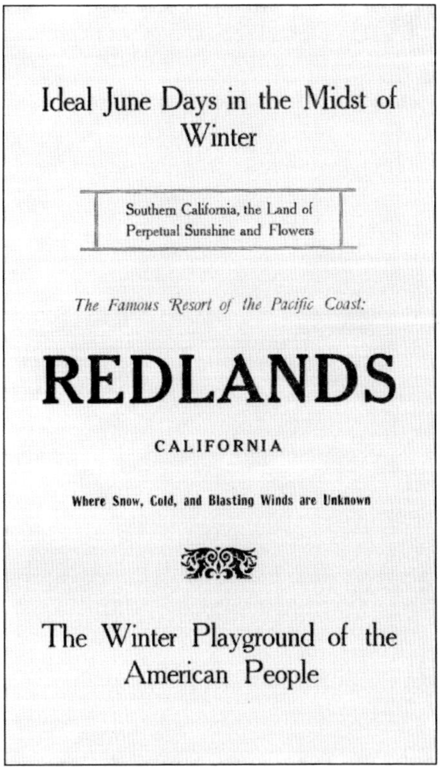

The promotion of Redlands started as soon as water and land were available for purchase. Winters were mild, but the comment "Where snow, cold, and blasting winds are unknown" was stretching it a bit, as residents discovered on the rare occasions when freezes killed and injured citrus trees. This advertisement for Redlands in the city directory of 1909–1910 fits in with the many efforts to bring tourists to town.

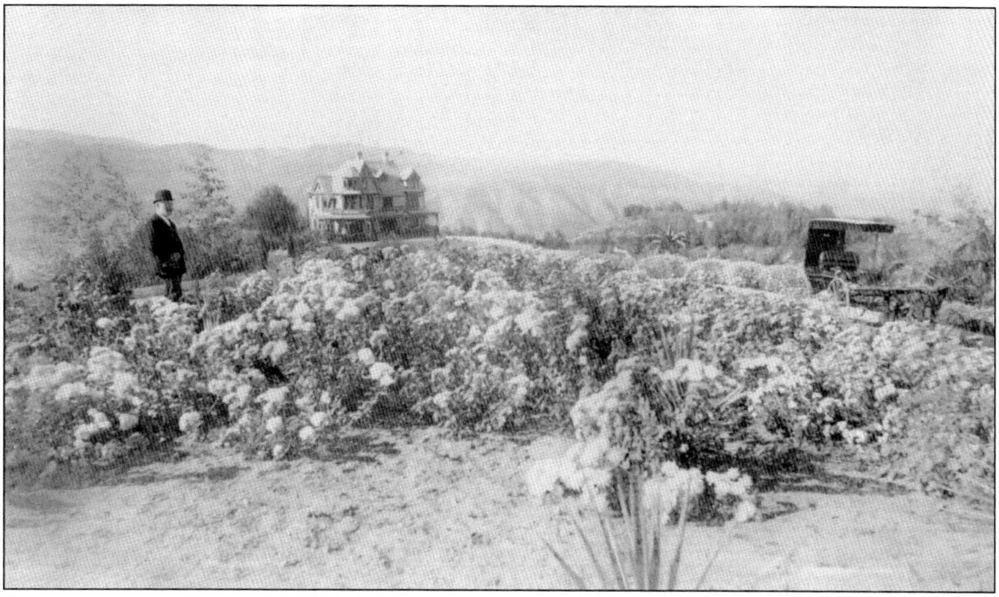

Between 1889 and 1891, the identical Smiley twins, Alfred and Albert, bought about 200 acres of land along a ridge two miles southwest of downtown Redlands. This would become Cañon Crest, a private park open to the public where the Smileys built their homes. The views attracted them to this nearly barren, waterless, and ridged land. Their experience landscaping their resort areas at Lake Mohonk and Lake Minnewaska in the Catskill Mountains of New York proved invaluable. The image above shows Albert's house, built on the southwest side of the park overlooking San Timoteo Canyon. Alfred built his home on the eastern side with a vista of the San Bernardino Valley, as seen below. These images, from about 1892, show incomplete landscaping on the grounds. The brothers wintered in Redlands, returning to their New York mountain resorts in the summers. (Photographer: Rudolph J. Philippi.)

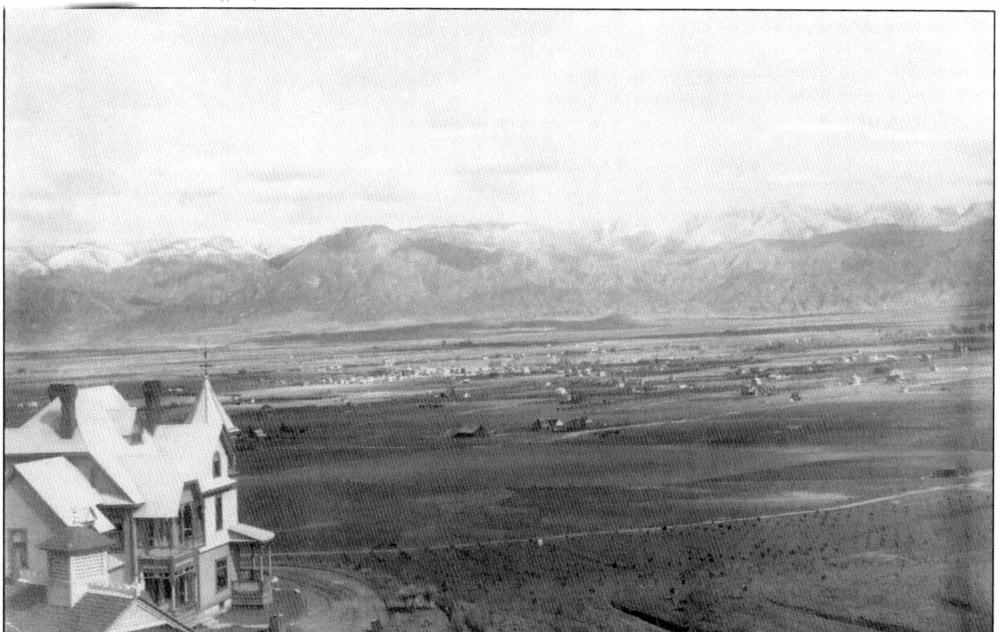

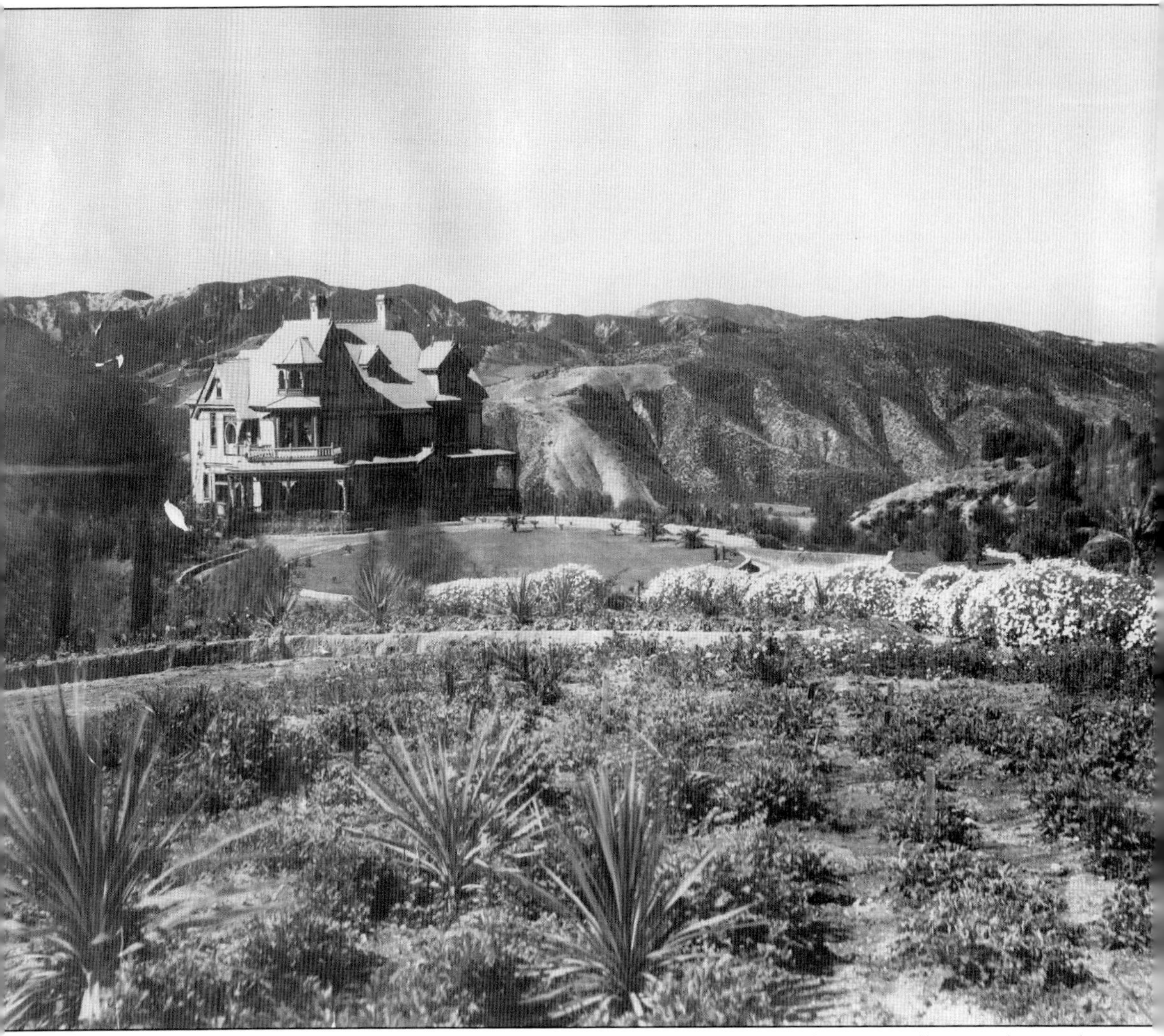

Taken from Cañon Crest Park around 1892, this view near Redlands is a small part of a much longer panoramic photograph that is believed to have belonged to Albert K. Smiley. Albert's house is at far left, in front of the mouth of San Timoteo Canyon and looking northwest to a valley vista. Note the barn on the right. This striking image is a testament to the beautiful views

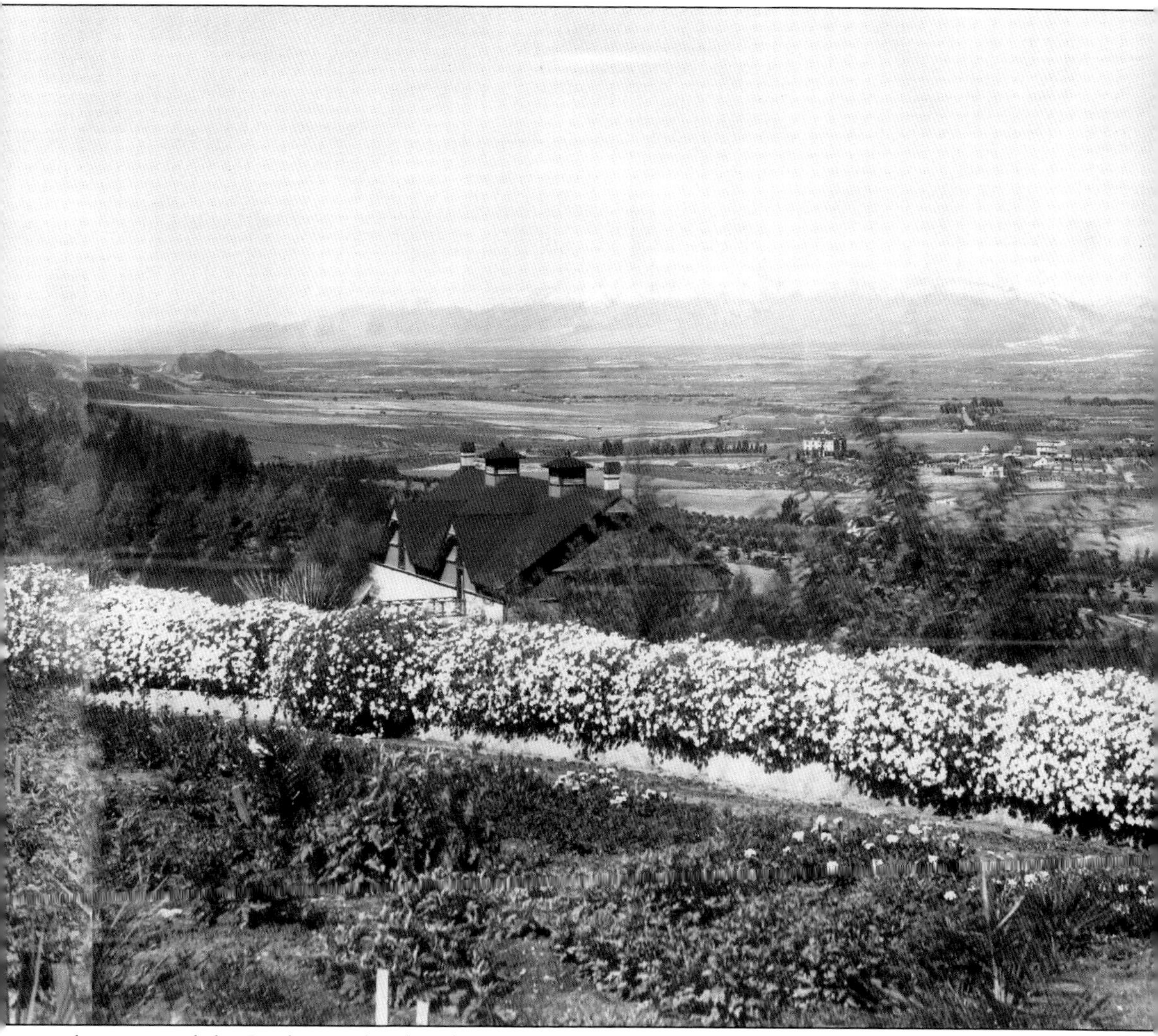

that inspired the Smileys to develop their park and open it to the public. Photographer Rudolph J. Philippi is responsible for many of the earliest views from Cañon Crest Park. (Photographer: Rudolph J. Philippi.)

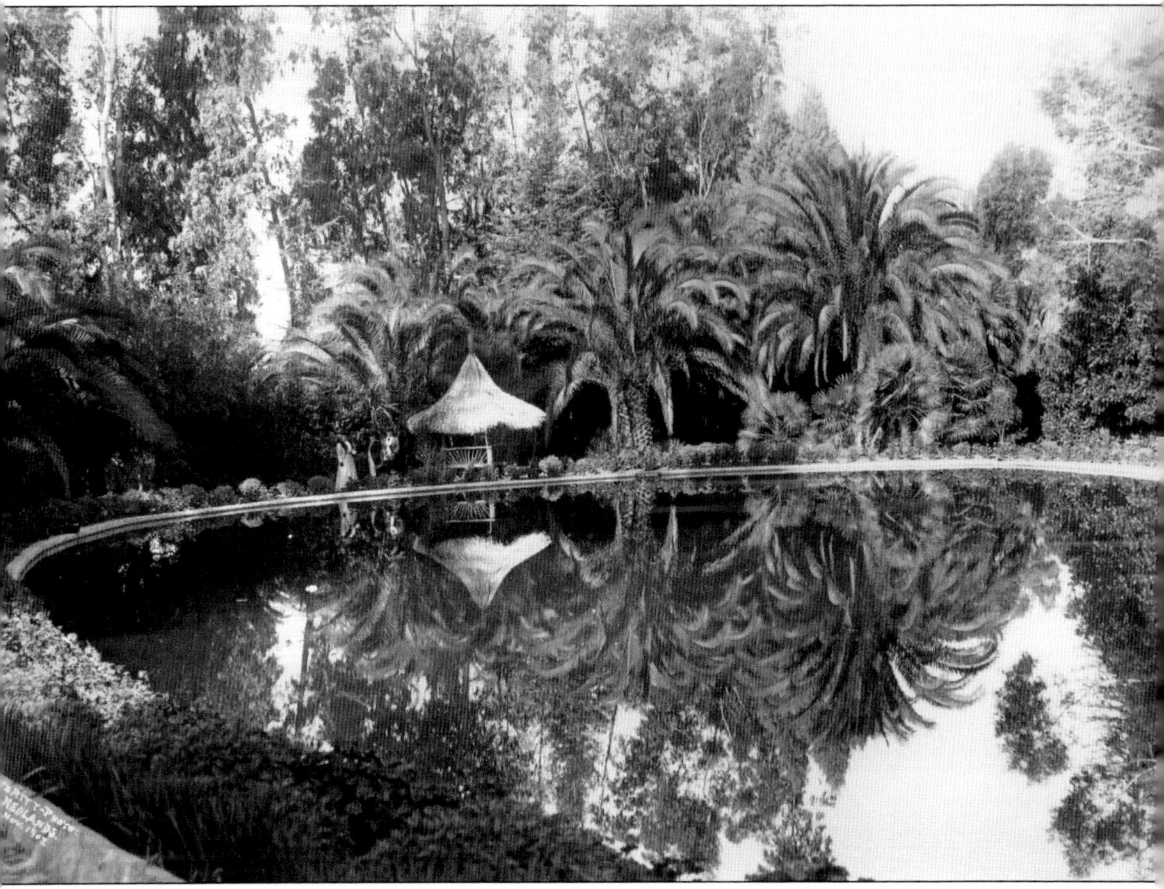

Cañon Crest Park, an appropriate name for a ridge park, was started in early 1890, soon after the Smileys bought the land. Soon, the park was also known as Smiley Heights. With low annual rainfall and no water on the ridge, the park needed a dependable year-round water source. About seven miles of pipes, mostly underground, were installed, water rights were purchased, and two large reservoirs were created. Mirror Lake, seen in this November 1907 image, served as one of the reservoirs but also became an attractive feature of the park, living up to its name. Sometimes, success was too much for the Smiley brothers. On December 30, 1899, they expressed their concerns to the public through *The Hour*, a local newspaper. Visitors were cutting flowers, even close to their homes, and they wrote, "They [tourists] drive through the grounds at a furious rate, they go scorching along on their bicycles at a dangerous pace, and they shout and sing at the top of their voices in the summer houses close to our dwellings." (Photographer: Elias F. Everitt.)

Longtime Redlands photographer Elias Everitt got heavily involved in photographing Cañon Crest Park, as noted in this 1901 advertisement from *Souvenir of Redlands* and by the number of park photographs attributed to him. Large and small photographs—some of them tinted—and postcards were sold in local stores, to railroads advertising for tourist trips, and for promotional handouts in Redlands, a good source of income for a professional photographer.

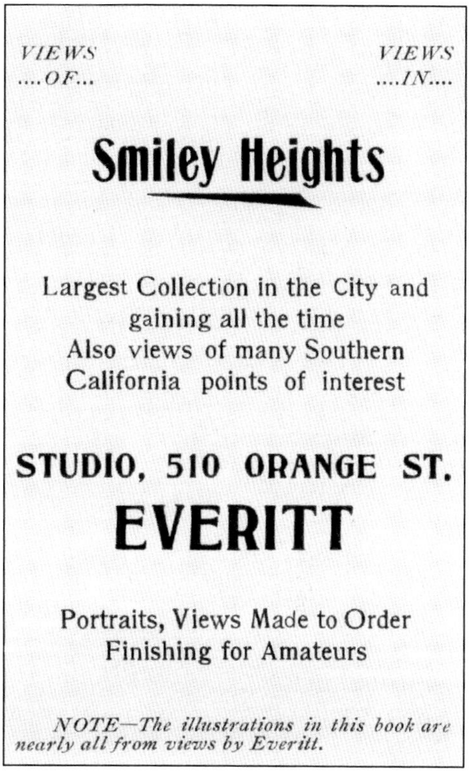

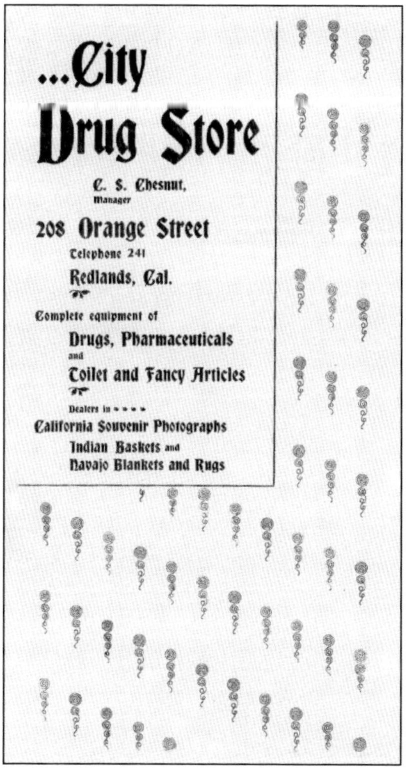

Like today's drugstores, those in early Redlands did not just sell pharmaceuticals. They also often had soda fountains, toiletries for sale, and souvenirs for the thousands of tourists flooding Redlands to see the area parks. This 1900 advertisement for the City Drug Store offered "California Souvenir Photographs," which probably included views of Cañon Crest Park.

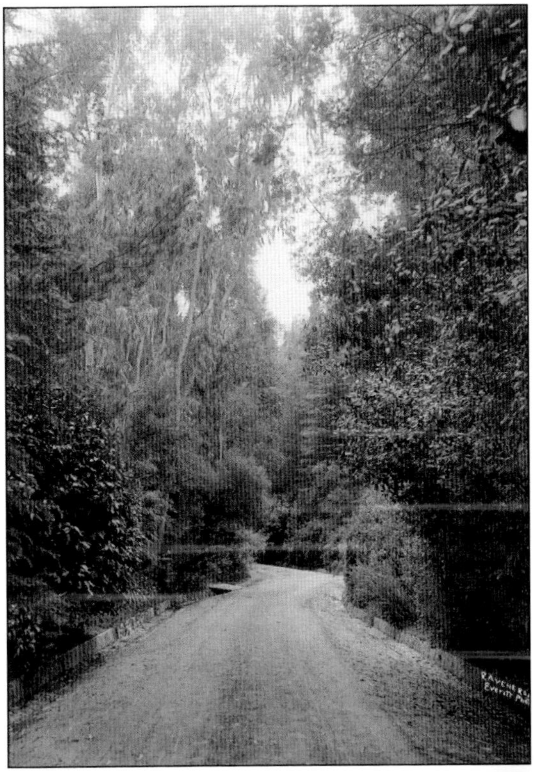

The Smileys meant for the park's narrow and curved roads, built before cars, to slow down visitors, bring them closer to the beautiful flowers, and surprise them with new scenes and views around each turn. About five miles of roadway in the park allowed many different vignettes, as seen at left. Additionally, at least three to four miles of stone masonry was created in the park for curbing and retaining walls, as seen in the 1897 footpath below. The rock for this work came from the Santa Ana riverbed, a good seven miles north and at least 300 feet downhill. In 1890, at least 12 teams worked to grade roads, and over 200 Chinese laborers also worked on the roads within the park. (Photographers: left, Elias F. Everitt; below, William J. Haskell.)

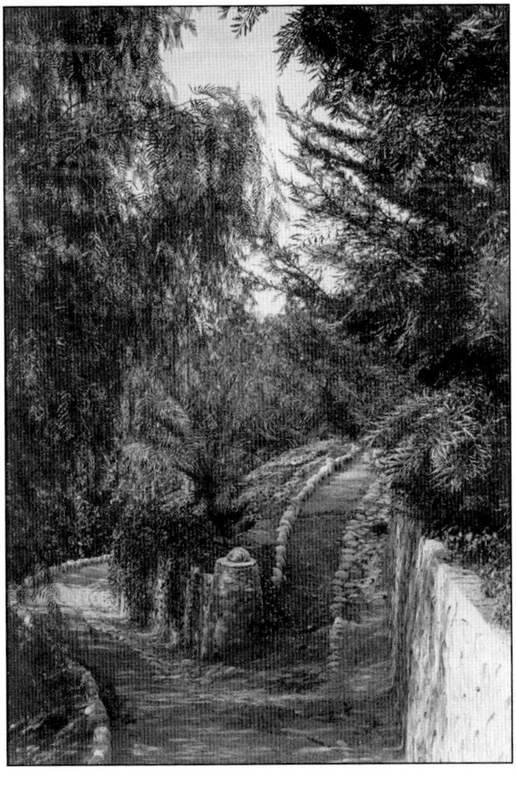

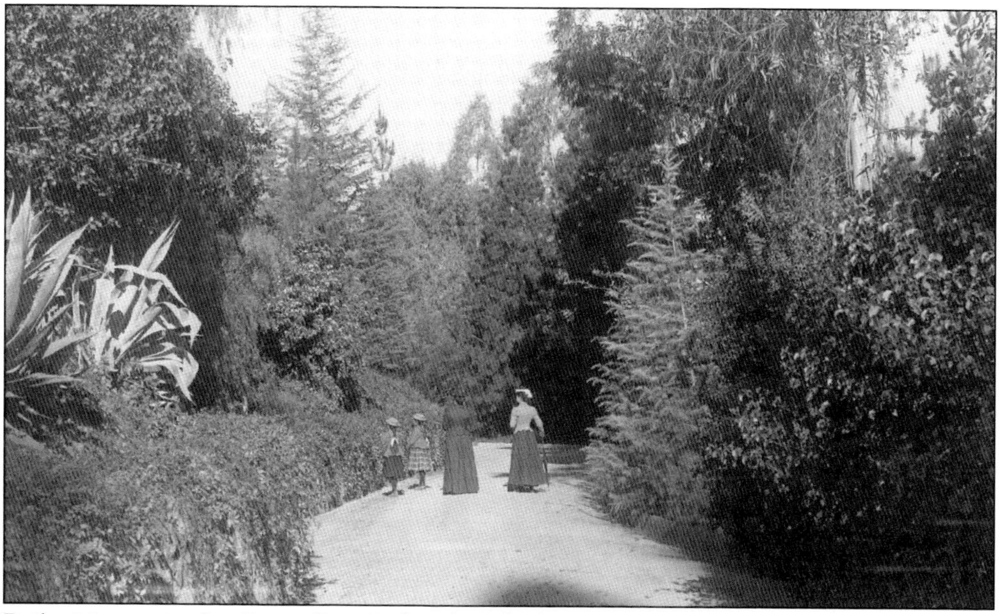

Daily visitors arrived at Cañon Crest Park on horseback, in private buggies, or in public conveyances, often from the train depots downtown. Being about two miles from the trains meant that most did not walk uphill to the park. Heartier visitors reached the park by riding the newly popular bicycles. But there was no better way to see Cañon Crest Park than on foot, as this group did about 1900. (Photographer: Elias F. Everitt.)

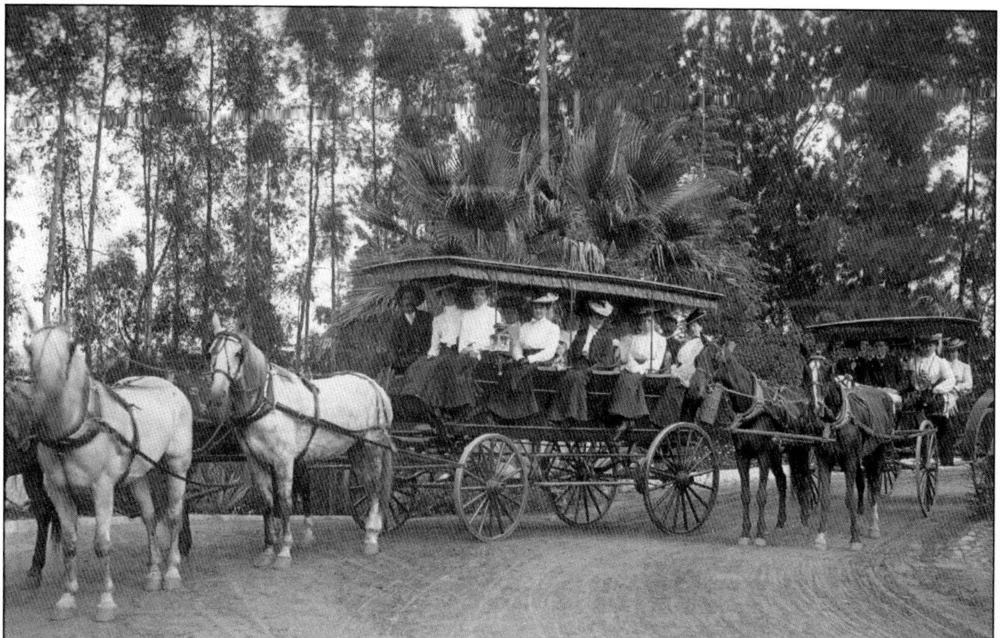

Tourists often came to Redlands from Los Angeles on special sightseeing trains. They would disembark, load up on large horse carriages called tally-hos, and clomp up the hill to the park. In one to two hours, they would return to their train and continue their day trip. Here, around 1900, four horses pull about 15 people in the tally-ho on the left. (Photographer: Elias F. Everitt.)

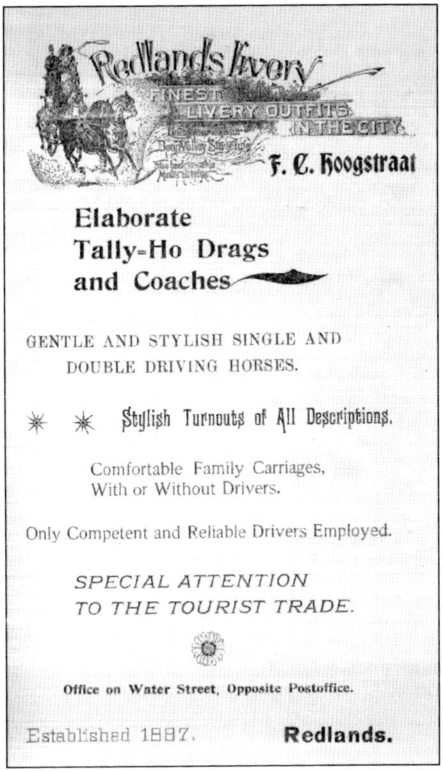

At least 15,000 tourists went through Cañon Crest Park in 1895, only five years after its development began. Redlands businesses such as the Redlands Livery benefited from these visitors, and, in 1896, the livery advertised tourist tally-ho rides. As early as 1896, the Redlands city directory acknowledged the town's debt to the Smileys: "Thousands of people come to Redlands for the express purpose of visiting Canyon Crest Park, and it has been an important factor in developing the town."

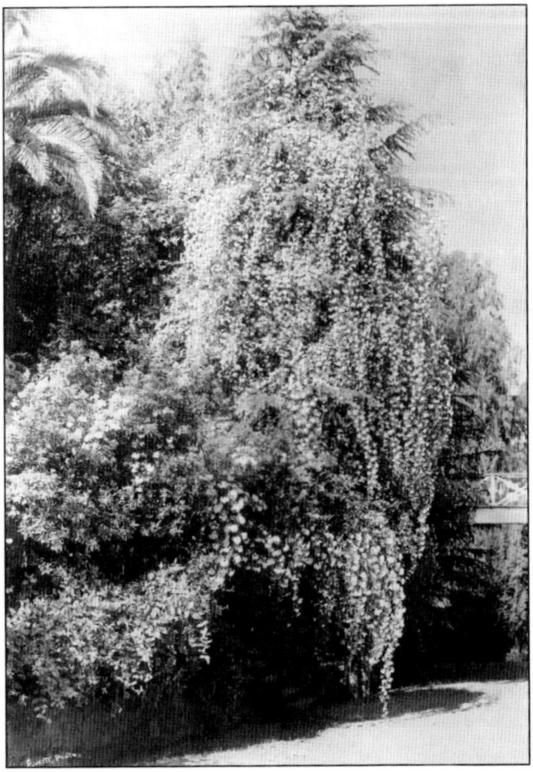

Multitudes of flowering trees, bushes, and smaller plants met the eyes of tourists as they turned corners on paths and roadways in Cañon Crest Park. Photographs were in black and white and did not do justice to the plantings, although the images were occasionally hand-tinted. Many semitropical plants shared the space with more common plants such as roses, geraniums, and pansies. Here, a banksia rose cascades down to a park roadway. (Photographer: Elias F. Everitt.)

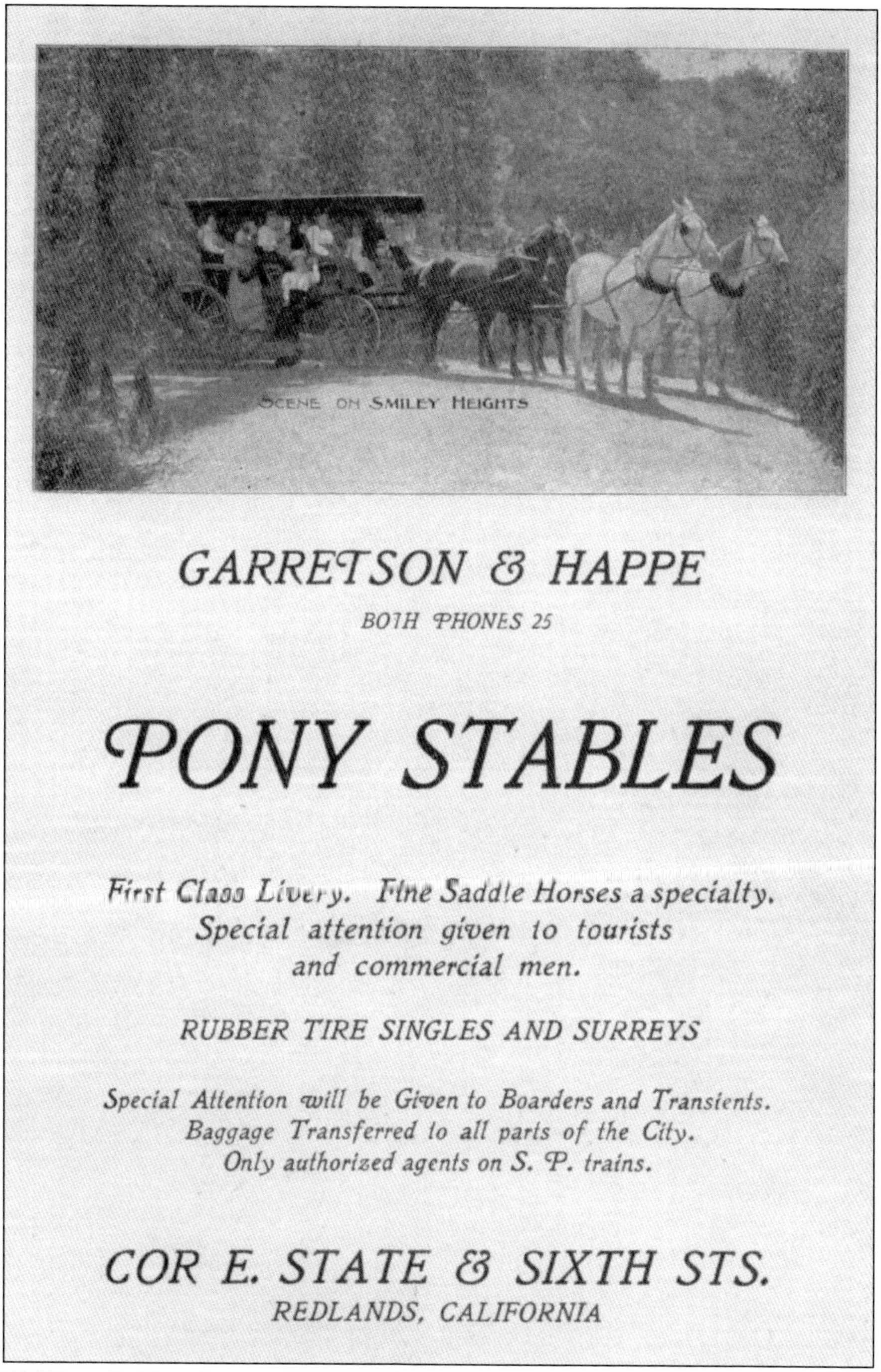

This 1905 Pony Stables advertisement included a photograph of a very crowded tally-ho in Cañon Crest Park, also known as Smiley Heights. Short- and long-term visitors were accommodated by Pony Stables, including tourists and businessmen, or, as they are called here, "commercial men." The "S.P." stands for Southern Pacific, whose depot was in downtown Redlands. The current use of the word "transient" has a negative connotation, but, in 1905, it likely meant a short-term visitor. Comfort was increasing with the use of rubber tires on horse-drawn carriages.

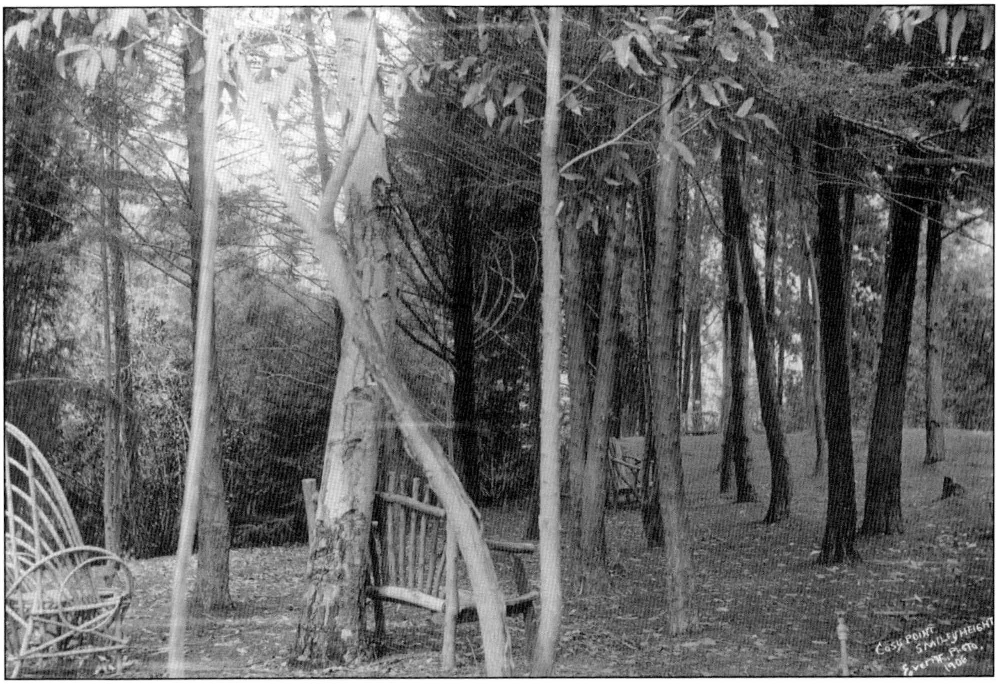

Cañon Crest Park included many locations for visitors to stop, rest, and contemplate views or landscaping. In 1906, Cosy Point provided benches made of branches in a cool, shady glade of trees. (Photographer: Elias F. Everitt.)

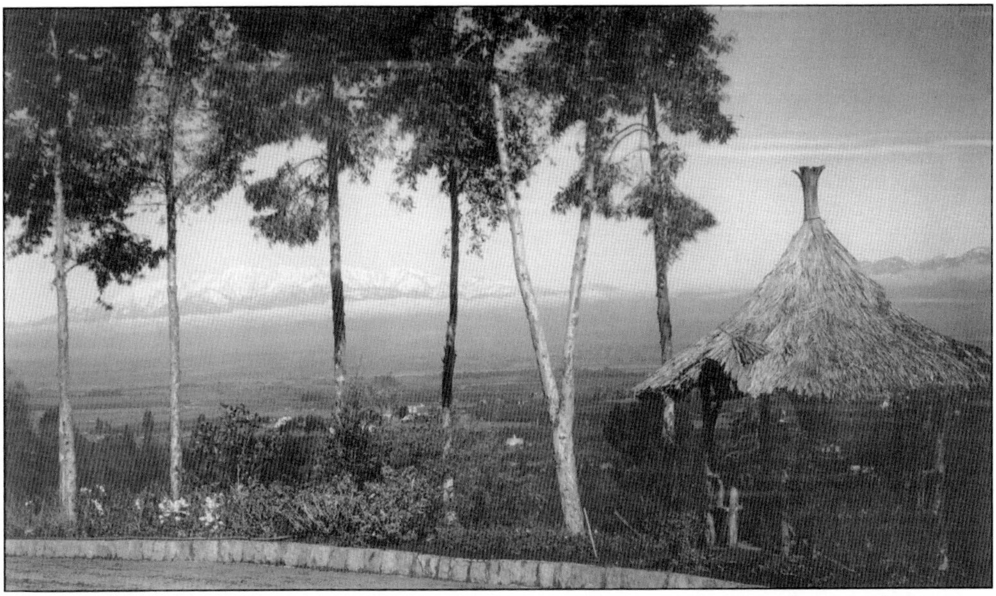

Palm-thatched summerhouses were placed where spectacular views could be admired. The Smileys had used similar structures in their resorts in New York. Here, the San Gabriel Mountains to the southwest appear to float with their cap of winter snow. Tourism in Redlands dropped during the Great Depression of the 1930s. The town could not afford to buy Cañon Crest when it was offered for sale in the 1930s, causing the Smiley family to close the expensive park. It was finally sold in the early 1960s and developed into housing. (Photographer: Elias F. Everitt.)

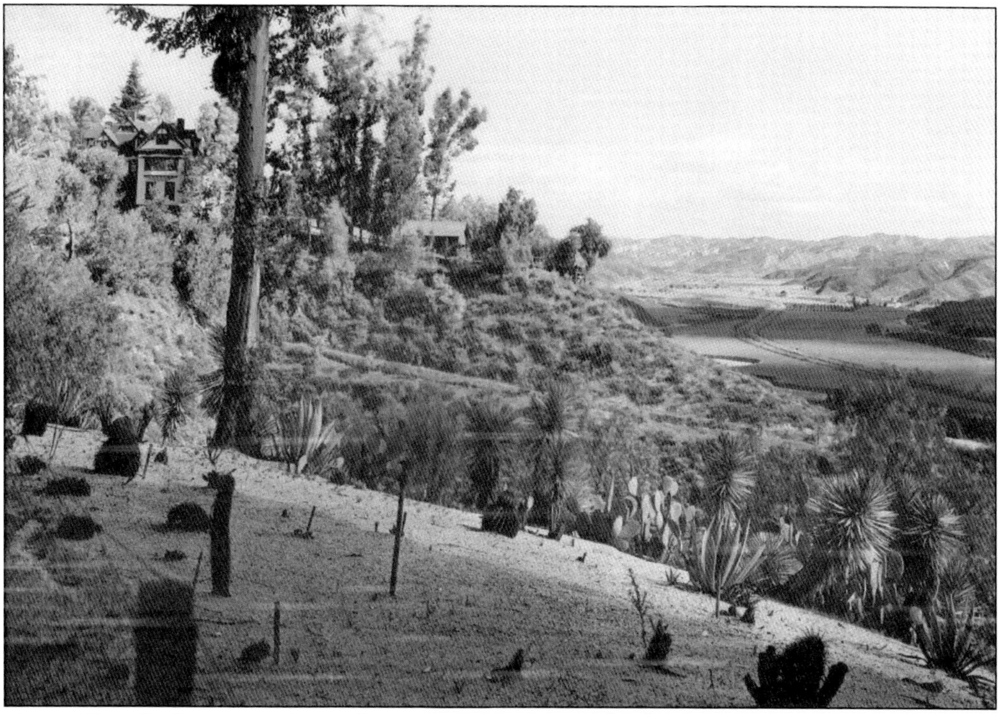

Cañon Crest Park sat on a ridge with stunning views not only of the San Bernardino Valley, where Redlands was situated, but also south and east into San Timoteo Canyon. These two photographs look east down San Timoteo Canyon. The photograph above, taken around 1910, shows Albert K. Smiley's home at far left, perched on a ridge. The view below shows the Southern Pacific Railroad tracks with a train going through the canyon about 1901. The small summerhouses, seen clinging to the slopes, offered panoramic views. (Photographer: Elias F. Everitt.)

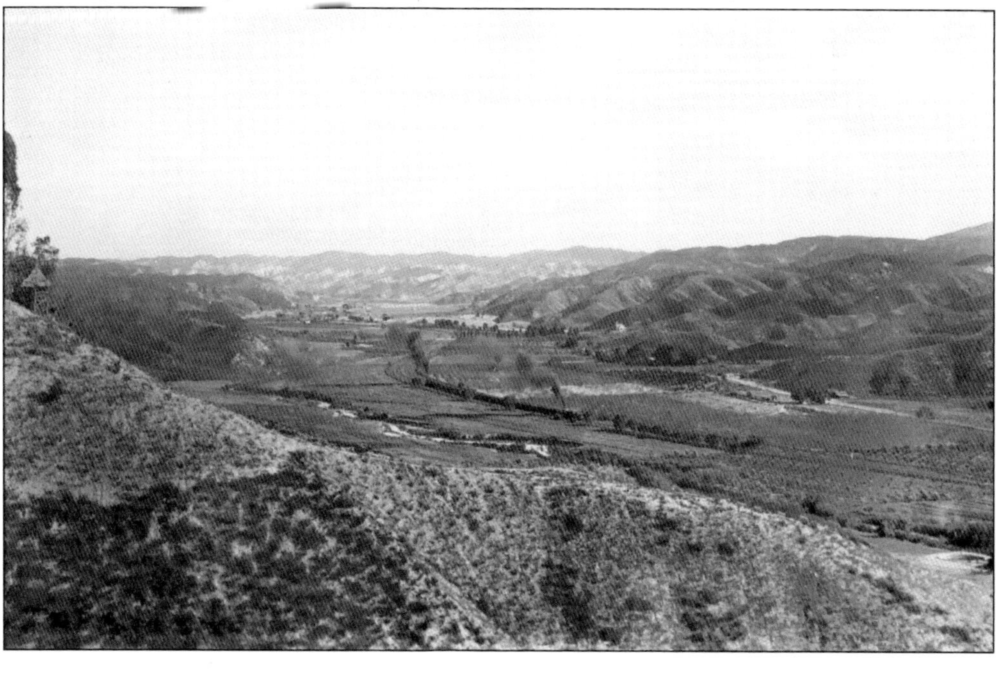

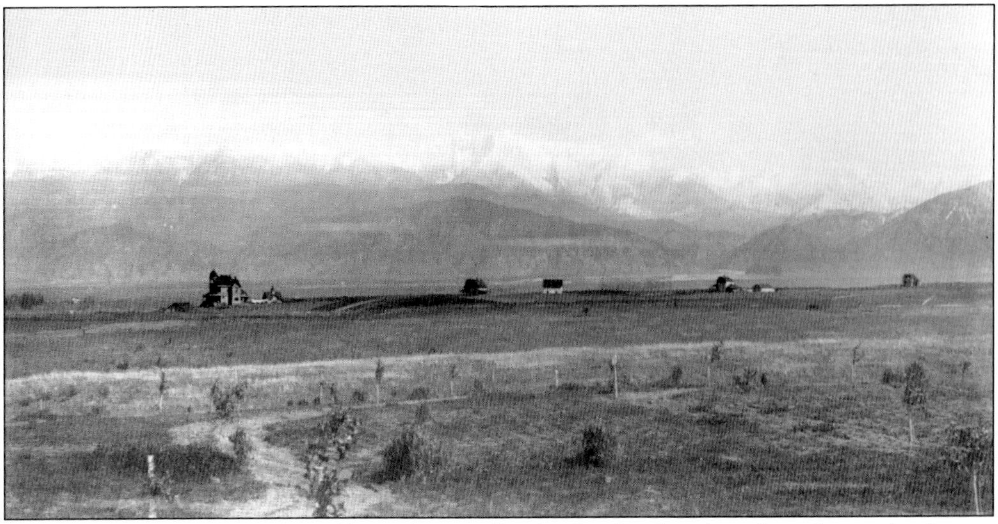

Prospect Hill Park, a second, smaller park in Redlands, also developed on the ridge south of town. Thomas Y. England and his family bought about 60 acres in the late 1800s and prepared it for visitors. Note how barren the ridge was before it had plantings in the photograph above, taken by Philippi about 1891, and how lush it had become by 1906 (below), with park plantings in the foreground. Philippi, known as a view photographer, worked from January 1890 until 1897, when he retired. In 1897, not even 10 years after Redlands was incorporated, a promotional book stated that Philippi's earlier views "preserve many scenes which have changed with different phases of growth and would be lost if his camera had not recorded them. Among these are the panoramic views of the city and valley, of which he made and sold a great number." Amazingly, more than 115 years later, many of these photographs still exist. The Everitt photograph below became one of the many postcard views of Redlands. (Photographers: above, Rudolph J. Philippi; below, Elias F. Everitt.)

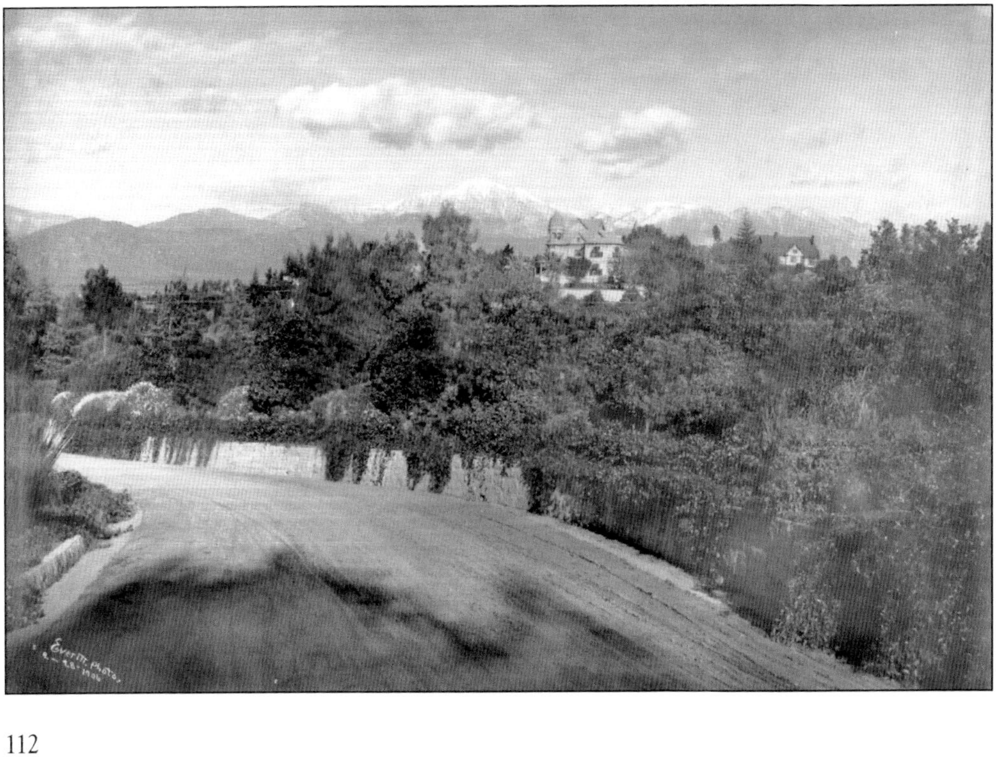

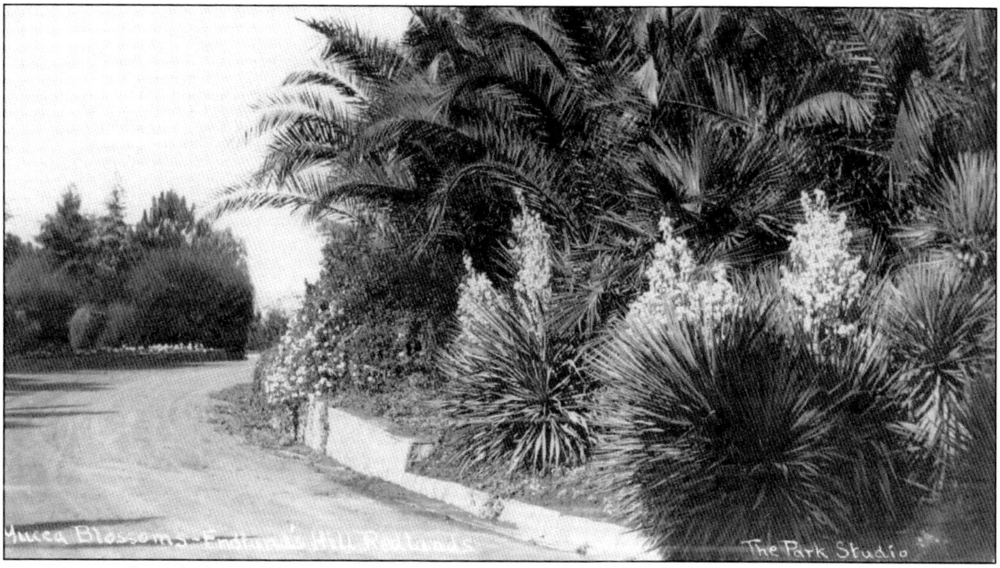

Prospect Hill Park, later called Prospect Park, became a Redlands city park in 1968 thanks to the hard work of many people who did not want to lose yet another of Redlands' famous parks. Today, it is still free for locals and tourists to visit and provides fabulous views of the San Bernardino Valley, Redlands, and mountains, and has intimate walks, beautiful plantings, and quiet picnic areas. This view from about 1904 looks very much like the park of today. (Photographer: Austin T. Park.)

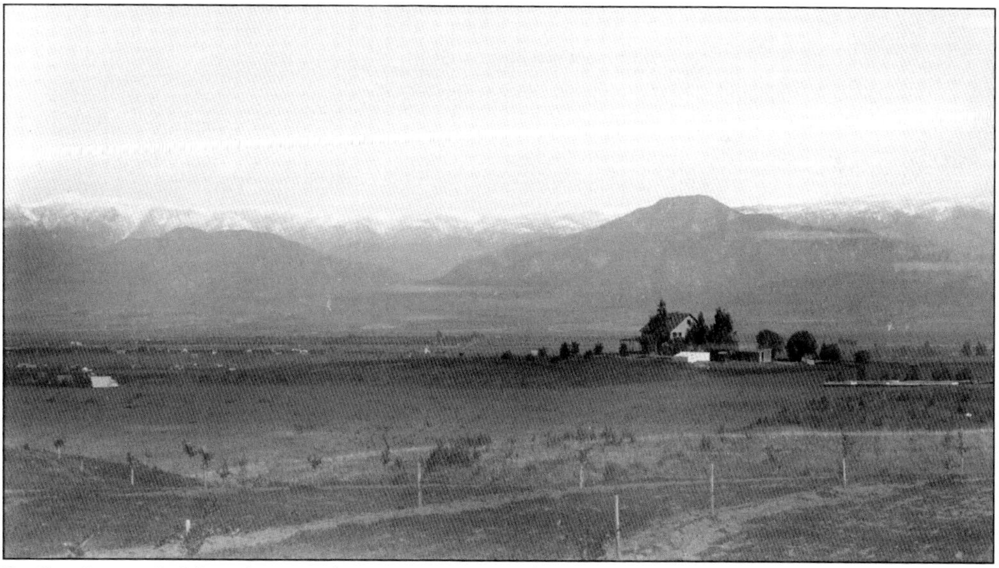

Redlands needed hotels to make tourism succeed. Redlands' first hotel, Prospect House, on Prospect Hill, filled a need from 1882 to 1888, hosting prospective land buyers, laborers, and businessmen. On a barren ridge south of Redlands, it had a spectacular view—or "prospect," hence the name—of the San Bernardino Mountains and Redlands. The lone house in this image is the original Prospect House, which was no longer a hotel by the time this photograph was taken around 1891. By 1888, Redlands had several downtown hotels, including the Sloan House and the Windsor Hotel, plus the Terracina Hotel, located on a bluff southwest of town. (Photographer: Rudolph J. Philippi.)

1892

Jan. 4. Steam Laundry started.
Jan. 12. Storm water bonds voted ($100,000); issued May 1, 1892.
Jan. 15. Terracina Hotel opened.
Jan. 17. Belt line, first train.
Jan. 30. Baker House opened, M. S. Lane, Prop.
Feb. S. H. Warren opened barber shop.
Feb. 1. Terracina street railway opened.
Feb. 16. Jas. A. Stone appointed superintendent of streets.
Feb. 17. Dog license ordinance passed.
Feb. 23. Lively earthquake.
Mar. 5. Terracina & Redlands Railway Co. incorporated.
Mar. 14. Southern Pacific R. R. regular service began.
Mar. 19. Visit of Los Angeles Chamber of Commerce.
Apr. 3. Old store, Colton avenue and Orange street, burned.
Apr. 11. City election; J. B. Glover, C. A. Kingsbury elected trustees; L. W. Clark, clerk; F. P. Morrison, treasurer; R. H. Kendall, marshal.
Apr. 27. City seal adopted.
Apr. 29. Barley mill burned.
May 5-6. Pomological Society met in Redlands.
May 15. Wilshire Bear Valley stage line started.
May 17. National Editorial Association's visit.
May 25. Sewer ordinance passed.
June. Orange shipments past season, 80 cars.
June. W. Howard White, civil engineer, opened office.
June 8. Street paving ordinance passed.
June 14. Heavy earthquake.
June 16. Redlands Guards organized.
June 18. Courthouse bonds defeated, second time.
July 14. Redlands Whist Club vs. Riverside.
July 23. Salvation Army permanently located.
July 27. Electric light and power franchise granted.
Aug. 3. Storm water ditch work commenced, zanja.
Aug. 3. Sewer system commenced.
Aug. 22. Hook and ladder truck arrived.
Oct. 1. Electric Light & Power Co. org., incorp. Oct. 6, '92.
Oct. 7. S. P. passenger depot changed to Motor depot.
Oct. 14. Sapphire Rebecca Degree Lodge, I. O. O. F., inst'd.
Oct. 31. *The Daily Facts*, first daily issued in Redlands, E. F. Howe publisher.
Nov. 24. Corner stone of Y. M. C. A. building laid.
Dec. 16. Club Stables opened.

1893

Jan. J. L. Stevenson purchased City Market.
Jan. 2. Postoffice moved to present location.
Jan. 5. K. of P., Redlands Lodge, No. 186, instituted.
Jan. 5. Harness shop opened by T. J. Kennard.
Jan. 11. Guards' first assembly.
Jan. 13. Work on zanja completed.
Feb. 3. Fraternal Aid Association organized.
Feb. 15. Street paving finished.
Feb. 16. Druggists acquitted, (see Dec. '91.)
Feb. 17. *The Facts* (weekly) discontinued.
Feb. 24. County division passed by legislature.
Mar. 8. Light snow, evening.

This *Chronological History of Redlands* was published in 1895 and stretched from 1820, far before the 1888 incorporation of Redlands, through 1894. This fascinating list provides data from the earliest days of the town, including a snowstorm of 12 inches on January 12, 1882, and a "very heavy earthquake" in November 1880, both of which later promotional literature seemed to ignore. Included in the history of January 1892, seen here, were the opening of the Baker House and the reopening of the large Terracina Hotel, which had been temporarily closed.

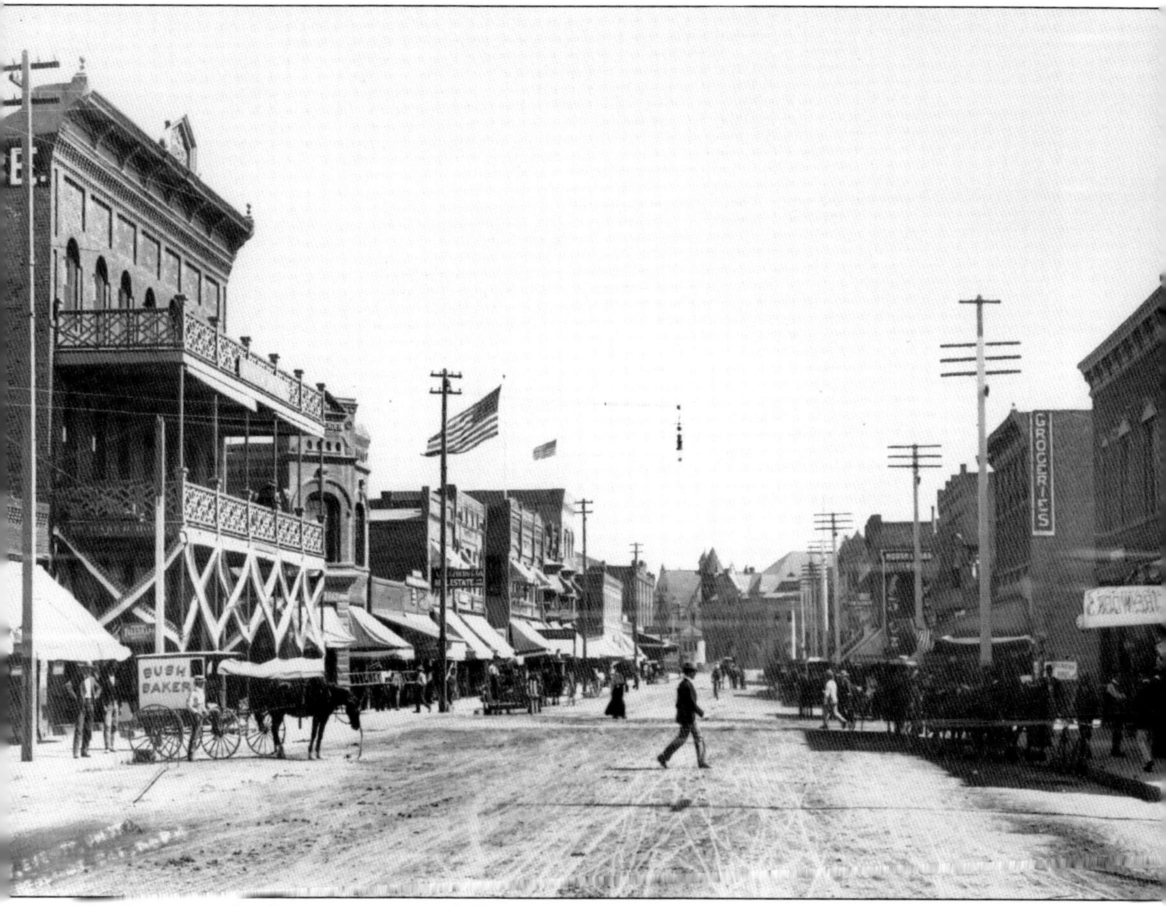

The three-story brick structure on the left was the Baker House, conveniently located in downtown Redlands at Orange Street and Water Street (now Redlands Boulevard). In this summer view from about 1898, the hotel was decorated with patriotic bunting and fireworks were for sale across the street. Business must have been brisk, as there was a drugstore, groceries, a bakery, and banks within a block or two of the hotel. The large YMCA building, which included the first library, is in the center distance. (Photographer: Elias F. Everitt.)

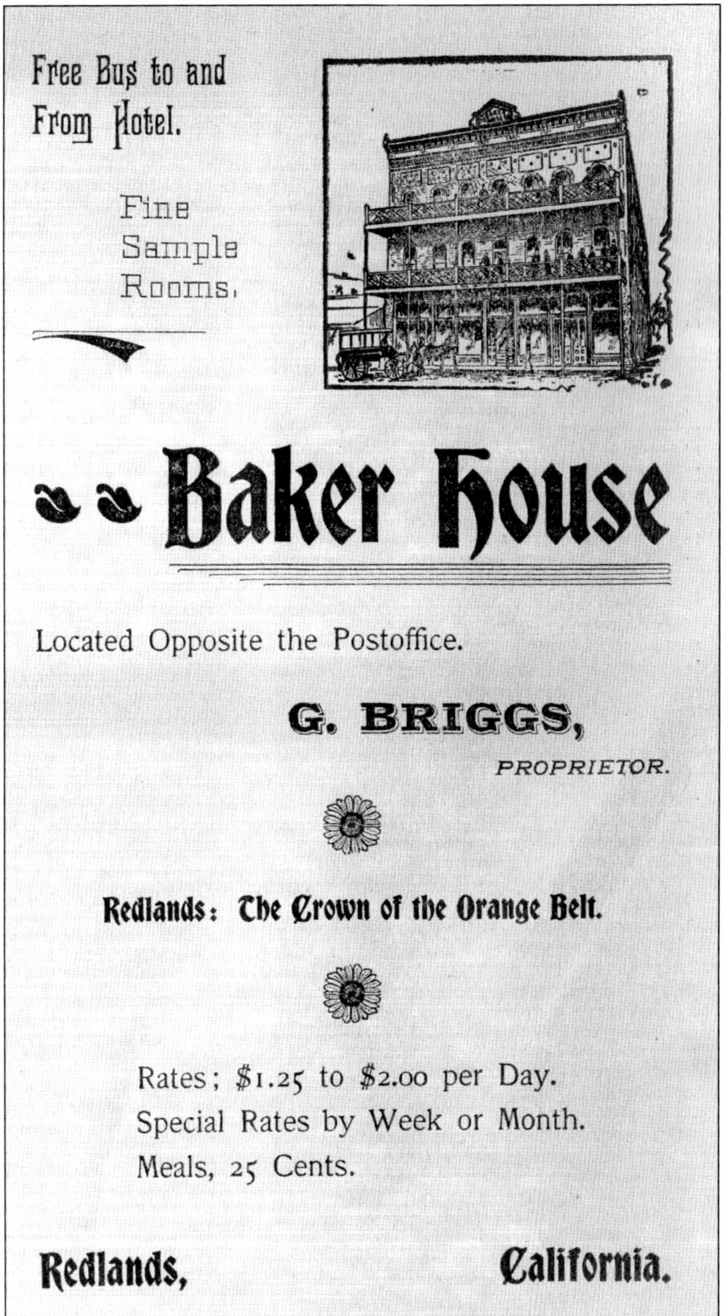

This 1896 city directory advertisement for the Baker House aimed to sell the hotel as well as Redlands itself, with the statement that the town was "The Crown of the Orange Belt." Popular with tourists, the Baker House also catered to businessmen. The "Fine Sample Rooms" provided space for salesmen to set out their samples as they conducted business. The "Free Bus to and from Hotel" was by horse carriage or mule-drawn streetcar, not by a motorized bus. Weekly and monthly rates were appreciated by winter residents or those coming for their health, who wanted longer stays.

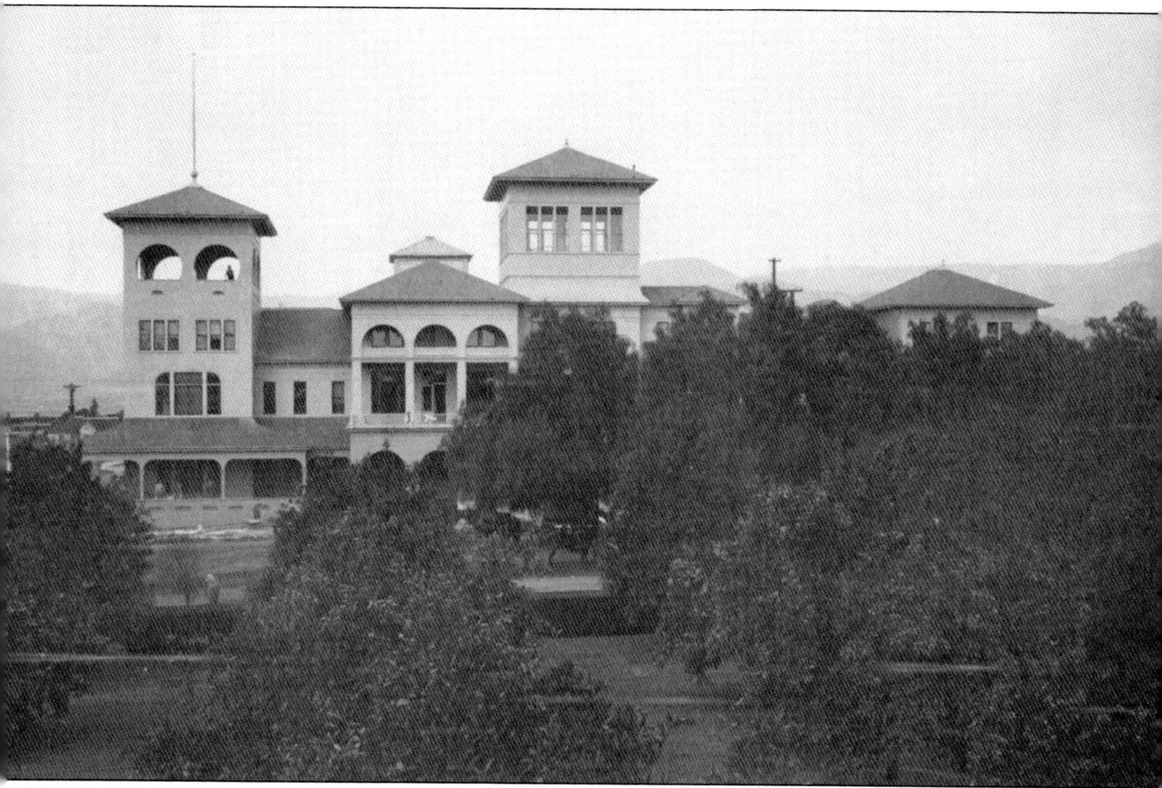

The Casa Loma Hotel opened on February 25, 1896. Located on the northeast corner of Colton Avenue and Orange Street, it was convenient to downtown and railroad stations. From 1904, the Wyatt Opera House was across the street to the northwest. Like many Redlands tourist hotels, it closed in the hot summer, until 1906, when it started summer service. Pres. William McKinley, in 1901, and Pres. Theodore Roosevelt, in 1903, used its balcony for their public speeches. (Photographer: John H. Young.)

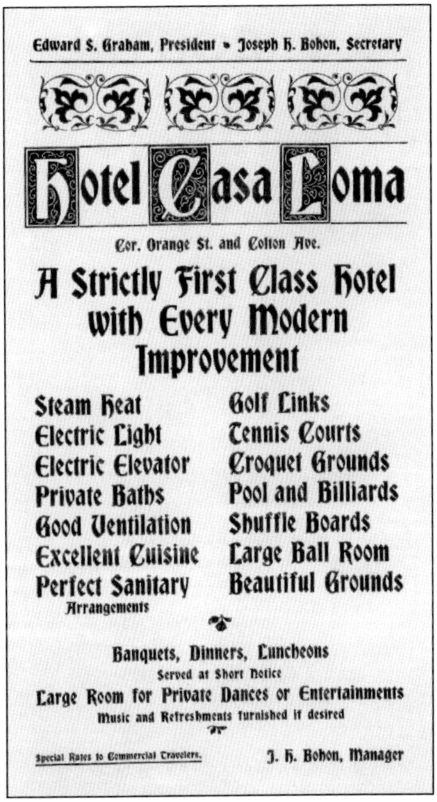

The 150-room Casa Loma Hotel required a large staff, many of whom resided in the hotel. In 1896, the year it opened, the Redlands city directory listed chambermaids, a dishwasher, bell boys, a steward, waitresses, a porter, a pantry girl, a bus driver, a chef, a pastry cook, and a cashier all working and living at the hotel. In 1900, this advertisement lists an electric elevator in the three-story Casa Loma, a nice feature for those visiting for their health.

A full-service hotel, the Casa Loma provided its guests with an elegant dining room. This photograph dates from between 1904 and 1915, when the photographer, Chase Thorn, was working in Redlands. (Photographer: Chase T. Thorn.)

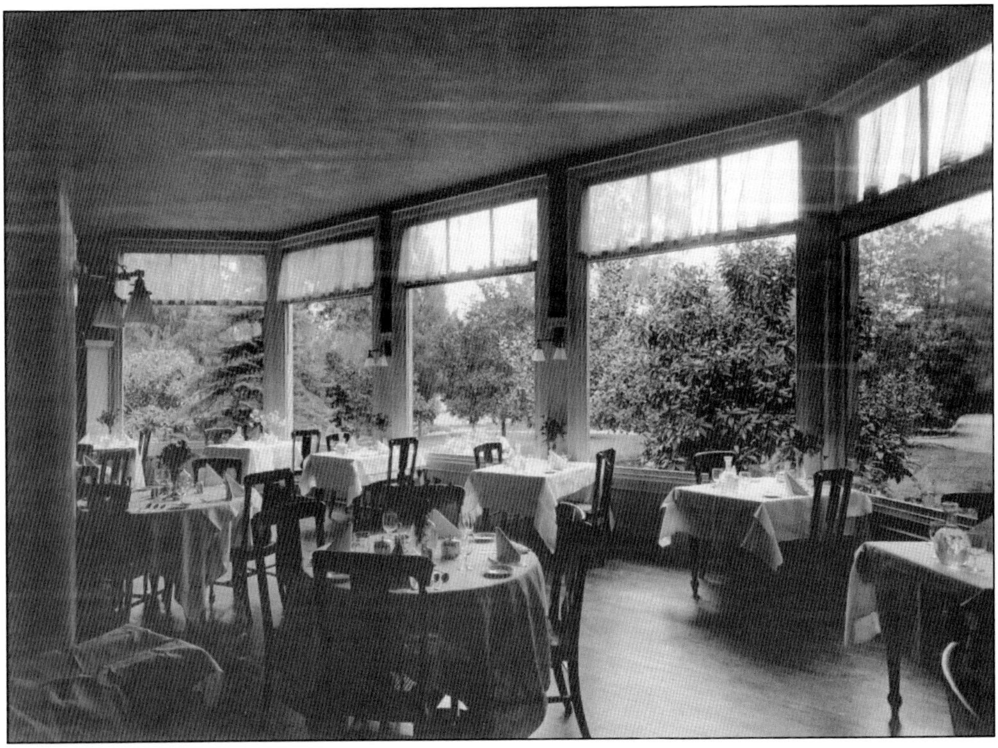

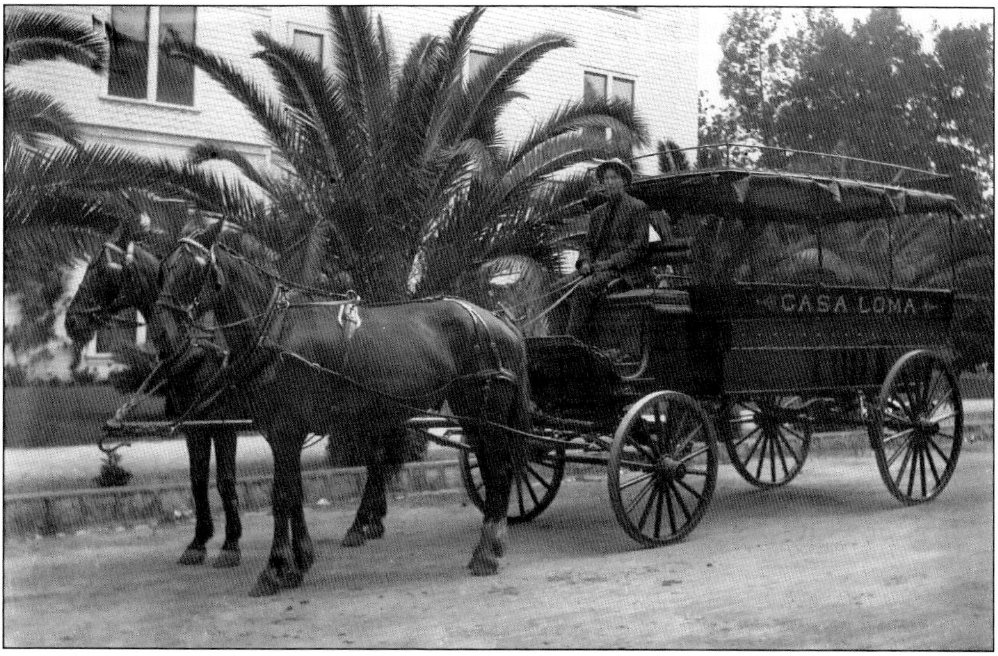

Several hotels, including the Casa Loma, had their own horse-drawn conveyances to ferry tourists between the railroad stations in Redlands and their hotel or up the hill to Cañon Crest and Prospect Hill Parks. This photograph was taken after the hotel opened in 1896 and before the end of the horse era, probably dating it between 1897 and 1910. (Photographer: Elias F. Everitt.)

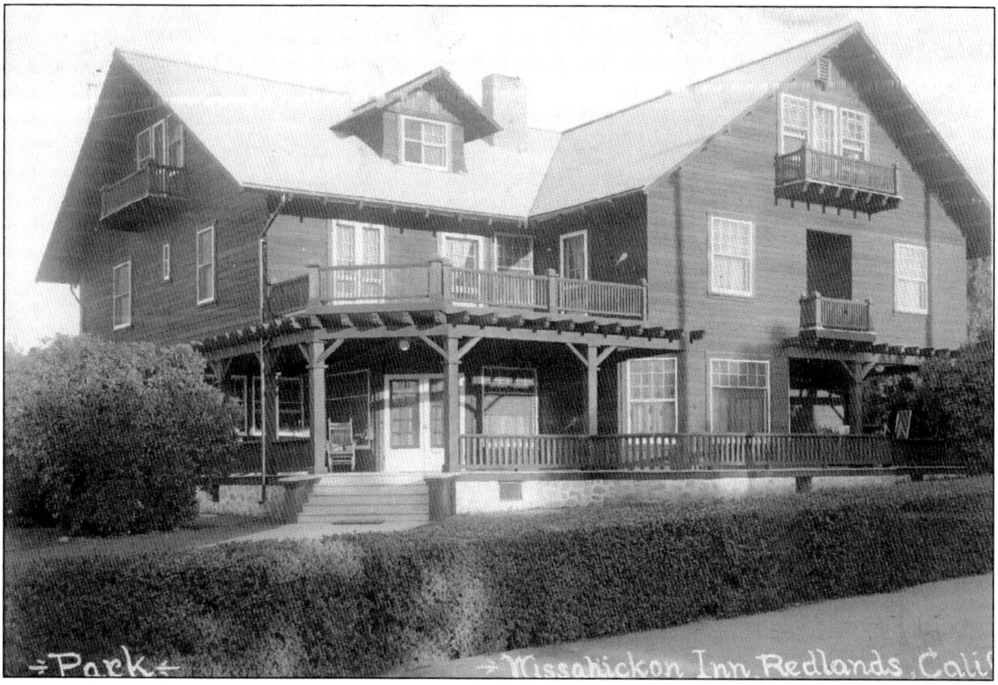

The Wissahickon Inn was on the southeast corner of Walnut Avenue and Center Street, south of downtown Redlands' noise and bustle. Catering to tourists and families, it opened in 1904. The name came from a Philadelphia creek that the owners had lived near. (Photographer: Austin T. Park.)

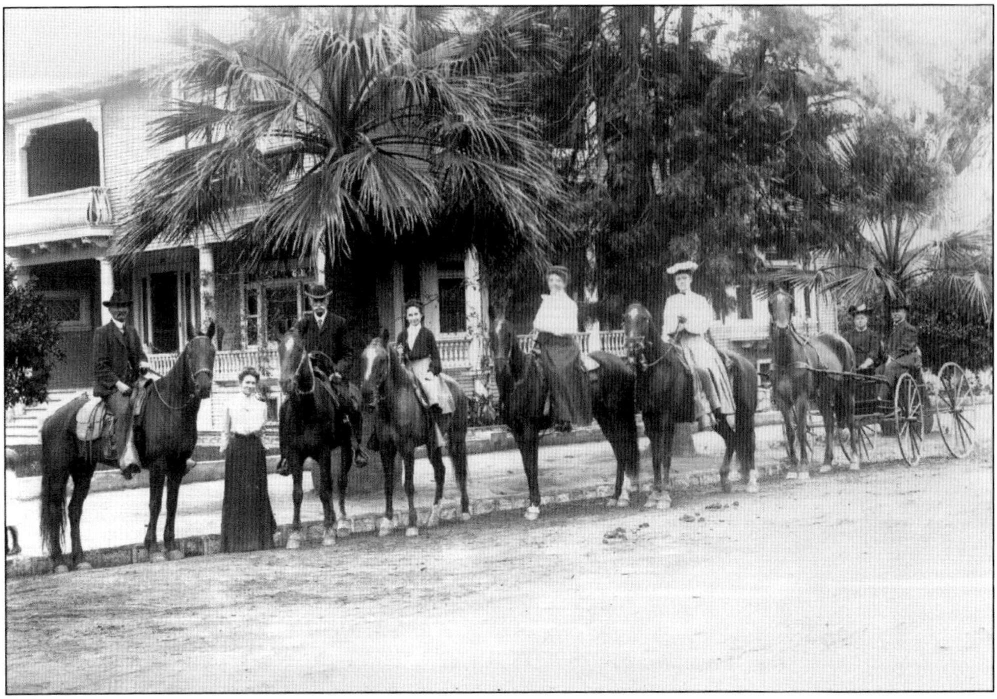

The Bennigsdorf Hotel, at 725 Orange Street, just across from the Casa Loma Hotel and the Wyatt Opera House, opened about 1904. These riders, gathered in front of the hotel in March 1904, were probably tourists renting rigs and horses to visit town landmarks like Cañon Crest and Prospect Hill Parks. (Photographer: Elias F. Everitt.)

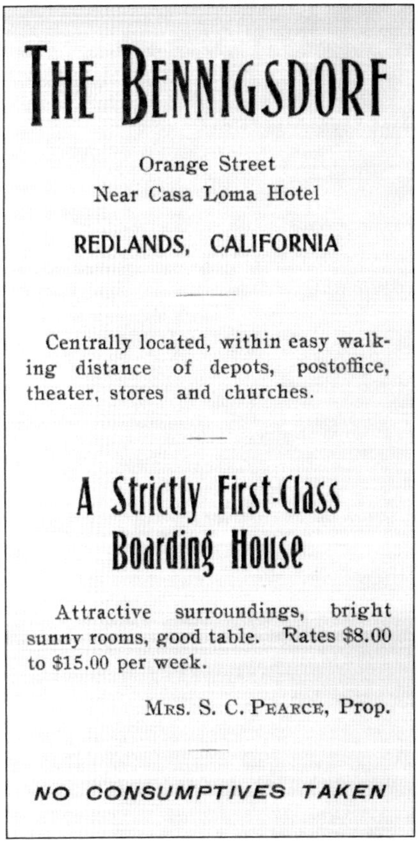

THE BENNIGSDORF

Orange Street
Near Casa Loma Hotel

REDLANDS, CALIFORNIA

Centrally located, within easy walking distance of depots, postoffice, theater, stores and churches.

A Strictly First-Class Boarding House

Attractive surroundings, bright sunny rooms, good table. Rates $8.00 to $15.00 per week.

MRS. S. C. PEARCE, Prop.

NO CONSUMPTIVES TAKEN

This advertisement for the Bennigsdorf appeared in a 1904 promotional brochure for Redlands. Called a "Boarding House" at this time, the Bennigsdorf provided meals and rooms, which was convenient for visitors. "No consumptives taken" meant that people with tuberculosis were not welcome, not quite matching the efforts to encourage those with poor health to come to Redlands for the climate.

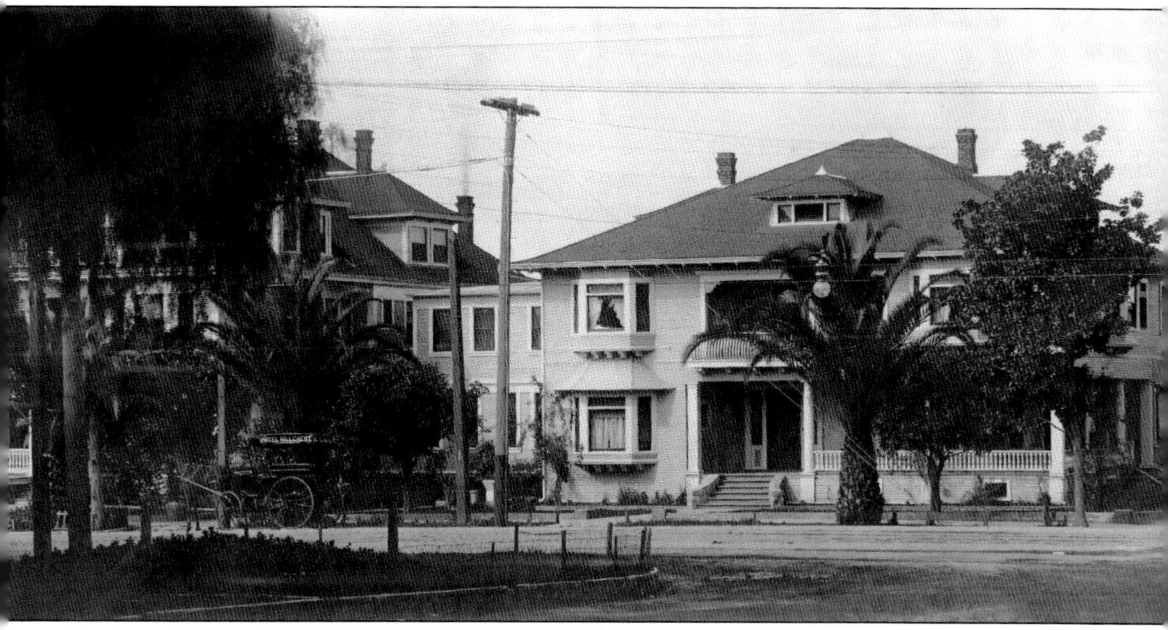

By about 1907, the Bennigsdorf was renamed the Hill Crest Inn. Although it was smaller than some hotels, it survived for over 50 years until about 1961, when it was torn down for the construction of Interstate 10. Note the horse-drawn carriage on the left with the Hill Crest name. (Photographer: Chase T. Thorn.)

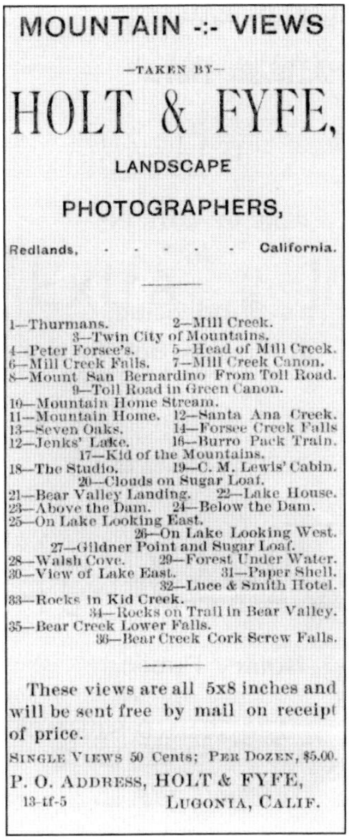

MOUNTAIN -:- VIEWS

—TAKEN BY—

HOLT & FYFE,

LANDSCAPE

PHOTOGRAPHERS,

Redlands, - - - - - - California.

1—Thurmans. 2—Mill Creek.
3—Twin City of Mountains.
4—Peter Forsee's. 5—Head of Mill Creek.
6—Mill Creek Falls. 7—Mill Creek Canon.
8—Mount San Bernardino From Toll Road.
9—Toll Road in Green Canon.
10—Mountain Home Stream.
11—Mountain Home. 12—Santa Ana Creek.
13—Seven Oaks. 14—Forsee Creek Falls
12—Jenks' Lake. 16—Burro Pack Train.
17—Kid of the Mountains.
18—The Studio. 19—C. M. Lewis' Cabin.
20—Clouds on Sugar Loaf.
21—Bear Valley Landing. 22—Lake House.
23—Above the Dam. 24—Below the Dam.
25—On Lake Looking East.
26—On Lake Looking West.
27—Gildner Point and Sugar Loaf.
28—Walsh Cove. 29—Forest Under Water.
30—View of Lake East. 31—Paper Shell.
32—Luce & Smith Hotel.
33—Rocks in Kid Creek.
34—Rocks on Trail in Bear Valley.
35—Bear Creek Lower Falls.
36—Bear Creek Cork Screw Falls.

These views are all 5x8 inches and will be sent free by mail on receipt of price.

SINGLE VIEWS 50 Cents; PER DOZEN, $5.00.

P. O. ADDRESS, HOLT & FYFE,
13-tf-5 LUGONIA, CALIF.

Summer excursions into the San Bernardino Mountains, which surround Redlands to the north and east, were popular with tourists and locals. Professional photographers saw a good source of income in taking images of mountain scenery and selling them to visitors. Professional photographer Daniel Holt and his short-term partner Mr. Fyfe—they were business partners from October to December 1887—took a two-month trip into the mountains in the summer of 1887. By October 1887, they advertised 36 views for sale in *The Citrograph*, as seen in the advertisement on the left. The photograph below was titled "Bear Creek Lower Falls." The October 8, 1887, *Citrograph* described what it took to capture these images: "The boys have had a rough time of it, scaling cliffs, penetrating almost inaccessible canons and wresting, by hard work, negatives of the beautiful and grand scenery that abounds in our mountains." (Photographers: Daniel Holt and Mr. Fyfe.)

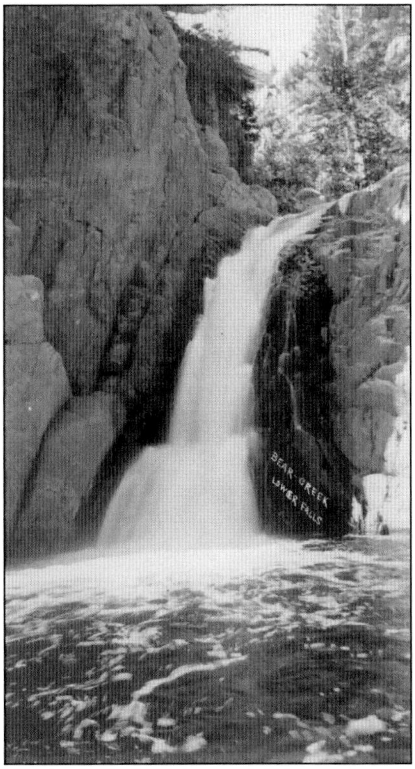

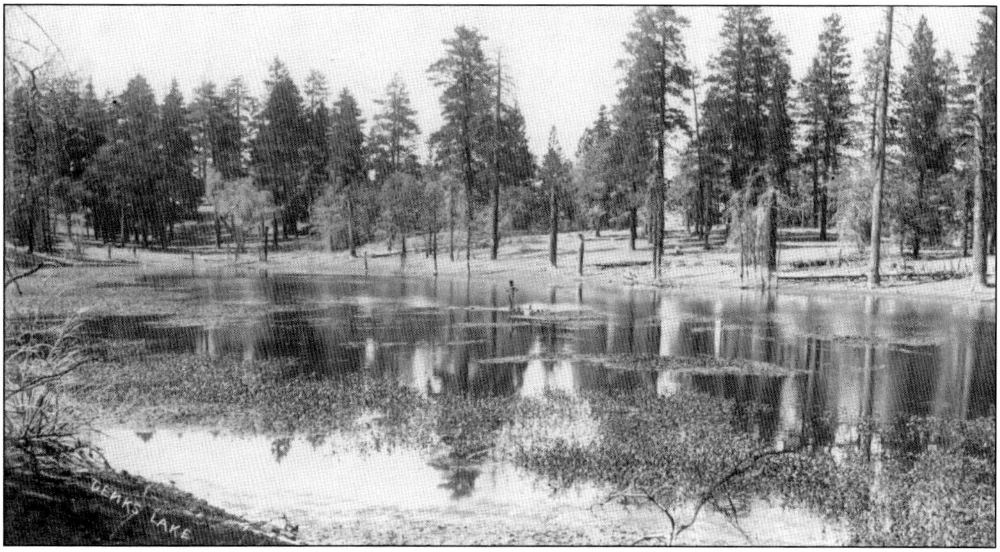

At least four of the 36 mountain views advertised by Holt & Fyfe in 1887 were later printed from their negatives and mounted on Rudolph Philippi's cardstock, a professional photographer in town from January 1890 to 1897. This likely indicates that Philippi bought Holt's negatives, a common practice at the time. Holt & Fyfe's view (above) of Jenks Lake in the San Bernardino Mountains is identical to the one mounted below on Philippi cardstock. The photograph on the opposite page, "Bear Creek Lower Falls," was another Holt & Fyfe photograph printed by Philippi. (Photographers: Daniel Holt and Mr. Fyfe.)

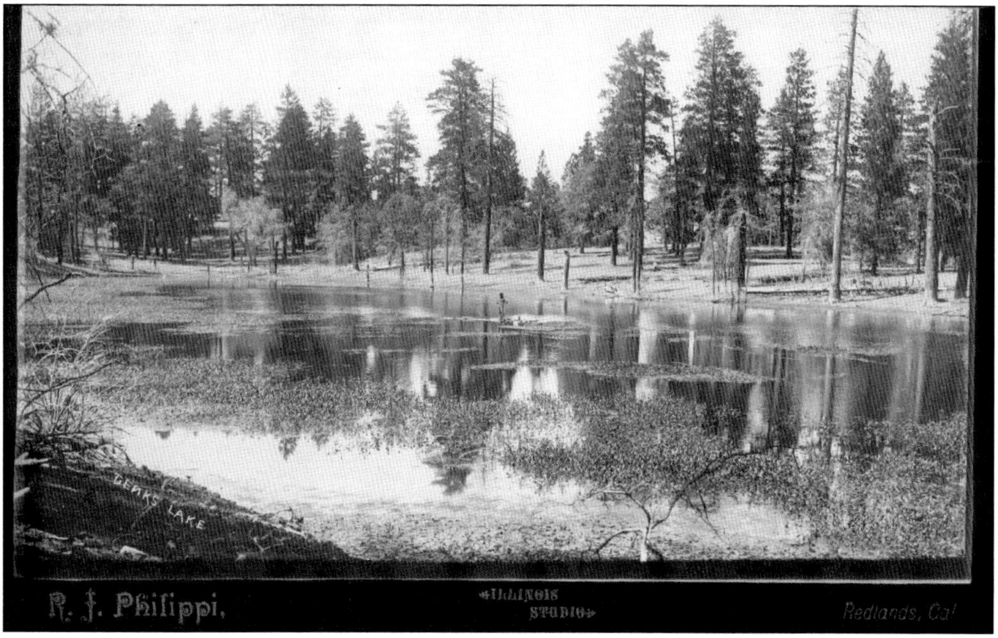

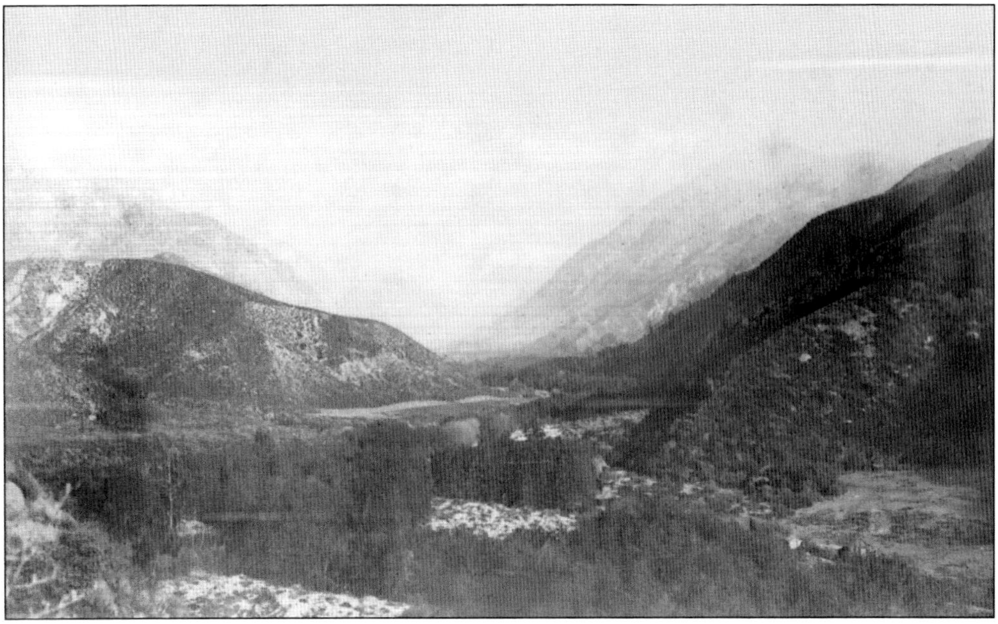

Two more 1887 Holt and Fyfe photographs show additional scenes in the San Bernardino Mountains. Mill Creek Canyon (above) was an entrance into the San Bernardino Mountains close to Redlands that led to the trails to Seven Oaks Resort. Mountain Home Stream (below) was within the canyon. (Photographer: Daniel Holt and Mr. Fyfe.)

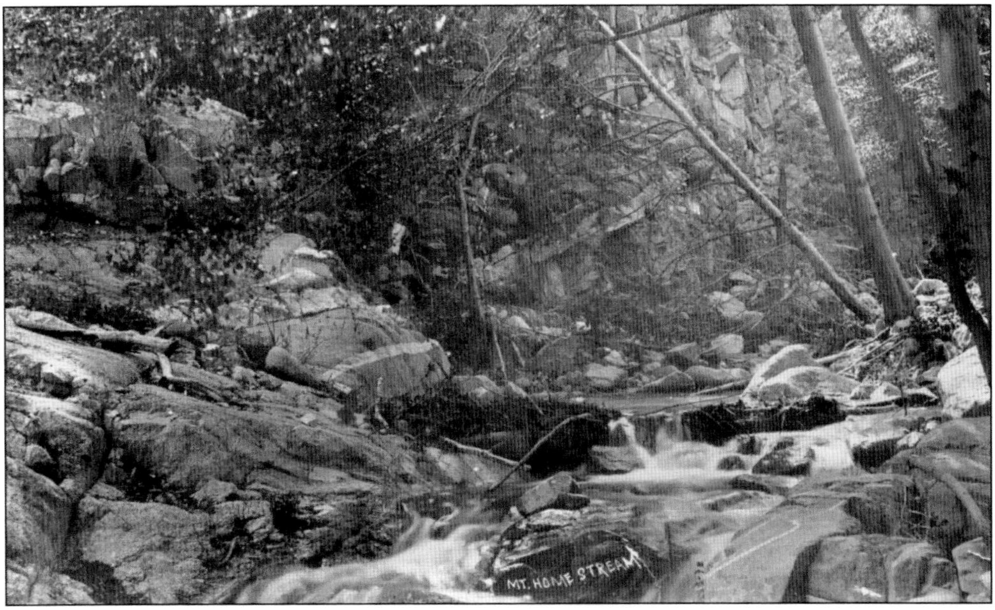

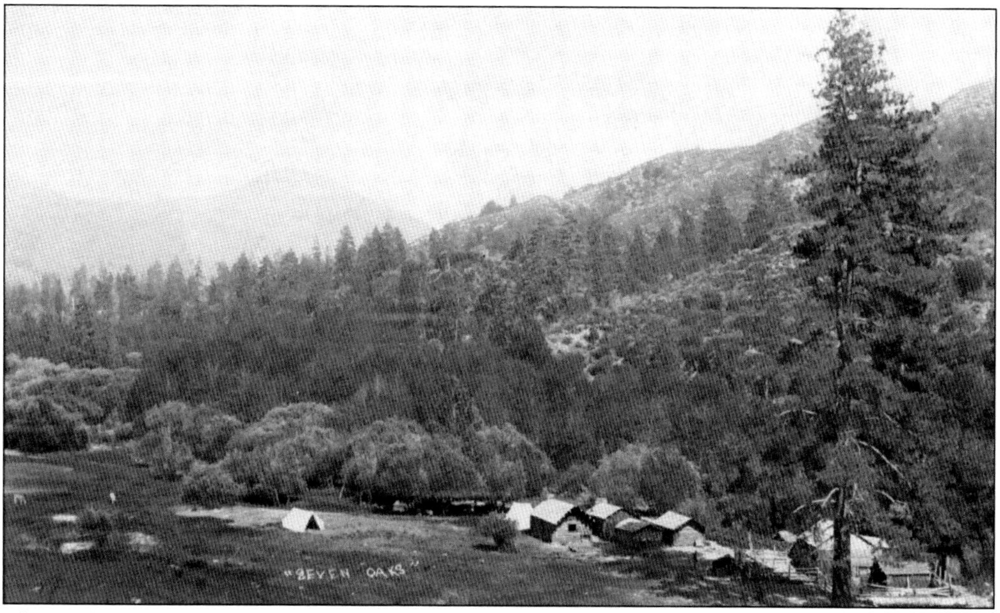

The cool air of the San Bernardino Mountains drew many people trying to beat the heat of a Redlands summer. At 4,800 feet, Seven Oaks Resort would have felt relaxing, along with the idea of fishing in a cold mountain stream. Above, another Holt & Fyfe view from 1887 shows tents and cabins at Seven Oaks. The 1896 Redlands city directory mentioned that the resort could hold 60 people with "commodious cabins, canvas houses and tents, plenty of hammocks and easy chairs under the shade trees." In 1896, traveling the 22 miles from Redlands to Seven Oaks meant taking a horse-drawn stage from Redlands to Mountain Home Canyon and then riding a burro or horse on up to Seven Oaks Resort, a long ride. (Photographers: Daniel Holt and Mr. Fyfe.)

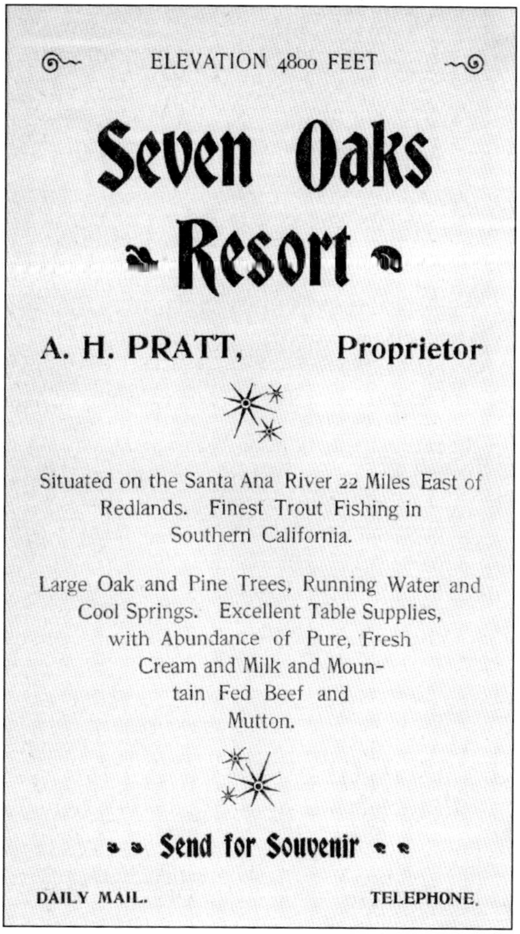
ELEVATION 4800 FEET

Seven Oaks Resort

A. H. PRATT, Proprietor

Situated on the Santa Ana River 22 Miles East of Redlands. Finest Trout Fishing in Southern California.

Large Oak and Pine Trees, Running Water and Cool Springs. Excellent Table Supplies, with Abundance of Pure, Fresh Cream and Milk and Mountain Fed Beef and Mutton.

Send for Souvenir

DAILY MAIL. TELEPHONE.

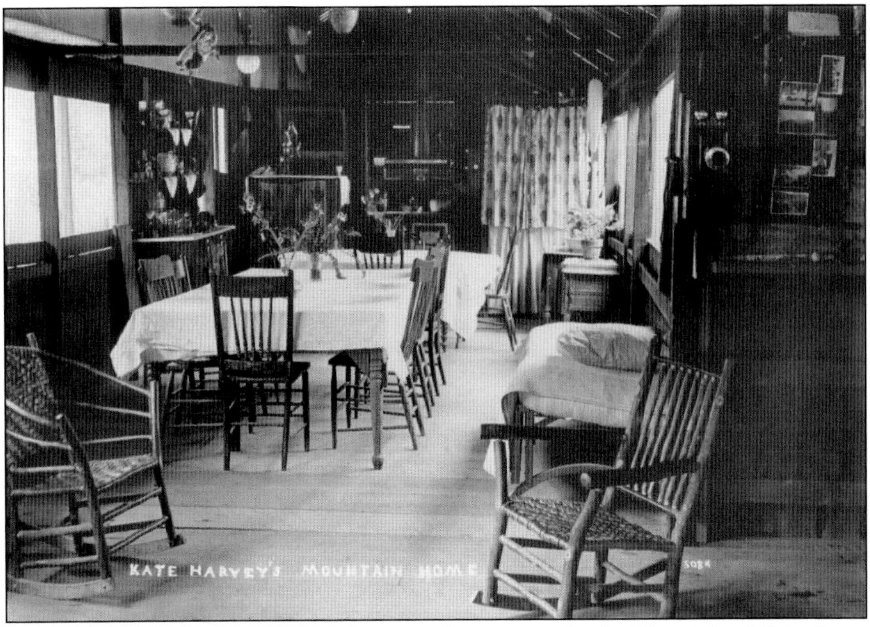

By 1912, many travelers to the mountains came by motor vehicle. The title of this photograph, "Kate Harvey's Mountain Home," at first sounds like someone's private cabin, but it was actually in the village of Mountain Home. The fact that postcards were being offered for sale in the upper right next to the telephone and the existence of two dining tables probably meant that it was a dining room for tourists. (Photographer: Clarence N. Jackson.)

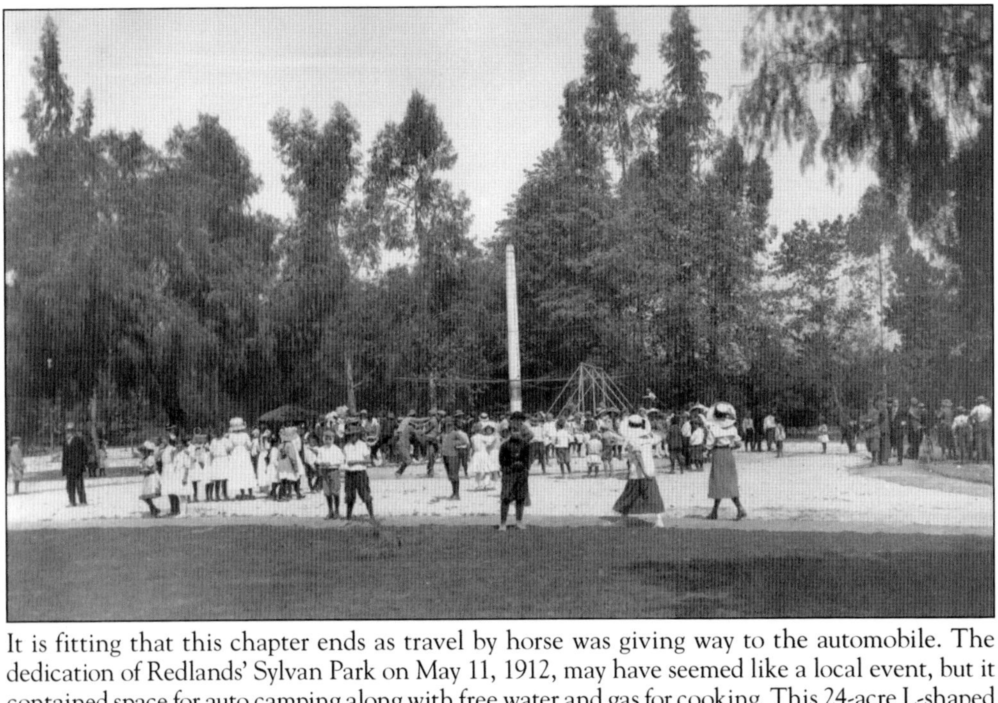

It is fitting that this chapter ends as travel by horse was giving way to the automobile. The dedication of Redlands' Sylvan Park on May 11, 1912, may have seemed like a local event, but it contained space for auto camping along with free water and gas for cooking. This 24-acre L-shaped park sits just west of the University of Redlands. In 1912, the playground contained a whirligig that spun around a tall pole. (Photographer: Charles O. Barnett.)

TABLE OF PHOTOGRAPHERS

Redlands Professional Photographers Who Started Between 1880 and 1920

NAME	DATE RANGE IN REDLANDS*
Barnett, Charles O.	1912–1923
Bird, Harry E.	1904–1906
Bunnell, Walter Alexander	1917
Butman, William C.	1906–1911
Carpenter, D.W. (male)	1900
Davis, Zelbert Louis	1909–1911
Everitt, Elias Foster	1897–1923
Everitt, Raymond Jacob	1900–1903, 1909–1919
Fairbanks, Guy Luke	1914–1941
Forrest, Lee Bagen (male)	1918–1923
Fryett, Frank C.	February 1892–September 1895
Fyfe, ? (male)	October 1887–December 1887 (see also Holt & Fyfe)
Hammond, Joseph F.	1891
Haskell, William J.	1896–1900
Herndon, Percy	1896 (see also Rogers & Herndon)
Holt, Daniel	1886–1889 (see also Holt & Fyfe)
Holt & Fyfe	October 1887–December 1887
Jackson, Clarence Newton	1912–1917
James, Edward Newell	May 1899–1907
Laney, Grace E.	November 1896–1904 (see also Laney & Melvin)
Laney & Melvin	November 1896–1899
Mee, Elbert Augustus	1912–1914
Mee, John Howard	1914–1916
Melvin, Charles Carroll	November 1896–1899 (see also Laney & Melvin)
Montee, James Wilson	1896–1900
Mudge, Katherine R.	1914–1925
O'Neil, R.C. (unknown gender)	1900
Park, Austin Trenor	1904–1907
Philippi, Rudolph Julius	January 1890–1897
Roessler, Edward E.	1900–1904
Rogers, Frederick Horace	1895–1896 (see also Rogers & Herndon)
Rogers & Herndon	1896
Rollins, Henry Harrison	1915
Shuford, Thomas Robert	1907–1914
Sutphen, Perry D. (male)	1904–1907
Thorn, Chase T.	1904–1915
Young, John H.	September 1895–November 1896

*Dates are within one year of these times and will become more precise with future research.